My Father's War

My Father's War

Fighting with the Buffalo Soldiers in World War II

Carolyn Ross Johnston

THE UNIVERSITY OF ALABAMA PRESS
Tuscaloosa

Typeface: Garamond

∞
The paper on which this book is printed meets the minimum requirements of American National Standard for Information Sciences—Permanence of Paper for Printed Library Materials, ANSI Z39.48-1984.

Library of Congress Cataloging-in-Publication Data

Johnston, Carolyn Ross.
My father's war : fighting with the Buffalo soldiers in World War II / Carolyn Ross Johnston.
p. cm.
Includes bibliographical references and index.
ISBN 978-0-8173-1768-3 (hardcover : alk. paper) — ISBN 978-0-8173-8620-7 (ebook)
1. United States. Army. Infantry Division, 92nd. 2. World War, 1939–1945—Campaigns—Italy. 3. World War, 1939–1945—Regimental histories—United States. 4. World War, 1939–1945—Participation, African American. 5. Johnson, Eugene Edwin, 1915–2006. 6. United States. Army—Officers—Biography. I. Title.
D769.3192nd J65 2012
940.54'1273092—dc23
[B]

2012005532

Cover photograph: Members of a Negro mortar company of the 92nd Division pass the ammunition and heave it over at the Germans in an almost endless stream near Massa, Italy. This company is credited with liquidating several machine gun nests. Ca. November 1944. Acme. 208-AA-47U-6. (african_americans_wwii_035.jpg). Courtesy of the U.S. Army, National Archives.

Cover design: Mary-Frances Burt/Burt&Burt

. . . the war occurred half a lifetime ago, and yet the remembering makes it now. And sometimes remembering will lead to a story, which makes it forever. That's what stories are for. Stories are for joining the past to the future. Stories are for those late hours in the night when you can't remember how you got from where you were to where you are. Stories are for eternity, when memory is erased, when there is nothing to remember except the story.

Tim O'Brien, *The Things They Carried*

Contents

Illustrations

Acknowledgments

In my search for my father's war over the past ten years, I have been indebted to many remarkable people. First, I want to thank my father, Eugene E. Johnston, for collaborating with me on this project. We spent endless hours recording oral history over many years. Regrettably he did not live to see the publication of this work, but he was able to review the transcripts of the interviews. Likewise, I wish to express my profound gratitude and admiration for my mother, Alta Ross Johnston. Sadly, she also did not live to see this book completed, but she would have been touched to relive so many moments described in these pages. To my amazing sister, Nancy Smith, and nieces, Jennifer and Patricia Smith, go my deepest thanks.

This book would not have been possible without the members of the 92nd Infantry Division who have shared their stories with me, their historical collections, and their friendship. I am especially indebted to Spencer Moore and A. William Perry, the historians of the 92nd Buffalo Association. Their unique collections are now housed in the Manuscript Division of the Library of Congress. I also wish to thank Charles Lancaster, Albert Burke, Joseph Stephenson, Joseph Hairston, Leonidas Williams, Richard Salmon, Harold Montgomery, Harold Fletcher, Spurgeon Burruss, Richard Johnson, Willie Green, Kermit Hancock, Jehu Hunter, Susie Moore, Helen Montgomery, Ivan Houston, Gordon Cohn, Jo Perry, Ralph Brown, Edward Brooke, and the children of the 92nd: Marian Johnson, Michael Moore, and Sharon Beckham. Tom Fergusson graciously shared the oral history of his grandfather General Ned Almond with me.

I am deeply grateful to Elie and Marion Wiesel for their thoughtful reading of and commentary on the manuscript, their enduring friendship, and relentless encouragement. Wayne Flynt, my mentor since 1966 when I entered college, read draft after draft of this manuscript, and his keen editorial eye was invaluable. He is a truly gifted historian and teacher. Maggi Morehouse gave me access to her extensive archives and over one hundred interviews of Buffalo Soldiers. She offered insightful criticism of my manuscript. She is the daughter of a white officer of the 93rd Division, Lee Quarterman, the author of *Fighting in the Jim Crow Army,* and she was the first person to receive a PhD in African Diaspora Studies at the University of California at Berkeley. Thomas C. Childers gave me tremendous help on the book with his brilliant criticism. His own highly imaginative literary nonfiction on World War II inspired me to take the plunge. I still marvel at his skill and lyricism. We both attended Bradley High School in Cleveland, Tennessee, and although we took similar paths, we did not meet again until over forty years later. I only hope I was able to follow half of his wonderful suggestions.

Leon Litwack, my mentor from Berkeley, beginning in 1970, has always inspired me with his groundbreaking scholarship and remains a cherished friend and colleague. I was so fortunate that he was working on his volume on African Americans during World War II during this time of my research and writing, and he generously shared his knowledge with me.

I wish to extend my profound thanks to Patricia Perez-Arce, Ed De Avila, and Jeffrey Kennedy. Patricia and Ed read numerous drafts of the manuscript. Along with Jeffrey, they traveled with me in retracing the steps of the Buffalo Soldiers in Italy. I am grateful to James McBride, a gifted writer, for *Song Yet Sung* and *The Color of Water,* for his work on the 92nd, *Miracle at St. Anna,* and for his friendship. I also want to thank Speaker Nancy Pelosi, who sponsored the event in the Capitol Rotunda commemorating the sixtieth anniversary of the integration of the military in the United States. I am grateful to John Lawrence, the Speaker's chief of staff, who greatly assisted in this venture. He has been a dear friend from the time we were graduate students together at Berkeley.

I wish to thank the following people who contributed greatly to this project: Jared Stark, who provided brilliant criticism; Jewel Spears Brooker; Margo and Rodney Fitzgerald; Nancy Wood; Catherine Griggs; Linda Lucas; John Hope Franklin; Henry Nash Smith; Lawrence Levine; Mara Soudakoff; Santiago Nunez; Claire Bell; Judith Green; David Woods; Christine Payne; John Galloway; Jim Goetsch; Constantina Rhodes; John McNeilly; Randy Browne; Katie Pfeiffer; Stephanie Wolfe; Vais Salikhov; Armando Solis; Bob England; Tiffany Boyd; Jimmy Nolan; Beth Zeeman; Paul Stern; General Barry McCaffrey; Richard Strilka; Jim Moore; April Bradley; Ross Cohen; Yasmin Uriel; Beth Kriebel; Jesse Sharpe; Joe Haley; Zoe Friedman; Tim and Clover Beal; Kip Curtis; Davina Lopez; Julie Empric; Jean Razor; Neel Desai; Lia Glovsky; Dick Lee; Mark Fennell; Josh Willitt; Joel Marantz; George Stovall; Bill Dickman; Jesus Subero; Xavier Landon; Margaret Rigg; Theresa Turner; Hollis Lynch; Dudley DeGroot; Vine Deloria; Abrasha and Peg Brainin; Lina Patridis; Judy and Bill Chandler; Janice Norton;

Joelle Collier; Greg Padgett; Jason Sears; Prentiss Willson; Xavier Gil; John Omlor; all my Ford students; Samson van Overwater; Peggy Newton; Peter Pav; Bill McKee; Bill Wilbur; Barney Hartston; Michael Solari; Lynn Carol Henderson; Stella Andersen; Ann Rittenberg; Bill Parsons; Andrew Chittick; Liz MacDonald; James Minor; John Edwards; Gary Meltzer; Diane Gladu; Michael J. Polley; and Faheem Bengazi.

I owe a special debt to Robert Patrick, director of the Veterans History Project at the Library of Congress; Adrienne Cannon, Manuscripts Division of the Library of Congress; Dr. James H. Billington, librarian of Congress; the librarians of the National Archives and Records Administration, especially those in charge of the World War II materials in College Park, Maryland; the librarians at Harvard University, University of California at Berkeley, the Western Historical Manuscript Collection—Columbia, Missouri (especially Bill Stolz); and the archivists at the Fort Huachuca Museum. I want to express my gratitude to James Rada of Howard University for sharing his filming of the members of the 92nd Division in numerous oral histories and at the World War II Memorial. His film *Deeds not Words* about the 92nd is a splendid contribution.

I want to also thank the staff of the Army Military History Institute in Carlisle, Pennsylvania, especially Michael Lynch, Dr. Conrad Crane, Rich Baker, and Arthur W. Bergeron Jr. I wish to thank Stuart Yamane for sharing the film about his father and the 442nd Division, and Fred Kuwornu who screened his excellent film *Inside Buffalo* at the 92nd Division Reunion in 2009. I am very grateful to the anonymous readers for The University of Alabama Press for their insightful critiques. Special thanks to Lloyd Chapin who has always believed in my work and generously supported it as the dean of the faculty at Eckerd College. I am also grateful to Betty Stewart, our new dean of the faculty. I wish to thank Don Eastman, Eckerd's president and outstanding leader. Special thanks to Karen Hallman for copyediting; Julie Maynard for indexing; and Joanna Jacobs, Dan Ross, and Dan Waterman of The University of Alabama Press, who have been editors that writers dream of having. To them I am very grateful.

My Father's War

I WAR AND MEMORY

1. Eugene E. Johnston. Photograph courtesy of Carolyn Johnston.

1

The Buffalo Soldiers at the World War II Memorial

The bus pulled up to the World War II Memorial in Washington, D.C., on October 9, 2004. One by one, the veterans of the 92nd Division, the Buffalo Soldiers, stepped out. They moved slowly toward the memorial, some carrying canes. To one side in the distance, the Lincoln Memorial sits on the horizon; to the other side, the Washington Monument pierces the sky. Entering the arena of the shining new World War II Memorial, unveiled just six months earlier, the black soldiers surveyed the Atlantic and Pacific Pavilions and the pillars representing the states of those who served. They stopped at the wall that is resplendent with a field of four thousand gold stars, representing the over four hundred thousand Americans who died in the war. The stars recalled to them a wartime practice, when families would place a blue star in the window if one of theirs was in the armed forces, and a gold star when a family member had been killed. They thought of those who lie buried in Italy where they fell, and those who have died since. As they passed the four American eagles holding a suspended laurel wreath, some spoke softly to their fellow veterans. Together, they slowly circled the memorial.[1]

Carl Proctor from Peoria, Illinois, had been in the 597th Field Artillery. On the visit to the memorial, he wore a shirt with buffaloes on it in commemoration of the 92nd Division. He was commemorating not only the war itself, but the battle to serve that African Americans had had to undergo to be able to fight in the war. Without the political pressure of the National Association for the Advancement of Colored People, other civil rights organizations, and Eleanor Roosevelt, the black soldiers would not have been assigned to two combat units, the 92nd and 93rd Divisions, known as the Buffalo Soldiers. They endured racial violence on the home front and experienced racism at home and abroad. Those who opposed black Americans in combat either suspected their abilities or somehow feared that once they had fought and died for their country they might demand democracy at home.

The Buffalo Soldiers of the Indian wars, the black soldiers who fought with Teddy Roosevelt in the Spanish-American War, and the Tuskegee airmen are well known. But many have never heard of the 92nd Division. Engaged in combat for nine months, often without a day off, they achieved their objectives in the Ital-

2. *Left to right:* A. William Perry and Spencer C. Moore at the World War II Memorial, 2004. Photograph courtesy of Carolyn Johnston.

ian campaign. They held the line in Italy, forcing the Germans to commit more troops than planned to the Gothic Line and drawing them away from the line in France. When the reorganized 92nd Division became multiracial with the addition of the Japanese American unit, the 442nd, and of a white unit, they broke through the Gothic line and achieved impressive results, liberating Massa, Carrara, Aulla, La Spezia, Pisa, Lucca, Viareggio, and Genoa.[2]

As they viewed the memorial, Spurgeon Burruss and Harold Montgomery remembered these battles, and how white soldiers segregated Lucca and Pisa right after the 92nd took them, making these cities off limits to the black soldiers who had just fought for their liberation. Segregation was not only the law of the land in the United States. It was also the rule for the Buffalo Soldiers of World War II, one of the last segregated units in the American military. Burruss was outraged that German prisoners had been better treated than black soldiers were, and that the prisoners were even permitted into the segregated officers' club. Leonidas Williams, who served in the 598th Field Artillery, also remembered the racism they faced. He thought of the time when he was on a troop train from Fort Huachuca that stopped at El Paso, where food was served to German prisoners, but not to the Buffalo Soldiers. And when they returned from the war, there were no parades for them. Instead, they confronted discrimination. Burruss recalled that even while

3. Lieutenant Doug Brown, 365th, Viareggio, Italy, 1945. Photograph courtesy of Spencer C. Moore.

4. *Left to right:* Joseph Stephenson and Spencer C. Moore at the World War II Memorial, 2004. Photograph courtesy of Carolyn Johnston.

still wearing his uniform, he had to give his seat to white people on public transportation. One war was won; another remained to be fought.

But now, on that crisp, sunny day in October, it was perhaps a different battle that was foremost in the minds of the Buffalo Soldiers, as they gathered at the large marble stone etched with the name of the Po Valley. The challenge was to remember their war. More than eleven hundred members of the "greatest generation" die each day—the silent passing of those who saved the world from Hitler. Of the over one million African Americans who served in World War II, seventy thousand are still alive today.[3] Of the Buffalo Soldiers, here stood twenty-five. Their minds went back to those days in Italy when they were sent into the front lines just hours after they landed. Perhaps some of them remembered a white Southern captain, Gene Johnston. Standing with them was his daughter. Why were she and the black soldiers of his division sharing such an intimate moment, and why did they hold her father, and by extension, her, in such esteem? She realized that in order to honor her father's memory, in order to tell their story, she would first need to uncover a different memory, a different history, a different story. This is that story.

2

"This Is Your Father"

My search for my father's war began long before that October day in Washington, D.C. It began, perhaps, as long ago as a sultry August day in 1953, with a five-year-old girl perched high on the swing set, her hair tangled and her clothes covered with the red clay of Georgia, holding a rubber knife in her mouth, a wolf-child, wild and wide-eyed, and with a handsome man in uniform suddenly materializing in her yard. "Come down from there," he called out. "You might fall." I just sat there watching him, puzzled and defiant.

"Carolyn, come down from there now," my mother ordered. "Listen to your father!"

I hesitated, looked down at the two of them, and took my precious knife out of my mouth. "No, he is not," I cried out. "My father is in the picture on the mantle in the living room."

Most of my life, my father remained inscrutable. Why was he always leaving, and why was he so deliriously happy when he returned? What did he do in the "war," a word that had the force for me of a great mystery? Over the years, both as a child and later as an historian trained in the methods of oral history, I asked questions about that war in an attempt to better understand his experience, his world, his war. And these questions led me on a journey: across the southern U.S., to places like Chattanooga, Tennessee; Cartersville, Georgia; and Aiken, South Carolina; but also to Washington, D.C.; Ft. Huachuca, Arizona; Carlisle, Pennsylvania; Magnolia, New Jersey; and to the hill towns and valleys of Tuscany. They also led to the political and social landscape of U.S. history, as I explored the ways in which my father's war was inextricably tied to the lives of the black Buffalo Soldiers and to the fraught terrain of race relations in the United States. Who was Eugene Edwin Johnston? Was he a bigot and racist, mired in the culture of segregation into which he was born? Was he a man of integrity and courage? A coward? What was his relation to the black Buffalo Soldiers? How was he shaped by that encounter, and how was he remembered? How should he be remembered? What began as a search for my father's war has become the story of the Buffalo Soldiers in the Second World War.

Like many of the children of the "greatest generation," I set out to learn, in the

5. *Left to right:* Sharon Knox and Carolyn Johnston, Cartersville, Georgia, ca. 1953. Photograph courtesy of Carolyn Johnston.

words of Stuart Yamane, the son of a soldier in the 100th/442nd: "What ordinary men were capable of, and in the context of history they became bigger than life, but their 'ordinariness' within that context is what's truly humbling . . . and in a strange way empowering. I can't help but wonder (hope?) that whatever it was in them might be in all of us."[1]

Yet my father, I would also learn, had an unusual vantage point as one of the three hundred white officers in the only African American division to engage in infantry combat in Europe during World War II. On his dress uniform were his medals: one Combat Infantry Badge, two Combat Medals for Gallantry, a Purple Heart, and a Bronze Star with an Oak Leaf Cluster. His long military career spanned the Italian campaign in World War II; intelligence work to smuggle a German rocket scientist out of Austria; further intelligence work in Eastern Europe during the Cold War; service in Taiwan, Quemoy, and Matsu in the late fifties; service on a ship going to Cuba during the Cuban Missile Crisis; and an extended mission in Thailand to prepare a staging base for the Vietnam War. He grew up poor in Chattanooga, Tennessee, and went on to meet Charles Lindberg, Franklin and Eleanor Roosevelt, John F. Kennedy, Chiang Kai-Shek, and the king and queen of Thailand. His life intersected with major turning points in U.S. foreign policy of the twentieth century. In this story of an ordinary soldier lie all the drama, turmoil, racial conflict, violence, and heroism of the century. But it was his experience in the 92nd Division that set his career in motion and that defined him as a soldier and as a man. For him, as for so many others, *the War,* the real war, was World War II.

For many years, my father was silent about his experiences with the 92nd Division. Why did he have such conflicted feelings about the war? How could he move from silence to testimony? One cannot capture the experience of all those in the 92nd Division, but one can search for the individual truths of those black and white soldiers. This work is not a military history of the 92nd Division; rather it seeks to illuminate the meaning and nature of the war for the Buffalo Soldiers, black and white.

II BECOMING A BUFFALO SOLDIER

3

The Road to War

In 1940, Gene Johnston cut a handsome figure in his new uniform. He was twenty-five years old and would soon go to war as a white commander of an all black unit of the Buffalo Soldiers. Like many black and white Americans, his first war was a war against poverty. The Great Depression hit Gene's family especially hard. They had food and shelter, but little more. Gene was born in 1915 and grew up in a segregated South. Gene's house was not far from the largest black community in Chattanooga, and the streetcar let out all those returning to the black neighborhood nearby, where they cut through his street to get home.

Black and white people in Chattanooga, Tennessee, had separate schools, churches, and restrooms, and they rarely associated with each other.[1] Segregation was a normal part of the young Gene's life. He grew up within the racist Southern culture and internalized many of its assumptions. Gene did not see a contradiction between the city's segregated facilities and playing with his black friends like Vann Dee and accepting them as equals. When Vann Dee died young, Gene and his friends went to the funeral and sat with his parents all night at his house.

Gene learned the polite term for his black companions was "colored." Southerners were used to this sort of racial blindness and being able to feel like they held no prejudices while at the same time believing certain racist assumptions.[2] Along with the experience of close childhood friendships with African Americans, he cherished the knowledge that one of his own ancestors freed his slaves. His strong faith in Christianity motivated him to treat everyone with respect.

A frightening incident made Gene sharply aware of how vulnerable African Americans were to violence by Southern whites. When he was in high school, he was part of a minstrel group and saw nothing odd about performing in blackface. One evening after a show, he and his friends decided to stop in Ducktown for something to eat. A sign in the town warned, "No niggers here. Stay out." While he was waiting in the car, a group of hoodlums pulled him out and began to beat him up, thinking he was black. Gene tried frantically to wipe off his face paint to convince them that he was white. Only when his friends returned did the gang back off.

But also a regular part of Gene's youth were the warm summer evenings when the Ku Klux Klan would gather on a large field in East Chattanooga. Gene and his white friends would drift over to hear their speeches. In fact, virtually everyone in his community attended, except the black families who sealed their windows and doors tightly shut. A number of Gene's neighbors were undoubtedly beneath those white hoods. He never actually saw any burning crosses, but he saw their charred remains.[3]

Gene's parents were poor working-class people. His mother, Julia, was the oldest of seven daughters. From the time she was only eleven years old, she would leave home each morning before sunrise with a lantern to find her way to the hosiery mill where she worked for many years. When she got older, she became a forelady at the mill. During the Depression, she lost her job and stayed home. Gene's father Fred was head machinist at the United Hosiery Mill. Gene, his brother, Walter, and his sister, Harriet, were all born at home. The Johnstons had scrimped and saved every dime to buy the property at 2500 Stuart Street. They built a shotgun house on the site, with plans to build a larger house when they could afford it. The Depression killed that dream.[4]

In high school, Gene joined the Reserve Officer Training Corps (ROTC), and became a captain of C Company, the winner in the 3rd Army competition for drill. Since Gene could not afford to attend a university, and he had no promising employment opportunities, he decided to join the army. The war was beginning in Europe, but the draft had not started yet.[5] Gene thought he was probably destined to be a soldier. One day he drove his shiny roadster car to Fort Oglethorpe, Georgia, which was ten miles from Chattanooga. The recruiting office was on the highway by the number two gate. While Gene was sitting in a little shack with a sergeant, he heard some recruits yelling in the building next door.

One of the men had tried to commit suicide by cutting his throat. When he came running out covered with blood, Gene rushed over to help him. Since he had been working for the H. L. Judd Company in the first-aid department, he knew what to do. He stopped the bleeding, and the next thing he knew he was sitting in an old timey ambulance with rubber tires, holding his thumb on the man's wound. When they arrived at the hospital they both had blood all over them. Gene stayed with the man all the way to the operating room.

After the patient's condition had stabilized, one of the doctors came out and said they wanted Gene in their unit. Gene washed the blood off his hands, and then directly went to be sworn into the army. It was the afternoon of September 9, 1940. He was assigned to the post hospital. The United States reinstated the military draft just a week later, on September 16, 1940. When Gene returned home, and told his mother and father that he had joined the army, they were both excited, but his mother had tears in her eyes.[6]

Still living at home with his parents, Gene drove to the post in the fancy Ford Sport Roadster he had built himself. He would lay the top back, put the windshield down, and then drop the wings onto the windshield. The car had chrome bars around the hood, and three or four lines of thick chrome bars around the front of the car. The Roadster would go fifty to eighty miles per hour, which seemed pretty fast at the time. He had a spare tire cover on the back of the car—a beautiful thing, painted bright yellow with "Happy Landings" written on it.

At Fort Oglethorpe, Gene worked in the operating room for about a year, and later as a ward boy, ward master, and a medical technician. As a medical technician, he began to take X-rays.[7] One morning, Gene had recruits lined up to start x-raying them when Captain Taylor, a draftee from somewhere in Georgia, came in and told Gene about Pearl Harbor. Taylor was shaking so hard his voice cracked. "That is why I joined the Army," Gene said. "I knew the United States would enter the war!" Some nurses from Fort Oglethorpe had recently retired in Hawaii; they had always dreamed of living in Pearl Harbor. As they were boarding evacuation aircraft, they suddenly heard a roar of engines. Japanese planes came in low and killed them right on the tarmac. Gene was stunned by the news and knew he might see combat.[8]

When Gene's commanding officer saw Gene marching the men, the CO said he was sending him to Officer Candidate School (OCS). Gene told him that he did not want to go, and he hid out for a couple of weeks, but the CO insisted. He marched him over to the office, filled out the papers, packed him up, and made sure he was on a train that night. Gene came out of OCS as a lieutenant. He just missed by one man being transferred to New Orleans in the transportation corps. He always thought that would have been a good job because he might have stayed there for the whole war. His job would have been to meet the troops, get them on the boat, and assign them quarters. Instead they assigned him to the all African American 92nd Division at Camp Robinson.

At first Gene was disappointed in the assignment. He and a group of white officers went to the colonel and asked why they were sent to a "colored" division. "You boys are all from the South," the colonel responded, "and you know how to handle these people and can get along with them." If anyone had told him when he was growing up he was going to be in a "colored" outfit, Gene would have told them they were lying. He had no idea what to expect and approached the assignment full of apprehension.[9]

After his initial shock, Gene took the new post in stride. Unlike a host of other white officers, he did not try to secure a transfer. Originally, all the officers in the division were white. In the spring of 1943, General Edward (Ned) Almond, commanding general of the 92nd Division, received the order from the War Department that every thirty days, thirty Negro lieutenants or captains would arrive as replacements, and thirty white lieutenants or captains would be released. "The officer personnel went from roughly 700 white officers to roughly 400 white officers and 300 Negro officers of low rank, 1st and 2nd lieutenants . . . ," Almond reported. By the time Gene shipped out, there were only around two hundred to three hundred white officers left in the 92nd Division.[10]

Gene Johnston reported to Camp Robinson in the fall of 1942 and began training. General Almond assigned the lieutenants to the company area and put some young West Point lieutenants in charge. A soldier from Louisiana wound up knocking down one of the West Point lieutenants because he insulted him. The general was amused at the "West Point" initiation. The West Pointers ran them all night long, sometimes having them run fast with one shoe off. When one man tripped over a hydrant, almost breaking his leg, the midnight exercises stopped. Finally, they assigned Gene to the 3rd Battalion as an operations officer, an S-3 of the battalion.[11]

On October 15, 1942, the 92nd Division was officially activated. On their uniforms, the soldiers wore a black buffalo on an olive disk with a black border. This symbol of the 92nd Division, the Buffalo Division, derived its name from the African American soldiers who fought Indians on the frontier in the nineteenth century. Because not one congressional delegation would allow 15,000 armed black men to train in its state, the units of the 92nd were split up for their initial training: the 365th and 597th at Camp Atterbury, Indiana; the 598th and 370th at Camp Breckinridge in Kentucky; the 599th and 371st at Camp Robinson in Arkansas; and headquarters and service companies at Fort McClellan, Alabama. From November 1942 until April 1943, the units remained separated.

The other all-black infantry division, the 93rd Division, the Blue Helmets, was activated before the 92nd, on May 15, 1942, and trained at Fort Huachuca. Then they were deployed January 24, 1944, to the South Pacific for the duration of the war. The soldiers of the 93rd saw combat while serving in New Guinea, Northern Solomons (Bougainville), and Bismarck Archipelago (Admiralty Islands). They were assigned to security, engineering, and construction operations. The Blue Helmets returned to the United States on February 1, 1946.[12]

When the 93rd Division was in training at Fort Huachuca, Gene Johnston and

Spencer Moore attended OCS. Moore was one of sixty black soldiers in his class at Fort Benning. Forty-five of them graduated. Spencer finished OCS just two months before he turned twenty-one, and so he was called the "boy lieutenant." Born in New Jersey in 1922, Spencer joined the 372nd, a National Guard regiment. He had attended the Camden Police Identification Department to learn fingerprinting, and for that he was promoted to private first class. He made $36 a month; the other privates made $30 a month. When called up for federal service on March 10, 1941, nine months before Pearl Harbor, Spencer trained at Fort Dix, New Jersey.

After entering the army on March 29, 1941, in Washington, D.C., Charles Lancaster joined Spencer Moore and the other members of the 372nd at Fort Dix. He quickly rose in rank from private to corporal, and then to sergeant. Lancaster developed a love for military life while he was in the Washington High School Cadet Corps.

After their training in New Jersey, the all black 372nd was stationed in New York City. They were housed in Harlem at 124th Street and 7th Avenue, around the block from the Apollo Theater. The soldiers were given passes to shows, attended the United Service Organizations downtown, where Moore jitterbugged with Linda Darnell as well as dozens of other New York girls. Many of their National Guard officers were ROTC and were senior in grade. However, no black soldiers were allowed to command a white soldier.[13]

German spies had been caught off the coast of Long Island. Along with the members of their unit, Moore and Lancaster went to Manhattan to guard the city during a bitterly cold December. While on duty in New York, they helped to guard an airfield and the ship SS *Normandie* (Normandy). Shortly after the troops were taken off that detail, the ship burned.[14]

> Spencer Moore was aware of racial discrimination, but as he said: "I was a kid. I was into having a good time; I wasn't trying to be a hero. I was just following orders. They'd say, 'Go here,' and I went there. If they said, 'Come back,' then I would come back. I mean, I didn't know anybody inside the Army who was an activist against the Jim Crow situation. We just felt that was the American way. My leaders were my commanding officers, not the race leaders at the time. . . . We would all say 'V for Victory,' but I wasn't thinking about my civil rights at home. I was thinking about keeping from getting killed, and from my men getting killed. I was thinking about victory abroad for me."[15]

Both Spencer Moore and Charles Lancaster went to OCS, but then went to different training locations. Moore went to Camp Breckinridge with the 370th on December 5, 1942. Charles Lancaster went to Camp Robinson with the 371st after his graduation from OCS on November 26, 1942. Fellow Buffalo A. William (Bill) Perry reported to Fort McClellan, Alabama, another training center for the 92nd. When Bill was eighteen, he volunteered for the draft. He ended up in the army because in the navy a black recruit could only be a mess man, a position he did not want. With limited opportunities in the air corps, most black draftees were assigned to the army. Bill Perry went to Fort McClellan by train. When he woke up one morning on the way, he saw a bus parked at a crossroads with a sign that said Rome. He said to himself, "Hell, I'm in Italy!" But, it was just Rome, Georgia, a small Southern town on the Alabama–Georgia border. That was the first time he had been south of the Ohio River. When he found out that all three of the commanders of the 92nd Division were white officers from Virginia Military Institute—Ned Almond, John E. Wood, and William H. Colburn—Perry felt like someone had slapped him.

While at Fort McClellan, Perry visited Anniston, a nearby town, but he only stayed there an hour and never returned due to the racism he encountered. When he arrived in town, he saw a theater that had a special entrance marked "blacks, colored." All black patrons had to go up a fire escape on the side of the building to get to the balcony. The white female ticket takers made the black soldiers put the money on the counter, and then they would rake it in, to avoid letting the soldiers touch them. Bill decided to return to camp because it would only mean trouble for him if he stayed in the town.

Perry's unit left Fort McClellan by truck in April 1943 and went to pick up the 371st and artillery units at Camp Robinson, Arkansas. The 600th Field Artillery, which had the 155-millimeter howitzer, stopped at an old air base along the way in Jackson, Mississippi, where they encountered a heavy rain, so heavy it caused the big guns to sink into the mud. They had a difficult time winching them out. After the struggle, some of the men went up the road to a restaurant to eat. When they got there, an employee told them to go to the back door. Perry and the other men got upset, and after a bitter exchange and threatening gestures, they made their way back to Camp Robinson hungry. These incidents were commonplace. At times, the troops ignored them, but sometimes they retaliated. Perry's unit stayed at Camp Robinson for a few weeks and then took a train to Arizona.[16]

Like Bill Perry, William McCaffrey, a white officer, reported to Fort McClellan. Upon graduation from West Point, he was commissioned as a second lieutenant in the infantry. He served for three years in Panama and became an assistant G-3 (assistant chief of staff, operations, and plans). McCaffrey was returning to the United States when the war broke out, and his ship was diverted from New Orleans to Tampa, where he experienced a long delay. After his thirty days on leave, he should have gone to New York or New Orleans and sought passage to Panama. But he was given the alternative of going to an officers' replacement pool in Little Rock, Arkansas. The post commander there called him in shortly after his arrival; he said that he needed a new G-3 and if McCaffrey did not have a new assignment within thirty days, he wanted to have him at the training center.[17]

McCaffrey wired a friend at Army Field Forces in Fort Monroe. About two days later he got a wire: "Headquarters Commandant, 92nd Division, best I can do, regards." When McCaffrey told the center commander, a major general, about his assignment, the commander asked, "Any experience with black troops?" McCaffrey did not have any, but he was grateful to be leaving the training center. He would eventually become chief of staff of the 92nd Division under General Almond during 1944–45.[18] The black soldiers held McCaffrey in high esteem because he was not racist.

Albert Burke also trained at Fort McClellan. Born and raised in Ohio, he had never been in a segregated situation before. He had been the only black student in his high school class, and he had attended Wilberforce University for a year and then went to Ohio University in Athens, Ohio. In 1939, Albert Burke got drafted in the middle of the school year, but he was allowed to finish the semester.

Burke's commanding officer at regimental headquarters, Colonel Fry, supported him, and designated him his personal sergeant. Fry let the officers who came there for training know that Burke was in charge. After a year, Burke was transferred to the 92nd Division and assigned to the 371st in the division headquarters. When he arrived, they did not exactly know where to place him, because there was no open position for a sergeant major in any of the regiments or battalions. So he was given a two-week furlough. Shortly after he returned, they left for Italy.[19]

Joseph Stephenson trained at Fort Atterbury, Indiana, another base for the 92nd Division. After graduating from North Carolina Agricultural and Technical, Stephenson found that his opportunities were limited. He could work in the lumber mills or on the tobacco farms. After Pearl Harbor, the whole nation had changed overnight. Men rushed to enlist. The government was slow in drafting Stephenson, but in the meantime, no one would hire him because he was 1-A and high on the list. As a result, he went to the draft board and signed up on February 28, 1942. He had uncles who were in the service during World War I, but that was not his reason for joining. He enlisted because he wanted a job, and he was eligible and free to serve. At this time, it was uncertain whether the black troops would be sent into combat. After Stephenson enlisted, he stopped by to see the dean and president of his college, both of whom were very proud of him.[20] He began his training at Fort Bragg, North Carolina.[21]

Stephenson encountered significant racial prejudice while in the military, but in an ironic twist, the prejudice of white soldiers toward the black soldiers at OCS worked to Stephenson's advantage. He was one of only two black candidates in his class at OCS. Due to segregation, he and his black classmates were housed with the five other black candidates from the previous class. With only seven soldiers in a barrack that usually housed forty, they were able to study much better than those in the all-white barracks. When the five graduated, only two black soldiers remained in the barracks. Stephenson and his classmates made high nineties on all their exams. The white soldiers then demanded that they move into their barracks. They ended up where they were supposed to be in the first place and studied with the white soldiers, even tutoring some of them. From OCS, Stephenson went to Fort Atterbury in Indiana, and then he and his platoon went to join the other men of the 92nd Division at Fort Huachuca.[22]

As in World War I, African American soldiers continuously faced racist treatment when in and out of uniform. They had to contend with resistance to their serving in the military and in combat and with the false stereotype that they were ineffective warriors. These attitudes of some Americans stemmed from deep racism and from fears of black men with guns. They also faced attempts to discredit black soldiers' contributions in previous wars because of a misleading interpretation of a World War I event.[23]

A total of 404,348 black men served in the U.S. military during World War I. The black troops who fought were largely successful in completing their tasks. General Pershing referred to the 92nd Division as "one of the best of the American Expeditionary Force." In fact, the 369th was the first to land in France and to join French forces, remaining in combat 191 days longer than any other unit. It was also the first Allied unit to reach the Rhine River. The French awarded the unit the *Croix de Guerre* in recognition of its heroism. In addition, many of the soldiers received medals for bravery.[24]

Nevertheless, a single incident led to disastrous and long-lasting stereotyping of black combatants. On September 28, 1918, one company of the 368th infantry disintegrated and failed in its objective during the Meuse-Argonne offensive. After regrouping, they failed again. Although Newton D. Baker, the secretary of war, stated that there was no evidence justifying the negative assessment of black soldiers, these incidents provided the opportunity for racists in the United States to claim that black troops were unfit for combat and were cowards. As a result of this incident, the 368th was demobilized in early 1919, and until the end of the war, black soldiers served in noncombatant roles.[25]

Consequently, when the Second World War began, opposition to black soldiers in combat was still fierce. Resistance was so strong that many opponents argued against any black soldiers being in combat, even the college-educated, high-scoring Tuskegee Airmen. On the other side, the National Association for the Advancement of Colored People, Congress of Racial Equality, and other civil rights organizations argued just as strongly for black soldiers to be allowed to fight for their country.[26]

Because of the strong political pressure to permit African Americans to fight in the combat units and lingering doubts stemming from misrepresentations of their record in World War I, the official army training literature presented contradictory views regarding black soldiers. Armed Service Manual M5, an officer training manual designed for white officers (like Gene Johnston and William McCaffrey) commanding black troops, included a section on "Rumors and the Negro Soldier." The authors of this manual presented a sociological explanation for racial differences. They insisted that "scientific knowledge does not support the idea of the inherent superiority of any one race over another." Instead, so-called "'Negro traits' in civilian life, such as lack of initiative, mental laziness, lack of ambition, and irresponsibility, may be traced back to the limited opportunities afforded the Negro to obtain information and to see the relevance of his job to some goal which has importance to him."[27]

The manual also assured white officers that if they showed their men respect and kept the channels of communication open, they would engender trust. The manual went on to say that if an officer thought his men were inherently inferior to any other group of men, he did not deserve their trust and devotion and would never earn their respect. It argued that the fighting ability of soldiers was "a matter of leadership, training, and motivation" and was not determined by race. If officers expected their black soldiers to perform well, they would. If they considered them inferior and expected little from them, they would not be disappointed either.[28]

As a black officer, Joe Stephenson demonstrated the tremendous power of expectations as he trained his men at Fort Atterbury. Because he believed in his men, they believed in themselves and trusted his leadership. He had a light weapons platoon. They handled 60-millimeter mortars, two light machine guns, and 150-caliber bazookas. He made his men believe that they had been especially picked for his platoon because they were different. He told them their weapons were different and required smart people to handle them, and they believed him. They trained at Atterbury that whole winter. Stephenson was able to transfer out a few underperforming men in exchange for strong replacements and get some fine people in. He did not care about their Army General Classification Test scores. He knew that most of his company had low scores, and to his horror, he discovered that nearly 80 percent of all the black soldiers were in the categories four and five, which were the lowest categories. The white troops also had a large number of illiterates, but not such a high percentage. Black units could not hide their low scorers or pretend they did not exist. Stephenson tried to motivate all the men in his company, regardless of their scores. He did not talk to his men about patriotism. Rather he told them: "You've got to learn to shoot because if you don't, you will be killed." Consequently, his men always fired well and scored high on all the tests they were given, whether for the mortar or the machine gun.[29]

Most white officers did not adopt Joe Stephenson's style of leadership. They continued to believe in stereotypes. Many believed racial stereotypes because they equated intrinsic ability of African Americans and their contemporary achievements. They failed to acknowledge the radically unequal education within the country based on race and, thus, assumed that the black soldiers were inferior if they performed poorly on standardized tests.[30]

Some soldiers who were believed to be unintelligent were actually a lot smarter than the white officers thought. For example, Spencer Moore observed one soldier's acting skills as he pretended to be crazy: "Some of those guys from the South weren't that dumb, because I had one in my platoon who was supposedly crazy. The company commander was going to give him a Section 8. Everyone was in agreement. When he got on the truck to go to the train station, he waved [knowingly] like this."[31]

Highly educated African Americans encountered racism along with those who were less educated. When the distinguished historian John Hope Franklin went to enlist in the navy, the recruiter asked him what his skills were. He said he could do office work, research, and write, and that he had a PhD from Harvard University. The recruiter said, "You have everything you need except your color." Franklin was so angry that he left and said the United States did not deserve his participation in the war.[32]

Future U.S. Senator Edward W. Brooke served in the 366th and trained at Fort Benning; Fort Devens, Sturbridge, Massachusetts; and then Atterbury, Indiana, where Stephenson began his first assignment. When he reported for training he was "often shocked by the lack of education in black soldiers from the South. Many came from extreme poverty and had never received a chance to develop their native intelligence. They had known nothing but a savage inequity between the races; only when it came time to die for their country was there a hint of equality."[33]

Like Joe Stephenson and Edward W. Brooke, Jehu Hunter went to OCS. Out of twelve in his class, he was one of three black soldiers who passed the course. Half of the white soldiers failed. Hunter was a native Washingtonian. He had graduated in 1939 from Armstrong High School as the valedictorian, then went on to receive a BS in Zoology from Howard University in 1943. He was in ROTC, entered the army in 1943, and left immediately for Fort Benning. When he was in OCS, he chose not to leave the post until he had completed the OCS, because of his fear of white military police. He was initially in the Mortar Platoon of M Company, 365th Infantry. After he went to signal school at Fort Benning, he returned to the 365th, and he was assigned as the communications officer for the 3rd Battalion from August 1944 to October 10, 1945.[34]

Gene Johnston and his unit went through basic training at Camp Robinson, Arkansas. From the moment he began his trip to Arkansas, Charles Lancaster's experiences differed greatly from Gene Johnston's. He described his treatment when he reported to duty and boarded a train bound for Camp Robinson. When he got outside of Woodbridge, Virginia, trouble began: "I was told that I was in the wrong place. I was pressured to move but I refused and the MPs confirmed that I was in the right place. The racist conductor was furious. Pretty soon the train was separated from my car and I was left on the tracks in the unattached car. I had to get a Trailways bus out in the middle of nowhere near Memphis. When I got to Arizona I was dumped off. I called the post and the commanding officer says, 'nigger, get your black ass out here by 1730 hours or you will face a Court Martial for disobedience of a direct order.'" The commanding officer, Colonel Sterling A. Wood then slammed the phone down. When Lancaster finally arrived at the camp, he reported to headquarters. Colonel Wood kept him standing, holding the salute for ten minutes at attention before he spoke. Then he told him his policies and expectations and said that he "didn't give a damn about customs of the service or any other customs when it came to Niggers."[35]

Joseph Hairston also trained at Camp Robinson and encountered Colonel Sterling Wood. He never forgot Wood's blatant racism and hostility toward black troops. Hairston joined the army in October 1940, attended OCS, graduated as a second lieutenant, and was assigned to the 92nd Division. Members of the Hairston family had taken a train from Virginia to Connellsville, Pennsylvania, in the 1920s, when Joseph was an infant.[36] Hairston's family was extremely poor, and in 1932, when Joseph was only ten, his mother died. His stepfather died shortly afterward. His stepfather's sister, Dorcas, took in Joseph and his brother. He and his brother delivered laundry and built the largest newspaper route in town. Hairston's entrepreneurial talent was obvious even at this early age. Because his town was predominantly white, he and his brother attended the white schools, but they were denied entrance to a local diner and other establishments. They were also forbidden to date white girls. His cousin was almost beaten to death for walking with a white female. So, even before his entrance into the army, Hairston knew the dangers of racial violence.[37]

At Camp Robinson, the troops were settling in for the night after a twenty-five–mile hike when William S. N. Banks heard the order: "'All colored officers report to Colonel Wood's tent' echoed through the area and shortly thereafter a large number of officers meeting the stated qualifications assembled outside the colonel's tent headquarters. Colonel [Sterling] Wood was sitting on the ground his legs folded under him like an Indian chief. . . . He began, 'My name,' I want to make sure you get this, 'my name is Colonel Sterling A. Wood.' Pause. 'And I understand colored people. I had a plantation in Alabama.'" This reference to the days of slavery was emotionally charged because many of the Buffalo Soldiers were born around fifty years after emancipation. Therefore, some of their grandparents had been slaves.

Joseph Hairston's life was profoundly affected by another speech that Colonel Wood made. Wood was disappointed with the OCS officers, whom he saw as "ninety-day wonders," and insisted that they undergo three months of extra West Point–style training sessions. One Sunday, he called the white and black officers into the theater. After he dismissed the white officers, he told the black officers: "You people constitute ten percent of the population of this country, and I'm going to see to it you suffer ten percent of the casualties." Silence fell over the room. Hairston and the other officers were stunned. When Wood left, the chaplain, who was the highest ranking black officer, walked out on to the stage reciting 1 Corinthians 13. These words about love touched Hairston deeply, and he internalized their meaning, but he still held on to his anger and outrage toward Colonel Wood.[38]

Wood's attitudes were shared by many of the white officers. When white officers took their responsibilities seriously, they sometimes were ridiculed by their fellow officers. One who spoke of his plan for training a black unit was told, "No need for that. We're just here to baby-sit Eleanor Roosevelt's niggers."[39] The Roosevelts actually came to visit Camp Robinson. Gene Johnston had gone home for Christmas and was returning on the train through Arkansas and Georgia. He saw troops stationed at every railroad crossing. When he arrived late one night in Little Rock, he took a cab to the camp and learned that an important visitor was arriving the next day. The cab driver said he did not know who it was, but that it might be President Roosevelt.

The next morning, it started to rain heavily. Gene was leading calisthenics for thousands of men out in the field. They stood in the rain in their good uniforms. Pretty soon, an open sedan came wheeling onto the field. Sitting up in the back were President and Mrs. Roosevelt. Some people called the members of the 92nd Eleanor Roosevelt's "running rifles." She was influential in advancing the rights of African Americans and supporting their entrance into the military.[40]

The Roosevelts drove up to the stand where Gene had been leading the troops in calisthenics. Gene Johnston saluted him, and the president nodded. Some colonel told him to go on with the exercises. The president sat there for a while as Gene led the exercises. Finally, Roosevelt waved his hand and drove off. Nine thousand troops stood in the rain on review.[41]

From Arkansas, Johnston, Lancaster, Hairston, and the rest of the battalion boarded a train to Fort Huachuca, Arizona, where they would join the other units of the 92nd Division coming from Kentucky, Indiana, and Alabama. They were apprehensive about what lay ahead for black *and* white Buffalo Soldiers.

4

Training at Fort Huachuca

> The Buffalo Soldiers of World War II were in segregated units with white officers who did not want to be there. They were subject to discrimination at home. They served nobly and they served with courage. They were treated as second-class citizens. They are an example of service and courage that should inspire us now.
>
> Colin Powell

When Johnston, Lancaster, Moore, Perry, Hairston, Stephenson, Burke, McCaffrey, and all the other members of the 92nd Division arrived at Fort Huachuca in April and May 1943, they found themselves in a remote area. Fort Huachuca, a place with deep roots for black soldiers, is located in southeastern Arizona at the base of the Huachuca Mountains near Bisbee, seventy-three miles southeast of Tucson and fifteen miles from the border with Mexico. The fort was home to the 10th U.S. Cavalry Regiment, the Buffalo Soldiers of the nineteenth century who squared off with the Chiricahua Apache. World War I Buffalo Soldiers also trained at Fort Huachuca.

The commanding officer of the 92nd Division at Fort Huachuca, General Edward "Ned" Almond, had a melodic Southern accent, but behind the Southern charm was an unreconstructed racist. He was a disastrous choice as the leader of the all-black division. When General Almond spoke at the activation of the 92nd Division on October 15, 1942, he pointed to the symbol of the buffalo:

> If you visit our headquarters you will see the living symbol of this division, the Black Buffalo. *You* must put the same pulsating, powerful life into *our* giant, this battle unit which we now call the 92nd division.
>
> Courage to face the facts and to conquer the foe is of paramount importance. Before considering a few factors which influence our creation of an efficient, fighting division, we must state our training objective. This objective is to produce a battlefield unit; it is devoid of racial, political or economic considerations. We desire to win the fight against the enemy which we are to meet on the battlefield. He who injects controversial ideas in our midst brands himself a fifth columnist bent upon giving comfort to the

> enemy. There is no worse crime than to sow dissension, discord, and disloyalty in the midst of a military unit. I promise fairness to every officer and man in this division, and I promise promotion for merit alone.[1]

Almond pledged his best and assured them that they would measure up to the task. He asked for "their loyalty, energy, and determination to labor unceasingly," and closed by saying, "You must sweat and give your blood; there is no other road to victory."[2]

General Almond was born in Luray, Virginia, in 1892. He married Margaret Crook before he went off to fight in World War I. He served with the 4th Division in France from June 1918 into the occupation period. From 1919 through 1928, he taught military science at Marion Institute, Alabama, with a year off to attend the U.S. Army Infantry School at Fort Benning, Georgia, in 1924. He graduated from the Command and General Staff School, Fort Leavenworth, Kansas, in 1930. Almond had a tour of duty in the Philippines and then attended the Army War College in 1934. From 1934 to 1938, he was with the Intelligence Division of the General Staff. He also completed the course at the U.S. Navy War College in 1940. Almond was assigned as assistant division commander of the other all-black division, the 93rd Blue Helmets from April to September 1942. Then he became Commander of the re-activated 92nd Division on October 15, 1942. By that time, he had only had one month's experience as commander of a combat unit.[3]

Almond believed that his friend Lloyd Brown, the G-3 of Army Ground Forces to General George Marshall, recommended him for the post. Marshall probably assumed that General Hall, who commanded the 93rd and was from Mississippi; General William Spence, artilleryman, who was from North Carolina; and General Almond from Virginia, all Southern white commanding officers, understood Southern customs and "Negro capabilities." Lieutenant General William P. Ennis Jr. confirmed that General Almond held racist views. Ennis thought that the only reason the Virginia Military Institute men were chosen to lead the 92nd was that they presumably knew more about "handling Negroes than anybody else." But he could not imagine why, because Ned Almond "just despised the ground they walked on."[4]

General Almond sometimes staged dramatic presentations. Joseph Stephenson described what a splendid actor Almond was at these ceremonies. He could really put on a show. He recalled one incident that was unforgettable and even touching:

> The whole Division was lined up. A big stand was set up holding something covered with a cloth, and we couldn't see what it was. Almond got up

> to speak and he was very, very eloquent and very dramatic. So I always looked for him to do something unusual. He loved the Infantry but he could never pronounce that word Infantry. "Infanry. Infanry," he said. The artillery fired over our heads and all around and hit on that mountain over there. And then when that was over he said, "The artillery can fire." And then the airplanes flew over. And he said, "Airplanes can fly over. They can strafe and they can bomb. But that hill, but that hill will never be taken."
>
> As he said that the scarf slowly came off, and there was a great big statue of an infantryman standing there with a rifle. He never looked around at it. He said, "But that hill will never be taken until the Inframan has put his boots on that hill."

Stephenson asked Colonel (later General) McCaffrey, the person who planned the occasion, why General Almond did not turn around. He said, "He knew that that thing had better be coming off at that moment!"[5] Almond was also dramatic in his approach to training at Fort Huachuca. The general went out with company commanders in their jeeps and drove at top speed in a line over rough terrain. He would pull up on a peak, stop, give the officers his critique, and then take off again with the dust flying. Sometimes he drove around with them for hours.[6]

General Almond was greatly impressed by Harold Montgomery. Montgomery was one of only seven African Americans who commanded black combat companies in the three battalions of the 370th. Montgomery enlisted in the army because he knew he was going to be drafted. When he entered the military, he fully realized that the army was segregated and that the leaders of the army were Southerners. He was determined to train the 197 men in his company and to save as many of them as possible. The army treated him well, and he often thought that the army was the best thing that ever happened to him.[7]

Montgomery refrained from making negative comments concerning senior officers in the army, but he fought racism and segregation throughout his career. He was grateful that the army gave him an education and an opportunity. He was recognized for his gifts and promoted on the spot from second lieutenant to first. When General Almond promoted him, he called him to his office. About nine days later, he was selected to go to staff officer's school. He had not been commissioned for more than nine months at that time. So the troops went on maneuvers, and he did not see his old company again. When he reported to headquarters of the division in January 1944, the sergeant major called him aside and said, "Look, Montgomery, don't tell anybody, but they are going to make you a company commander. You are going to take over Company H." Company H in the 370th was a heavy weapons company.[8]

6. Alta Johnston, ca. 1944. Photograph courtesy of Carolyn Johnston.

Gene Johnston's Company M had some really good, conscientious soldiers. Some of the men went to religious services on Wednesday night; others went every night, and they sang. They also listened to the Heavenly Gospel Singers, composed of members of the company. They were well-known and previously had a radio show in Arkansas. The group even composed a song about Gene, which they recorded. But he never heard the song. Whenever one man was absent, someone else could step in and sing. They had a lot of fun. Unlike many of the white officers, Gene got along well with his troops, and they treated each other with mutual respect. At first, Gene was on trial, but he worked hard to prove his dedication to the men, his fairness, and military carriage.[9]

The 92nd Division was commanded by a diverse group of people. Ned Almond, Joseph Stephenson, Harold Montgomery, and Gene Johnston revealed a wide variety of racial views. Almond held the most racist views of the four and believed that the black officers were incapable of leadership. Stephenson and Montgomery were highly educated black officers who had confidence in their men and held high expectations for their performance. Gene Johnston differed from many of the other white officers in his even-handed treatment of men in his unit. Still, whether he was out in the field training or listening to the Heavenly Gospel Singers, Gene could not stop thinking about a beautiful woman he had met in Tennessee. He was determined to marry her.

5

Marriage and Bisbee

When Gene Johnston met Alta Ross at the Eureka Baptist Church in Cleveland, Tennessee, it was love at first sight, for him at least. They only had three dates before they got married. When he went to see her at the University of Tennessee at Knoxville, she already had a date. She told him to meet her later, and he took her and her friends for a ride in his Ford Sport Roadster. When he moved to Fort Huachuca, he wrote frequently to Alta. She was a college girl, and he was a soldier; he seemed to have a wild, almost dangerous streak, coupled with a shyness that Alta found charismatic.

In the fall of 1943, Gene was home on leave and went to Cleveland to see Alta. He was walking downtown near the courthouse and ran into her sister Mildred, who told him that Alta was at Bradley High School where she taught, and would not get off until around three o'clock. He walked to the school, where one of the students took him to her classroom. Alta was shocked to see him smiling broadly at the door. That evening they went out to her house in the country and sat up all night talking. He must have been persuasive because the next day, November 26, 1943, they went to Rossville, Georgia, to get married.

Judge Crowe had his office right on the state line; half in Georgia and half in Tennessee. There was a line of people when Gene and Alta arrived, so they waited out in the main office. The judge was sitting at his desk, and as fast as one couple came through the swinging gates into his office, he would marry them. Alta, who was twenty-four at the time, did not want to reveal her age. The clerk kept asking how old she was, and Gene finally made up a number. After a short time, they called them in to see the judge, who quickly married them. Gene gave the clerk two dollars and they were on their way.[1]

The newly married couple went to Chattanooga, but had no time for a honeymoon because about thirty minutes later, Gene had to board a bus for Fort Huachuca. They sat at a restaurant at the bus depot on South Market Street in Chattanooga until he had to leave. The civil ceremony was barely over on that beautiful fall day in 1943 when Gene left his new bride; they both knew he would soon be going to war.

Shortly afterward, Alta quit her teaching job, packed a small suitcase, and boarded a bus to see him in the barren West. When she got off the bus, she began her search for a place to live. Her boldness and independence always served her well. Some women who worked at a restaurant told her about a place she could rent. Gene had only been back about a week when Alta called him around five o'clock one day. He said, "Where are you?" She told him she was just down the road in Bisbee, the little mining town about twenty-five miles from the fort. Gene said he would come as soon as he could; he caught a ride with one of the men who went back and forth daily from the fort to Bisbee. By that time, Alta had already moved into a place on the side of the mountain where they would live for three or four months.

Bisbee is down in a canyon with a creek running in the middle. The Copper Queen Hotel looked the same as when miners of the previous century stepped up to its bar. Six or seven thousand miners worked in the copper mines, with shifts going down all the time. From town, one could drive to the top of the hills on the level of the desert and see almost to the camp thirty-nine miles away (before the tunnel was built). Gene went to Bisbee each night, but had to be back on the post at Huachuca by five o'clock in the morning. Because he did not have a car, he had to catch a ride with someone, or on the side of a tanker truck, freezing from the cold, with black smoke billowing up all around him. If he did not make it to reveille, he would automatically be put on restriction and not allowed to go home.[2] At night from Bisbee, you could see the shimmer of lights from the fort.

III THE FIGHT TO FIGHT

6

Buffalo Soldiers in the Jim Crow Army

Racial tensions ran high at Fort Huachuca, and creating a sense of community proved to be difficult. The post mirrored the larger American society and had racially segregated facilities. White and black soldiers at Fort Huachuca rarely had any contact when off duty. There were two officers' clubs, the Lakeside Officers' Club for whites and the Mountain View Club for blacks. Gene Johnston would go to both on occasion. He sometimes regaled the other officers, like Richard Salmon, Ray Zobel, and Curtis Ivey, with tall tales, some risqué, but always hilarious. However, because segregation extended to billeting practices and seating at meals, bonding of the troops with their white officers was highly unlikely.[1]

The policy of segregation extended to the contingent of black members of the Women's Auxiliary Army Corps (WAAC) assigned to Fort Huachuca. Madine Davis Lane went to Fort Huachuca as a WAAC nurse. Her first job had been on Staten Island, New York, in a tuberculosis hospital. Then she applied to the military and was commissioned at Governor's Island, New York. She and three other women went first to Jersey City, New Jersey, and from there by train to Fort Huachuca, Arizona. On the trip, they nervously thought about what lay at the far end of those railroad tracks. Lane's first military assignment at Fort Huachuca involved basic training for nurses and military communication. They learned the insignia, map reading, proper flag protocols, and whom to salute, as well as survival training.[2]

Lane had a challenging time at Fort Huachuca, but she also had a tremendous amount of fun. She told her friends that with over 15,000 men and so few women, "things were hot and lively every night." She played tennis in the mornings or went horseback riding. When off duty, she played tennis and went to the club, then danced from nine at night to two in the morning. The nurses stayed in the newer compound. Lane helped the hospital staff cope with the illnesses that ran through the fort, including an epidemic of meningitis. During that time, six soldiers died in a twenty-four–hour period. They also had an outbreak of a kind of tuberculosis, which they finally found out was silicosis, most likely caused by irritation from the fierce dust storms there.[3]

In one segregated sector, the medical sector, African American doctors were in charge. The hospital and staff at Fort Huachuca were unusual. Lieutenant Colonel Midian O. Bousfield, a black doctor, was the head of the hospital. He had been head of Provident Hospital in Chicago, an outstanding, historically black institution. Most of the residents at Huachuca had come with him, so a number of the doctors were people that he had worked with previously. They were all black doctors who were commissioned when they came into the military as colonels, majors, captains, and first lieutenants, depending on their years of experience.[4]

The hospital at Fort Huachuca was divided into white and black sections. Not surprisingly, the white side of the hospital, with 222 beds, received better treatment than the black side, with 944 beds. Lieutenant Colonel M. O. Bousfield reported regularly on problems at the fort to Truman Gibson, civilian aide to the secretary of war. Bousfield told him about an incident when a black chaplain, Chaplain Louis J. Beasley, and his wife were insulted when they went to a post restaurant. Previously, they had eaten at the same restaurant and sat with white officers without incident, but this time, a white colonel at another table told them to move. Bousfield also reported that General Almond's wife had purportedly called a telephone operator with the WAAC "a nigger" and said that she thought separate shopping days should be set aside for the races at the post exchange.[5]

The 92nd Division went through nineteen months of training instead of the usual ten to twelve months because many of the men of the division were illiterate or had not received the benefit of a good education in the separate and unequal U.S. school systems. General Almond said that he would do everything he could to see that everyone went overseas and into a combat area, but at one point it looked as though only a portion of the 92nd would go.[6] Almond believed that while there might be a few exceptions, certain characteristics such as undependability and laziness were typical of *all* African Americans. Although he thought that they should be employed in the defense of the nation, he thought that it would be foolish to expect them to exercise characteristics that were "abnormal to their race."[7] Albert Burke encountered this racist mentality when he was at Fort Huachuca. An officer called him "boy." Burke did not answer him. He said, "Don't you know I am talking to you." Finally, Burke said, "Look at the stripes up my arm. Does that look like a boy? You recognize my rank and I'll recognize yours."[8]

Despite Almond's racist assumptions, the beginning of his tenure with the 92nd seemed auspicious when the units of the division were still at four different locations. General Benjamin Davis Sr., the first black general in the American Army, visited Fort McClellan, Alabama, in February 1943. On February 5,

7. Major General Edward M. Almond, 92nd Infantry Division publication, Fort Huachuca, Arizona, 1942. Courtesy of Eugene E. Johnston.

8. 92nd Infantry Division publication, Fort Huachuca, Arizona, 1942. Courtesy of Eugene E. Johnston.

1943, Davis wrote a highly laudatory report. He said that the morale on the post was exceedingly high, the recreation facilities good, and the chaplain's work excellent. He pointed to the troops' great interest in group singing, and the fine division newspaper.

Since activation, fourteen "colored" officers had been promoted, with ten promotions pending. Davis even praised Almond, whom he said was "most active and efficient," and that Almond "has shown a special aptitude for a command composed of colored and white officers and colored enlisted personnel." Overall, he thought that "the 92nd Division at Fort McClellan was being administered and trained in a superior manner." The only area that he cited for improvement was that more guest house facilities for "colored troops" needed to be provided.[9]

When General Davis visited the 371st and 599th at Camp Robinson, Arkansas, he did not find its racial relations as positive as those at Fort McClellan. He reported that the "morale, though very satisfactory, does not appear as high as that of other units of the 92nd Division, which were recently inspected." When Davis visited Camp Atterbury, the commanding officer ordered the mess hall and other sections integrated while Davis was inspecting. As soon as he left, segregation was reestablished. Evidently other camps did not prepare for Davis's visit "so thoroughly."[10] Morale at the four training sites suffered from the widespread belief that the two black divisions were not going to be committed to combat.

As racial relations deteriorated at Fort Huachuca, General Davis and Truman Gibson came to investigate the complaints about discrimination and low morale among the black troops. Even Eleanor Roosevelt became involved. Almond reported an incident when a soldier who had been confined to quarters was found out of his quarters by a white senior officer. The black soldier told him, "I'm not out of quarters, you sonofabitch. Now hit me." Almond had him sent to the guard house. This triggered Davis's visit. General Almond denied the presence of any serious racial tension.[11]

All of the black officers gathered at the field house to hear General Davis. Some of the officers wore red handkerchiefs, and one of them addressed the general as he was on the way to the podium, saying, "General Davis, as one handkerchief head to another, we greet you." Naturally, the military police immediately grabbed him. In his speech, Davis emphasized his own struggle to succeed and ended by saying, "You're in this Army. You do what you're told. Never mind the background or the feelings that these white officers have for you. You toe the line." He added, "I just want to tell you that you're my color but you're not my kind." General Davis noted that the morale of the 92nd was low, but in his final report he wrote that there were no complaints or reports of racial discrimination.[12]

One of the issues under investigation was Almond's allegedly using the expression *nigger* in remarks before a school of the division's cooks and bakers. After interviewing several men, Davis and Gibson could not get any of them to state that the general had used the epithet *nigger.* No white officers were present during these interviews. General Almond used the Southern pronunciation of *Negro,* which sounds like *Negra.* Therefore, they urged him to use the term *colored,* which could not under any circumstances be confused with *nigger.*[13]

Officers at the highest levels in the army were concerned about the race riots and disaffection among black troops. George C. Marshall wrote a memorandum to the "Commanding Generals, Army Air Forces, Army Ground Forces, and Army Service Forces" about the serious nature of the racial violence throughout the country affecting "negro" soldiers. He pointed to riots of a racial nature at Camp Van Dorn, Mississippi; Camp Stewart, Georgia; March Field, California; Fort Bliss, Texas; Camp Breckinridge, Kentucky; and San Luis Obispo, California. He stated that all of the reported disturbances followed a pattern: "Unrest and disaffection begin with real or fancied incidents of discrimination and segregation. No positive action is taken to overcome the causes of unrest. Gossip or rumor of a nature designed to excite the men circulates among the units and a minor incident brings on a general outbreak." Commanding officers sometimes did not realize the seriousness of the problem and their responsibility regarding the matters. He urged uncompromising discipline for black and white soldiers.[14]

One commanding officer who did realize the seriousness of the problems regarding racial discrimination was Edwin N. Hardy, the post commander at Huachuca. Hardy was around sixty-five and could be seen riding a majestic white horse. He believed a special effort was necessary for administering and commanding African American troops. He tried to implement the principles of fairness, tolerance, good manners, humility, and self-sacrifice, especially in regard to them.[15]

Hardy was aware of widespread disaffection within the 92nd Division. He believed that the black officers and enlisted men of the division had lost confidence in their white officers. White and black junior officers bore responsibility for poor morale on the post. White officers sometimes displayed improper racial attitudes, and black officers generally failed to cooperate with their white counterparts. Hardy thought it might help to transfer any white officer who felt he could not associate closely with black soldiers. As General Davis had advised Almond, Hardy counseled white officers from the South to refrain from using the term *Negro,* which was prone to mispronunciation and interpretation as a racial epithet. Throughout the training period of the 92nd, Hardy tried to counsel Almond to be more sensitive to racial dynamics.[16]

In the summer of 1943, Colonel Hardy had a "heart-to-heart talk" with Almond, telling him that the troops resented the fact that he had sent so many black officers to the remedial proficiency school. Hardy did not share Almond's racist views and tried to promote more interaction between black and white officers. He sponsored an art exhibition in the black officers' club, a barbecue, and a reception, all intended to "draw white and colored officers closer together." At the barbecue, he issued instructions to white and black officers that they were to mix and not to bunch up in separate groups. Sadly, nothing significantly changed from these attempts to engender camaraderie across the races.[17]

A letter from an anonymous "noncom in the 92nd Division" sent to Mr. C. A. Scott, general manager of the *Atlanta Daily World,* on November 23, 1943, concerned the "appalling conditions in the division":

> General Almond is rotten. Possibly the news never reached you but there are several rumors that he has been fired at by soldiers who despise him. Whenever he is introduced, there is the usual, "Boo." When General Davis inspects the P.T.U [physical training uniform], our cripples are hidden. These are men who are walked "to death" and are physically unfit to carry on. They are really sapping the life out of the fellows. The morale is at as low an ebb as in a whore-house. Nobody gives a d—— about what happens. Unless something is done there will be an internal revolution. They are afraid for us to have our rifles after we leave the field. They search daily for ammunition. I swear to God it is pathetic.[18]

Vernon J. Baker, who won the Medal of Honor for his courageous actions in the Italian campaign with the 92nd Division, described the white Southerners like Almond in charge of all-black units: "These white heirs of the plantation era commanded black men whom they were raised to disdain and distrust. At the same time, blacks who had been persecuted, whipped, and spit upon as soldiers had to defend these commanders and their culture to the death. An unpalatable, unworkable mandate."[19] Challenging Jim Crow had serious consequences. Colonel Reuben L. Horner III, one of the most decorated officers of the 92nd Division in World War II, agreed with Baker that Almond was a liability as a commanding officer. Horner said that Almond was "egotistical, bigoted, and racist," and that he "considered himself lord god almighty and never lost a chance to degrade Negro officers in command positions."[20]

Apparently, General Almond did not acknowledge the extent of discontent among his troops. Reuben Horner found that the 92nd Division was the most racist outfit he ever encountered. Horner's father was in the original Buffalo Soldier unit. On one occasion, Reuben sat with the other company officers in the 3rd Battalion at Fort Huachuca. Not all the white officers had shown up. The battalion executive officer, who was white, came over to him and said, "Boy, run up and tell the Captain that we're waiting on him and his officer and to get over here immediately!" Horner looked around and said, "Are you addressing me?" He said, "Yes I am. Get up there!" He told the major that he was commissioned as a second lieutenant in the U.S. Army, and to his knowledge that had not changed. Thus, he should be addressed as lieutenant, not boy. They punished him by assigning him to be a battalion trash officer. He had to check all the garbage bags to see if any GI issue or equipment had been thrown away. Shortly thereafter, someone put an artillery shell into the trash and blew out the incinerator. Naturally, they suspected Horner. They put him on duty checking uniforms at the theater to see if the soldiers' military blouses were buttoned and ties were on properly.[21]

After training in Alabama, at first, A. William (Bill) Perry found Fort Huachuca beautiful, with all the red-roofed buildings and purple mountains. However, dissension soon arose between the officers and enlisted men. If a soldier asked too many questions, he got busted and transferred rather than court-martialed. Bill Perry learned this the hard way. He got into trouble at Fort Huachuca because he had a difficult time adjusting to the segregated post. His attitude deteriorated, and he started laughing at some people. He was not exactly defiant, but insubordinate enough to get him transferred.[22]

Eventually Perry made the adjustment to calling people "sir." Bill went to K Company in the 370th and reported to Captain Elmer F. Reedy, nicknamed "Iron Jaw" Reedy. Because Perry was a high school graduate, they soon sent him over to work with the supply sergeant, who was responsible for the weapons. At the end of each day, all the weapons and ammunition had to be counted and stored. Shortly after Perry went to K Company, there was a violent incident. One night as the men were going to sleep, someone stabbed Robert Randolph, the platoon sergeant of the Second Platoon in K Company, in the back of the head with a bayonet. The perpetrator jumped from the second floor and escaped. Luckily, Randolph recovered. The attacker was not identified. Randolph was liked by generally everyone, so it was a surprise that someone had attacked him. Later in Italy, the attacker evidently confessed to the deed in the middle of combat.[23]

While at Fort Huachuca, the soldiers spent a lot of time training in the field. After one of the maneuvers, Bill Perry and the other ten thousand men stopped and prepared for General Almond's inspection. They polished up everything and laid their gear out on field blankets in the proper fashion. Sometimes, the soldiers waited for four or five hours in the sun and then General Almond would fly by in his little plane, look down, and blow sand and debris in their faces; that was his kind of inspection. On other occasions, the general would walk the line. He would often say to one of the men: "Where are you from, son?" Sometimes he called him "soldier." The man would say something like, "Birmingham, Alabama, sir." Then the General would say, "Oh, do you know Mr. So-and-so down there?" The soldier would reply, "Yes, sir; yes, sir," because he knew that Almond liked that. Because Almond was not keen about Yankees, he did not bother to ask a soldier where he was from if he did not have a Southern accent.[24]

Almond made an exception for the Yankee William (Bill) McCaffrey, who became the G-3 of the 92nd. McCaffrey lacked any racial prejudice and was straightforward with General Almond from the start. One time at Fort Huachuca when Almond did not allow sufficient time to disseminate the marching orders for the units, the troops ended up spread over a good part of Arizona. He blamed this on Staten Ralls, so Almond fired him and then hired McCaffrey as the G-3 and First Lieutenant Edward L. Rowny as his assistant. Soon after McCaffrey began in his new position, he received a call to report to General Almond's office. He arrived to find two red-faced regimental commanders standing in front of his desk. General Almond said to him, "Bill, you gave this live firing zone to both the 370th and 371st Infantry and they almost shot each other up. What happened?" McCaffrey said, "I don't know." After checking, he told Almond, "Well, the 370th is the one I gave it to. I don't know what the 371st was doing there."[25]

Almond said, "I told the 371st they could use it." McCaffrey then said, "Well, if you're going to be the G-3 you don't need me. I'd like to go to one of the Regiments." After Almond excused the colonels, he said, "You shouldn't talk to me that way. I am the Division Commander." McCaffrey said, "You can't be Division Commander and G-3; it won't work. If you're going to be G-3, you don't need me." Almond started to laugh and said, "Okay, you're G-3." After that, McCaffrey told him exactly what he thought. They sometimes had fiery exchanges, but Almond liked him immensely and trusted him.[26]

Along with General Almond's shortcomings, one had to acknowledge that he was seemingly fearless. He was the first to take a jeep over an impossibly steep ridge and the first to jump in a foxhole and let a tank run over his position. Once, he was the lead man in a ten-mile hike along the skyline of the Huachuca Mountains. He meant it when he said, "Follow me!" Almond had his senior officers go through the obstacle course. The officers crawled on the ground under live machine-gun fire, and with nitro-starch bombs bursting around them, they struggled under seven-strand barbed wire. The dirty, sweating senior officers finished the course to the cheers of their admiring soldiers.[27]

By the summer of 1943, Fort Huachuca was experiencing considerable unrest. In one instance, a white captain had been attacked and severely beaten. Widespread anger and disaffection existed among the African American enlisted men. Despite many incidents reflecting racial tensions on the base at Fort Huachuca, General Almond denied that there were any serious problems.[28]

Almond tried to cover it up when the 371st instituted a segregated officers' mess. The black officers walked out in a body and arranged to take their meals in the Negro officers' club. Almond denied that his policy was to segregate the officers' mess for "colored officers by designating certain tables." He claimed that the incident occurred in violation of his stated policy. After a group of officers left the mess in protest, the commanding officer of the regiment called all the officers together and said, "all officers (white and colored) were urged to return to their regimental mess, which they did within two days"(the time set for the reopening of the mess on June 9, 1943).[29]

Almond claimed that no resentment lingered. The white officers of the division blamed the post command, and particularly the Negro officers in Station Hospital, as well as the inefficiency and poor performance of the Negro officers for the poor racial relations. The Negro officers resented their inability to obtain promotions and blamed the bad racial attitudes of the white officers of the division. Almond denied any unfair treatment in the promotion system and claimed that Negro officers were fairly promoted. He acknowledged that the towns of Tucson and Bisbee were off limits to the black soldiers of the 92nd and all troops at Fort Huachuca. Previously, there had been racial disturbances in those cities, and in order to avoid any future incidents, the policy remained in place.[30]

One incident revealed the depth of the turmoil and near crisis level of race relations at Fort Huachuca. Truman Gibson and General Davis accompanied General Almond to the dedication of a new baseball field and the game that followed. When Almond started to address the ten thousand soldiers, mostly black enlisted men, in attendance, they greeted him with disorder, boos, and catcalls. Truman Gibson could not resist saying, "General, such popularity must be deserved." Almond did not say a word and waited for the roar to die down. He was shocked by the incident.[31]

A dramatic change and decline in morale occurred when the 92nd settled into Fort Huachuca. Almond did nothing to promote racial understanding between whites and African Americans. Some of the black officers and men believed that

Almond tended to focus on "mechanical perfection in the execution of training missions, overlooking the human element." Davis found that Almond misinterpreted smart execution of military exercises as indicative of high morale. While the men might seem to have a calm demeanor, resentment over their unfair treatment seethed beneath the surface in the black soldiers. This explained the explosion of violence on occasion when they confronted racism.[32]

To improve morale, numerous recreational facilities and activities were available at Fort Huachuca. Soldiers could attend one of four motion picture theaters, and see such films as *Song of Nevada* with Roy Rogers and Dale Evans, *Bathing Beauty* with Red Skelton and Esther Williams, *Double Indemnity* with Barbara Stanwyck, *Battle for New Britain, Goodnight Sweetheart, Johnny Doesn't Live Here Anymore, and Mark of Dimitrios.* They could play sports like baseball and football, participate in religious services, frequent the territory occupied by the WAACs if invited, and attend talent shows and other entertainment provided by visiting celebrities.[33]

A song, the "Battle Hymn of the Buffalo Division," was intended to inspire the soldiers:

I
We're the Buffalo Division
By the government's decree
We offer up our lives today
For truth and liberty
And to our God and country
II
Our parents, wives and sweethearts
Live in cities far away;
And in the hands of God we know
They will forever stay.
We pledge them peace and victory;
For these to God we pray;
The 92nd rolls along.[34]

The newspaper, the *Buffalo,* was published weekly by the Special Services Office and Public Relations while the troops were in training. Its purpose was to create a sense of community; inculcate values of discipline, patriotism, and morality; inform soldiers about the progress of the war and activities on the base; and recognize individual achievements. Virtually every issue of the *Buffalo* featured a visit by a prominent black celebrity, such as Joe Louis, the famous boxer. Louis was pictured with the division's mascot, a live buffalo named Buffalo Bill. The paper quoted Louis as saying, "If all the 92nd is as tough as the Buffalo, they'll be a real Division."

Buffalo Bill was intended to raise the morale of the troops, but he also managed to cause disruption. Buffalo Bill evidently relieved himself at the most inappropriate times and in the most inappropriate places, including the middle of the road in any parade he was in. If the wind was right, Buffalo Bill's aroma, soldiers remembered, was strong enough to fell an entire platoon. In May 1943, Buffalo Bill was there to greet them when the entire division assembled. Once, when he broke away from Sergeant Valentine, his handler, the animal wandered back and forth over the parade ground until they finally corralled him. The whole division broke into uncontrollable laughter, including General Almond and the other dignitaries on the reviewing stand.[35]

Hattie McDaniel, who won an Academy Award for her performance in *Gone with the Wind,* visited the fort. Lena Horne was "the sweetheart of the 92nd Infantry Division." A front page picture of Horne appeared in the *Buffalo,* with the caption: "Lovely, luscious Lena Horne leaves us lyrical. . . . She came, she saw, she conquered and gave us something MORE to fight for." Lena Horne's uncle was Sergeant John B. Horne, who was at Fort Huachuca. Eddie Anderson, "Rochester" of Jack Benny fame, also came to the fort for a two-day visit and put on shows for the troops. Louis Armstrong came to perform for the troops and played to a wildly enthusiastic audience. Eventually, they cleared the benches to make room for dancing.[36]

Regardless of the extensive recreational opportunities and numerous visits by famous black entertainers, racial tensions persisted at Fort Huachuca, and low morale remained a problem. Some senior white leadership including General Almond viewed black soldiers as second-class citizens primarily fit for menial labor. This tended to create a climate of distrust and undermine cohesion within the unit.[37]

African American soldiers faced violence against them throughout the war at home, as well as abroad. In July 1943, police in Beaumont, Texas, shot Private Charles Reid in the back. A similar incident occurred in El Paso when a policeman killed Private Willie Jullis.[38] The stage had been set across the South for violent confrontations. Often African Americans faced courts-martial, beatings, and murder.[39] In April 1941, a black soldier with his arms and legs bound was hanged in Georgia in a wooded area of Fort Benning. Racial violence erupted in Tampa, Florida; Fayetteville, North Carolina; and Gurdon, Arkansas.[40] Sergeant Lester

Duane Simons, a member of an all-black 94th Engineers unit, said that the Tennessee state police beat one of the soldiers "unmercifully" at the maneuvers near Murfreesboro, Tennessee. Simons added that even the white officers were also discriminated against and not permitted to stay in the downtown hotels.[41]

When Joseph Hairston first enlisted in the army and was assigned to the 150th Field Artillery Regiment Medical Detachment near Alexandria, Louisiana, he inadvertently ended up right in the middle of a riot:

> I was at the corner when the white police, civilian police, came down the street to this mob of people. As they got to the corner I just happened to be standing there. A white policeman pushed me in the chest and he said, "Get out of my way, nigger." A moment later he opened fire, point blank into the crowd. Well, when I heard the gunfire I left and went several blocks away into a movie. When I came out of the movie that night all the blacks were cleared out of town and I was immediately sent back to Camp Livingston. We were restricted to the post for 30 days before we could go to town. General Davis investigated that, but you'll find very little in the archives as to what really happened. Nobody really knows how many people died. But I saw the point blank firing into that crowd. They [white policemen] were shoulder to shoulder across the street marching abreast of each other and shooting point blank into that crowd.[42]

Jim Williams experienced hostility and racism on the home front on his way back to OCS on a furlough when his train stopped in Richmond, Virginia. He ran up to the station to go to the restroom. Williams recalled:

> I'm standing at the urinal relieving myself and I heard this, "Hey, boy. We've got a place for you over there." And I ignored it. I didn't know who he was talking to.
>
> He said, "I'm talking to you, nigger." Boy, every ounce of blood just drained out of my body. So he started to turn like he was gonna come to me, and I didn't turn. But I figured if he's coming over I'm gonna stick his head right in the urinal. Right then another man's voice said to me, "Sergeant, get over here." He said, "I said get over here." When I turned his way I noticed he was a major. He asked me, "What's your name?" and I told him, and he said, "Where's your outfit?" I told him that too. And he said, "I see you have the OCS patch on." And I said, "Yes, sir, that's where I'm going now." He said, "Now are you gonna let an incident like this spoil your

> chances for becoming an officer?" I said, "No, sir." He said, "Well, you get back on your train and go on now. And good luck." And as I went I noticed he had been drying his hands and he had torn the paper towel to shreds and the vein in his head was standing out. And that guy must have noticed how angry the major was because he walked out quickly. He was mad, but I think that guy knew if he said one more thing that major would have killed him in there. He was that mad, that angry. And I never forgot that he said, "You're gonna face more incidents like this and you're supposed to know how to handle them."[43]

Violence against black soldiers in uniform persisted throughout the war. Daily incidents and fights occurred on public transportation. African Americans from the North sometimes refused to honor Southern racial practices of segregation and sometimes white Southerners who had migrated to the North objected to close contact with blacks on urban buses and trains. Verbal exchanges might escalate into violence or even riots. While white and black soldiers were instructed to abide by the local practices regarding racial segregation, conflict was frequent.[44]

Corporal Rupert Trimmingham wrote to *Yank,* the weekly army paper, describing his trip from Camp Claiborne, Louisiana, to the hospital at Fort Huachuca. He was outraged that German prisoners of war were treated with more respect than he and the other African American soldiers:

> Dear *Yank:*
>
> Here is a question that each Negro soldier is asking. What is the Negro soldier fighting for? On whose team are we playing? Myself and eight other soldiers were on our way from Camp Claiborne, La., to the hospital here at Fort Huachuca. We had to lay over until the next day for our train. On the next day we could not purchase a cup of coffee at any of the lunchrooms around there. As you know, Old Man Jim Crow rules. The only place where we could be served was at the lunchroom at the railroad station but, of course, we had to go into the kitchen. But, that's not all; 11:30 a.m. about two dozen German prisoners of war, with two American guards, came to the station. They entered the lunchroom, sat at the tables, had their meals served, talked, smoked, in fact had quite a swell time. I stood on the outside looking on, and I could not help but ask myself these questions: Are these men sworn enemies of this country? Are they not taught to hate and destroy . . . all democratic governments? Are we not American soldiers, sworn to fight for and die if need be for this

> our country? Then why are they treated better than we are? Why are we pushed around like cattle? If we are fighting for the same thing, if we are to die for our country, then why does the Government allow such things to go on? Some of the boys are saying that you will not print this letter. I am saying that you will.[45]

Training for the Buffalo Soldiers at Fort Huachuca reflected the racial tensions in the broader society. Before shipping out for overseas, the 92nd Division went on maneuvers in Louisiana, where they encountered an unforgiving landscape and the unforgiving racism of the Deep South.

7

Maneuvers in Louisiana

The maneuvers in Louisiana involved fives phases: division exercises, river crossings, advance to combat, defense on a wide front, and meeting engagements. The area stretched sixty miles long and forty miles wide. This realistic training took place from February 8 to April 3, 1944.[1] While on maneuvers in Louisiana, Gene Johnston's battalion commander was Colonel Arthur Walker, whom he greatly admired. Walker was like a father to him; he was a reserve officer who had taught horticulture at the University of Arizona and lived in Phoenix. Gene alternated as an operations officer for the battalion and a heavy weapons commander. During the maneuvers, Gene and the captain had gone without a bath for about six weeks, and finally they went to get one. They found a place where they could bathe and then went to a restaurant at the edge of a Louisiana town.

While they were eating, a member of the military police (MP) came in and said, "Is that your jeep? We just arrested your driver and we're taking over your jeep." His driver, a black soldier, claimed that he had the authority to drive around in Gene's jeep. Gene went over to investigate, and as soon as he got there, the lieutenant saw Gene and began apologizing. His driver confessed that he did not have any authorization to take the jeep. The MPs took the offender over to the jail where they had a number of soldiers. Gene's friend almost got in a fight with the MP lieutenant, who was furious. He and the MP were screaming at each other, so Gene said, "I will wait outside while you finish arguing." When he walked over to the gate, one of the soldiers said, "Hey, buddy, come over here. There are about fifty of us in here, and we all belong to the same outfit. Why don't you pull that pin for us in the gate?"

When Gene pulled the pin, all fifty ran out of the jail. Then, he just got in his jeep and when his friend came out they drove off. The MPs came out and took off to find the escapees. Most of the soldiers who were sober went back to their camp. The next morning, a report went to their colonel, who then punished those involved by restricting them to camp for two or three weeks. Fortunately, they did not want to go to town anyway because they did not have any money. Gene sided with the men in the stockade by releasing them, an action that helped to bridge the racial divide while on maneuvers in Louisiana.[2]

Gene's letters to Alta reveal his frustrations and his dreams for life with her after the war. They also provide a window on the complexities of the racial dynamics of the division.

On February 1, 1944, Gene wrote to Alta from near Knight, Louisiana: "It's warm enough that the men are sitting around in their shirt sleeves—the camp fires make it look very cheerful—some of the men are singing and that is a good sign. Honestly, I'd practically made up my mind to marry you ever since the first Saturday night I dated you, remember?" He also acknowledged how the wives of the soldiers suffered: "It's easy for me to see that not all of the fighting and suffering is done by the soldiers but the wives of the men back home suffer just as much or more. As far as the physical hardship is concerned I can take it all in a stride but the yearning for you is something that just keeps gnawing away."[3]

One night Gene and his company were trying to meet up with a convoy in pitch blackness, and everyone was lost in the Louisiana swampland. He pulled out his compass and told the battalion to follow him across the swamp. His superior objected and thought they should go in another direction. When Gene insisted that he knew how to get them to safety, the superior officer reluctantly followed, but said it was against his advice, and that Gene would have to take responsibility if he was wrong. They walked all night through the swamp, and in the morning, they emerged from the swamp within yards of the expected meeting place. When recalling the incident, Gene added, "You just have to have confidence if you are a leader." In his letter to Alta of February 4, 1944, from near Knight, Louisiana, Gene told the story of following the compass course through the swamps about ten miles and winding up within thirty-five yards of their destination.[4]

Throughout his time in Louisiana, Gene continued to reassure Alta of his love. On February 9, 1944, he wrote to her from Burrs Ferry, Louisiana: "Darling, believe me when I say I love you more than anything in the world. My only ambition now is making you happy the rest of your life."

A few days later, on February 14, he confided to Alta that without her he would not want to live.[5] They were involved in an experience that would last their whole lives. While their love was blossoming, Gene was experiencing the command of an all-black company, a unique time in history that would mark them both.

At times, Gene conveyed his frustrations with the division: "I'm sure disappointed at the way things have gone down here, although I half-expected it, for this Division never does things like the other divisions do."

However, he wrote that he was pleased that his unit won over the 75th Division, a white unit, in the maneuvers.[6]

On February 24, 1944, from Pearson, Louisiana, he continued to explain the difficulties of the racial dynamics in the division: "Well we came, we saw, we conquered—after 5 solid days and 4 nights of constant driving we completely licked the entire 75th Div (white troop) and compelled them to ask for an Armistice—About 8 more white officers were shipped out today leaving myself and two other white officers in the battalion gee, I hate to see my old buddies leave, for some of them I've been soldiering with for nearly three years."[7]

Gene commented on all the white officers who were leaving. At one point, he and two others were the only white officers in the battalion. Yet, revealingly, Gene did not attempt to leave himself. But in a letter of March 4, 1944, he confessed that he would like to leave the unit. He seemed critical of his superior officers rather than of the racial composition of his troops:

> March 4, 1944, Vic Alco, La
>
> Why, I'd be tickled to death to be transferred to any white outfit as a buck private—and that's the truth—so help me—this is really a rotten outfit—there is absolutely no coordination of the staffs of the higher echelon—consequently we are often times sent off on wild goose chases—just because of some numbskull's inefficiency.[8]

From Fisherville, Louisiana, Gene wrote to Alta about the departure of white officers on March 12, 1944: "All the officers are doing all they can to get transferred, many are going A.W.O.L. and taking chances on reclassification and court-martial so you can imagine how serious it is getting to be. There aren't but a few white officers left and it sure seems funny not to see any of the fellows around." He anticipated major changes in the division when he wrote on March 20, 1944, from Caney, Louisiana: "If I am not badly mistaken, there will be some changes in the command personnel after this problem (maneuver)—I just have a feeling that way. I've never seen or heard tell of so many wrong decisions made since being in the Army."[9]

Even though Gene mentioned the bad decisions and mismanagement by his superiors, he did not convey to Alta the full extent of the racial tension present in Louisiana among the white and black soldiers. While the troops were on maneuvers in Louisiana, a number of racist incidents took place and the soldiers fought back. Nelson Peery related a time when the black soldiers were not served at a small store at a crossroads and some trouble had broken out. Later that week, all the trucks were moving out in a convoy. So, the first truck went by this store "taking the corner and takes the corner just a little wide and kind of rips up the front part of the porch out on the front. Next truck rips some more off and then the 30 trucks totally ripped up the front of that porch."[10]

In another dramatic incident, the black soldiers refused to take racist treatment and fought back. Staff Sergeant David Cason Jr. eventually went overseas in the 370th and was later transferred to the 365th. Cason went to the swamps of Louisiana to join the 92nd Division on maneuvers. After defending a bridge all day, one of the soldiers spotted a place with an ice cream sign on it. Cason recalled:

> We were all young and hot and wanted some ice cream. The jeep driver must have had the same idea for he turned in at the sign and our carrier followed. Jumping down we headed for the door. Just as the first fellows off the truck reached the door somebody inside hooked the screen, stepped back, and stood looking at us. The usual shot-gun totin' cracker was suddenly standing in the back door. Not a word had been exchanged; [the] silence was deafening! The fellows closest to the screen wheeled and headed back to the carrier. Others followed as a few climbed aboard and one pulled back the canvas covering the 50 mm machine gun it concealed. The team that operated the gun pulled a belt of ammunition out of its box, slapped it into place, and the trigger man swung that machine gun around to cover the doorway of the ice cream parlor. The only sound was the activities of the men, no words. When I heard the gunner slide the bolt into firing position, with the rest of the men, I stepped back to the carrier, picked up my rifle, removed the slip with soap in the shell, reached in my pocket and pulled out the real thing. All of our clips being slapped into place at the same time sounded like a cannon going off.
>
> Fortunately for all concerned, the crackers inside realized this was for real; these were not "niggers" playing soldier, these were black men who planned to kill and die for that right. The cracker in the back door disappeared; we could see his hasty retreat. The figure, which stood looking at us like we were a new species of animal, reached out and unhooked the screen. As we filed in we learned the silent figure was a waitress. Tears were streaming down her face as she scooped up the ice cream with trembling hands. Sitting in a cluster not far away crying and shaking like leaves in a breeze were several other women and a couple of kids.[11]

The man in the store never reported them. This sort of violent defensive reaction to racist treatment took place within a context of numerous racist incidents throughout the South in which black soldiers were injured and sometimes lost their lives.

The 92nd Division Returns to Fort Huachuca

Racial tensions persisted when the 92nd returned to Fort Huachuca. Once back in Arizona, training continued with intensity. Gene took his machine gun company out and taught them how to displace: to have two guns up above, one to cover the other, and move back to the rear. He trained his men individually to protect each other with covering fire. They complained about it, but he told them that what they were learning could save their lives in combat. He stayed in a barracks near the black officers' club, Mountain View. One night when he was at Mountain View, a black lieutenant told him about a racist incident. He came down from New York and when he stopped at some town, they would not feed him unless he went around to the back of the restaurant. Many of the other soldiers encountered similar incidents and worse. Gene was aware of the racism his men faced.

At times, Gene expressed his frustrations and anger over racial dynamics within the division and blamed the politicians for forcing them into the situation. With so many white officers transferring out, he began to feel increasingly isolated and under pressure. Fights were breaking out between white and black officers. On July 29, 1944, he wrote to Alta:

> Darling, regardless of what happens always remember you are all I live for and am fighting for.
>
> In all my life I've never seen a bunch of white men under more pressure and take more insults than the few we have left here. It can't last much longer at the rate it's going. I think the only reason they're taking it is because they want to show they've got the "guts" to take it. We figure that all dogs have their day sometime. I'm convinced we white officers are not here to fight for our country, but for the Negroes and the dirty politicians behind them.

On the next day, July 30, 1944, he wrote about a fight that occurred: "We had another little skirmish last night; one of our white officers got into a fight with one of the colored officers."[12]

One Saturday, Gene was working with his company, a heavy mortar outfit, out in the field firing 81-millimeter mortars. When they got down to the last rounds, he was going to take them in. His men were complaining because they could see the main gate and people walking around down there. When they were firing away, they did not realize that only about a thousand yards away was Fry, a town on the edge of the camp, just outside the gate. Finally, just as they were getting ready to quit, Gene gave the order to "fire at will." He said, "We're going to fire all the ammunition we have left and then we're going to go in. Fire for effect." They looked down the field and started pumping shells in the mortars, and fired all their remaining ammunition, about twenty-five rounds just as fast as they could fire them. They kept waiting for them to land. Then it got very quiet. About that time they saw smoke rising down among the tents in Fry, and people started running in all directions.

They practically wrecked that town and terrified everyone there. Because they had not changed the sights on the guns and just dropped in the mortars, pandemonium ensued. Prostitutes and their customers were running in all directions. Gene was afraid to go to the white officers' club that night because he was afraid they had killed some people. Fortunately, no one was hurt. General Almond found out who was responsible, and he called Gene over. Gene did not say a word and Almond said "I understand you were out shooting today." Gene said, "Yes, we shot. We were shooting." After a long pause, the general said, "You did a good job of it, young man—particularly because you moved those people out down there."[13]

When the mortars fell, the people who were running were not all prostitutes and their clients. Prostitutes, soldiers, and families lived in the Hook. When Joseph Hairston went to Fort Huachuca, he and his wife Ann lived in a brothel. Next to the beer tavern called the Green Top, right outside the post, was a four-sided structure with fifty rooms called The Hook that housed prostitutes. General Almond told the owner that he had to rent half of the rooms to his black officers, or he would place the property off limits. So the owner rented rooms to twenty-five couples. The rooms had two cots, a hot plate, and a bathroom in the hall. The officers were on one side and the prostitutes on the other.

Initially, they put the men's restrooms on one end and the women's on the other. When Hairston went to take a shower he realized that there was a woman taking a shower next to him. So he stayed a little longer. He did not know how to get out of there unnoticed. When he told the other men, they all went to take a shower. When their wives wondered what was going on, they checked and then made that area off limits to the husbands. They put a sign saying "men" or "women" on the restrooms, which would rotate.[14]

Soon after the firing on the prostitutes' tents, Gene was trying to inject realism into his training exercises. Outside one of the headquarters buildings, there was a pond about seven feet deep and forty feet around, surrounded by bushes. As the S-3, Gene was in charge of training, and he wanted to simulate battle conditions as much as possible. He had his men use the pond to practice river crossings. Upstairs, the generals watched as the men erratically paddled across the pond. They saw two men who were paddling going around and around in circles, swearing all the while. Gene was sitting up in the bushes on the side of the pond watching them. Meanwhile, he had some men hidden along the edge of the bank who put some fuses in a quarter pound of nitric starch, lit them, and threw them into the water. Some of the men had never been in a boat in their lives. The boat glided right over the top of the starch and when it went off, the explosion lifted the men right out of the water.

A minute later all you saw was a bunch of helmets floating on top of the water. Gene thought he had killed all of them. Pretty soon the soldiers crawled out of the water, and ran after the men who threw the starch, chasing them all the way to the other side of the post. The general saw it all from the window and he thought it was the funniest thing in the world. But it was a dangerous thing; Gene could have killed every one of them.[15]

Another white officer in Gene's unit, John Runyon, remained at Fort Huachuca after many other white officers left. He and his wife, Corinne, were enchanted with Fort Huachuca. They found a small cottage at Nicksville, one of perhaps twenty near the camp grounds. All of them were occupied by officers and their wives, and they formed a young, friendly community. They were next to a large cattle ranch. Corinne said that "Nicksville was like a motel, with a general store, an office, a bar, and some little houses around a pretty little garden with oleanders and cottonwoods." The Runyons spent time with Ed and Rita Rowny and Mary and Bill McCaffrey at the white officers' club, next to a beautiful pond with swans gliding by. While at Huachuca, Corinne had a daughter named Gail, who was premature and weighed barely five pounds. They put her in a shoe box, packed it with cotton, and kept her under the electric light in the hospital.[16]

Runyon tried to gain the trust and confidence of his men by being open with them and inviting their input. He said, "It was, and still is, amazing how much can be accomplished when you praise a group." Morale improved, and the officers, the enlisted men, and the noncommissioned officers started working together. Together they went into the field and camped on the breeding grounds of rattlesnakes and giant tarantulas. While on maneuvers there, they killed 152 rattlesnakes in seven days.[17]

Spencer and Susie Moore, an African American couple, lived at a motor court in Benson, Arizona, just forty-two miles northeast of Nicksville, where the Runyons lived. Spencer fell in love with Susie and married her when she was still a senior in high school. She was nineteen when she joined him at Fort Huachuca after she finished her senior year. She had never made a trip of such distance by herself. Her train trip from Indiana through Missouri was uneventful, but she was surprised that all the black women were removed from the train in Texas to make room for white soldiers.[18]

Susie lost her berth to a white major and had to find another train out of El Paso to Hereford, Arizona, the depot for the fort. Spencer had waited a long time for Susie at Hereford, but when he was told there were no more trains that day, he left and went to bed. When she finally arrived, she was dropped off at the gate of the fort in the red light district and had to fend for herself among the prostitutes and their customers. Finally, an MP called Susie's brother-in-law, Clifford, who was also at the fort. He came and escorted her to her lodging.

Once Susie and Spencer settled in, they had several joyful months before Spencer went off to fight in Italy. They lived in one room in a motor court constructed of adobe in Benson, which they shared with a friend, Jack Miles. The room had a little stove and orange crates with skirts around them for their night stands. There was also a big brass bed. Susie smiled mischievously as she listened to the popular song "Put Me in Your Big Brass Bed until My Face Turns Cherry Red." She thought those motor court parties at Huachuca were the "closest thing to heaven." When Spencer left for Italy, Susie was pregnant.[19]

Gene Johnston, John Runyon, Spencer Moore, Reuben Horner, Bill Perry, Joseph Hairston, Jehu Hunter, Albert Burke, Joseph Stephenson, William McCaffrey, General Ned Almond, Edward Brooke, Harold Montgomery, Charles Lancaster, and all the other members of the 92nd Division boarded trains bound for Newport News, Virginia. When Gene Johnston left, they backed up the train all the way over to Bisbee. He stood on the back steps of that train and saluted. He saluted old Fort Huachuca, and said, "I hope I never see this place again."[20]

IV WOMEN WAITING

8

"I'll Be Seeing You"

The Long Wait

Those months at Fort Huachuca were like a honeymoon for many of the soldiers and their wives. It helped when Alta Johnston could forget that Gene would be shipping out soon, and they could just enjoy one another. Sometimes they would go to dance at the cantinas at night. Gene was an award-winning jitterbug enthusiast, and Alta loved dancing with him. Then they had to make the long climb up the hundred steps to their little house in Bisbee, Arizona. Carrying groceries was a major ordeal. When word came that the troops were ordered to maneuvers, and then to the war, Alta drove with three other wives back to Tennessee. She had to say too many goodbyes.[1]

Returning from Fort Huachuca to her mother's house on the farm, Alta began the long period of waiting. Waiting to hear from Gene that he was still alive. Waiting for news of the war. Waiting in line to buy rationed goods. And waiting for a dreaded telegram saying that Gene had been killed—a telegram that, thankfully, never came.

Life on the home front meant living under stress. At least food was more plentiful on a farm than it might have been for those in the city, and probably better than desert fare around Bisbee. Alta continued to teach school while Gene was away, which helped pass the long days with something meaningful. She read a lot, books like *The Robe* by Lloyd C. Douglas and *For Whom the Bell Tolls* by Ernest Hemingway. Listening to the radio, she heard *The Shadow, Amos and Andy,* and the news, along with the music of the big bands. "Is You Is or Is You Ain't My Baby," and "Don't Sit under the Apple Tree with Anyone Else But Me" were songs that tormented her and the others left behind, as they wondered if their husbands would be faithful to them. Many of the wives would wonder and worry about that for the rest of their lives. But mainly the fear was whether their husbands would come back or come back whole.

Alta hardly knew Gene when she married him, and she was pregnant with their first child when he left for the war. Their daughter Nancy Jean was born in January 1945, when Gene was fighting his way up the Apennine Mountains against the

Germans. During those lonely days, Alta smoked Lucky Strikes and tried to control her fear. A few letters would get through from Gene. Many others never made it. Waiting for the mail carrier with such longing and expectation was torturous; she waited by the window with a sense of dread.

Like all of her neighbors, Alta prayed a lot and went to church a lot. Any hardships on the home front seemed insignificant in view of the suffering of the soldiers in Europe and the Pacific. Sometimes she unconsciously relished her freedom and was proud that she could cope with any situation alone; yet having been raised with the expectation of having a man to take care of her, she resented having to carry such a heavy burden. The independence that she experienced during the war and afterward made her unable to be truly submissive again. A whole generation of women later revolted, largely as a result of the war experiences and their educations.[2]

Alta wondered whether Gene would ever see his child, and whether their child would see her handsome father. How did she ever end up marrying such a wild man, fond of fast cars and the jitterbug? But his shy manner was irresistible. Gene knew if he were going to stay married to Alta, he could not have even an occasional beer; he had to be a teetotaler or no deal. When she married him, she never dreamed she would be an army wife for her whole marriage, moving every two years, always packing and always leaving friends, and spending so many years alone.

Alta's family had already known sorrow. Her father was robbed and murdered in 1939. Her mother, Margaret Ross, a healer, midwife, and clairvoyant, was part Cherokee. She had a premonition of her husband's death because an owl appeared in the daylight near the house. Aldon, Alta's brother, who was a Marine, was killed in the Philippines on the way from China. The Marines tried to claim it was a suicide rather than a murder. Two of her baby sisters died shortly after birth in terrible accidents, and another sister died during the war. So, Alta was accustomed to sadness. She was a walking contradiction; she was short, but named Alta. She was dedicated to the needs of other people, but secretly longed to be in control and have real power. She was frail looking, but tough as steel. Everyone was always surprised that at the times of crises or deaths she did not fall apart. She was used to having to pull it all together and go on. Alta kept Gene's precious letters through every move that they made, and she waited.[3]

Susie Moore got up around five in the morning the day the husbands all left Fort Huachuca. Spencer Moore told her, "Don't worry about me. I'll be back. The bad penny always comes back." The other men told her not to worry, and that they would bring him back. The sun was coming up over the mountain. It was a gorgeous sunrise. The men told their wives goodbye and half of them were crying. Susie did not cry; she was not a crier. She worried in other ways. Everybody looked like they were in a photograph. Then the men started walking to their rides without looking back. They just left. The couples had developed such closeness over those weeks. Now they were all dispersing, the men to war and the women to their homes back east.[4]

V FACING THE GOTHIC LINE

War Stories in Black and White

9

Combat in Italy

September 1944–January 1945

The war experiences of black and white soldiers took place in parallel universes. The 370th Combat Team left the United States on July 15, 1944, and arrived in Italy on August 1, 1944. The 371st arrived on October 18, 1944. As a member of the 370th Combat Team, Spencer Moore arrived in Italy before Gene Johnston. After Spencer and Susie Moore, his young bride, spent time at Fort Huachuca, Spencer went to Newport News to board the *Mariposa,* a cruise ship, which had been converted to transport troops. Nine to twelve soldiers occupied each of the staterooms. Some of the soldiers brushed their teeth in the French bidets in the rooms, not knowing their purpose. The others teased them about that for a long time.[1]

Moore went up to the bridge frequently and talked to the captain. One day, he asked Colonel Sherman, the commander, "Are we going to work or going to fight?" Moore knew that when the 9th and 10th cavalries had landed in North Africa, they were converted to quartermaster and engineer regiments. Sherman replied, "We're going to fight."[2]

Racial tensions persisted during the passage to Italy. When morale deteriorated on the ship, a white officer planned a party and tried to coerce the troops to attend. When they refused, tensions mounted. The officer felt threatened and talked a man into sleeping in his bunk. The man slept with his feet where his head usually was and was found shot in the foot the next morning. The colonel who had been the intended target died overseas.[3] In a similar incident, a cruel captain forced the black soldiers to do extra duty and on hot days put them through calisthenics with rifles. Later on when they were in Italy, someone shot and killed him in his tent and threw the rifle in on top of him.[4]

The 370th Combat Team

Arrival

The 370th Combat Team (CT) landed in Oran, North Africa. When they arrived, the officers told the troops to stay away from the women onshore or they would be found dead. From Oran, they went by convoy to Naples in July 1944; when they arrived, the harbor was full of sunken ships. A ramp had been built resting on the sunken ships, stretching all the way out to where the ship docked. When Harold Montgomery walked ashore in Naples, he and the other men heard a new sound "like the roar of a crowd in a ballpark. Hundreds of black service troops—cooks, stewards, and laborers—had gathered to cheer the arrival of the first black combat soldiers in Italy." That night, they stayed at the crater camp near Mount Vesuvius, which had erupted on March 14, 1944. Would lava flow down on the Buffalo Soldiers as it had on Pompeii? During the night, the Germans bombed the harbor, but Spencer Moore was so tired he slept through it.[5]

The black press and politicians had pushed to get black troops into combat. When the 370th CT arrived in Italy, this goal was quickly achieved. They began to see action as soon as the last week in August. The 92nd Division was sent to Italy to put pressure on the Germans, so they had to keep troops there. The more troops the Germans had to commit, the fewer troops the Allies had to put in Normandy. This Allied holding action involved thousands of black soldiers engaged in a three-pronged attack on the Germans: along the coast, they crossed the Cinquale Canal toward the town of Massa; to the east they assaulted the Strettoia hills; and further east, they went into the mountains and attempted to capture German defensive positions. The Gothic Line extended from the coastal plain in the west to the Strettoia hills in the east and then on to the Apennine Mountains, also called the Apuan Alps. The barrier that confronted the 92nd Division and the entire 5th Army was virtually insurmountable that winter in 1945.[6]

Numerous trenches with seemingly invisible gun emplacements and a labyrinth of escape tunnels gave the Germans extraordinary advantages. They also used camouflage expertly. Their steel and concrete fortifications were high in the mountains, such as at Castle Aghinolfi near Massa, which the Germans used to control the passes through the Apennine Mountains. Barbed wire, minefields, and trip wires abounded. From these posts, mortars and machine-gun fire relentlessly poured down on the Buffalo Soldiers. The Mount Folgorito–Mount Cauala area was ideal for defensive purposes because deep ravines cut through the peaks with nearly perpendicular rock walls.[7]

Two gigantic guns that had been taken off an Axis warship were mounted on rails at Punta Bianca near the naval facility at La Spezia. They were on a rocky cliff that proved impervious to Allied bombers until the very end of the war. For the entire war, they rained unmerciful fire onto the Buffalo Soldiers. These guns were superior to any weaponry that the Allied fleet had in the Ligurian Sea. The Germans targeted Highway 1 (called by the soldiers the "Purple Heart Highway"), and wiped out troops as they advanced up the road on the west coast of Italy.[8]

Spencer Moore knew how vulnerable the troops were on Highway 1. Once deployed overseas in the 370th, he saw combat virtually continuously for months. He was anxious to see action, but once it began, he told his fellow soldiers, he "wished to hell he'd never seen it." He questioned the company commander during an officer's meeting about his failure to follow orders from the battalion commander about selecting the duty officer. Being young and naïve, he did not understand the ramifications of questioning a racist officer, and so he paid with his career. Moore remained a second lieutenant throughout the war. At the age of only twenty-one, he led forty men in his company. He was wounded, frostbitten twice so badly that he was hospitalized, bitten by a German shepherd, and kicked by a mule. He fought in three battles: the Rome/Arno, the Apennines, and the Po Valley.[9]

Moore saved the life of his friend Kermit Hancock when he had a very close call because of a haystack. Soldiers sometimes got in haystacks to keep cool from the sun, and the Italians often hid things in the haystacks.[10] Moore told Hancock to go down by the river and get behind a stone wall. He was supposed to listen for the patrol and then start firing. Instead, Hancock got inside the haystack that the Germans used for target practice. Shortly, Moore heard, "Help, Help," and saw the aid man dragging his wounded friend. The Italians had hidden a Fiat in the haystack, and when a shell hit, the car blew up and shrapnel flew everywhere. Hancock's calf was pretty nearly gone, and blood was spurting from a severed artery. Moore kept him from bleeding to death. Kermit Hancock had to spend a year in the hospital.[11]

Moore himself was badly wounded near Seravezza when the Germans started firing machine-gun bullets at him. He narrowly missed being cut down when he made a quick move and avoided a stream of bullets. As he and Beringer were crawling up the hill, the Germans turned the mortars on them. They jumped in a culvert and were both wounded. A bullet graced Beringer's scalp, but did not kill him. Moore did not realize he too had been hit. The back of his boot was torn off and his heel was bleeding profusely. Medics put sulfanilamide powder in the wound and wrapped it up. Because he needed a new pair of boots, he slid down the hill to the aid station. He made it across to a big tree riddled with bullet marks and crossed the canal to the medics. After they bandaged his heel and gave him a tetanus shot, the jeep took him to where the ambulance would pick him up.[12]

Finally the ambulance came and they took Spencer down the Purple Heart Highway to Pisa, with mortar shells hitting to the right and left. He just missed getting hit by a shell. Moore drank some brandy, which made him woozy because he had been awake almost the entire night. Half asleep when they arrived at the hospital, Spencer saw a huge face before him and pulled his pistol. It turned out to be an outdoor movie screen. He was in the hospital at Pisa for twenty-eight days.[13]

After he left the hospital, he was released to a replacement depot, where he almost froze from lying on his cot without enough blankets. On his way back to the 92nd in the ambulance, an aid man came running out; the medic stopped and went down to see what happened. The medic was excited, even hysterical. He said, "Come down here; help me." Four engineers had tried to disarm an antitank mine and it had exploded. The men were blown to pieces. There was a head here, and eyeballs blown out of their heads. They did not have faces, and there were body parts everywhere. It was horrible. "Son, we can't help them," the ambulance driver said. Someone on graves registration had to pick up the parts.[14]

None of the soldiers who experienced combat would ever be the same after what they had endured. They would carry the memories of the fear, terror, and shock for the rest of their lives, and those back home would never be able to understand why they could not forget. The scene of all those men blown to pieces haunted Spencer Moore's nightmares. Another time in combat, he was especially distraught over his men's fears. Headquarters called him one night and ordered him to take a combat patrol out. Moore recounted a harrowing night: "I just started out with Lieutenant Case's platoon [at Mallazano]. But his platoon was scared, and we had a bombardment one night. The Germans shelled us pretty heavy, and the men ran off and left me. Only Sgt. Ball, Wes Taylor, and Oza Brown stayed with me. The rest ran down. A platoon is supposed to be about 36 men. But I guess it must have been 20 or 25 of them that were leaving us. I went down on my knees and begged them not to leave me. Together we can beat them. They will pick us off separately. I got them back up there."[15]

Like Spencer Moore, Bill Perry crossed the Atlantic on the *Mariposa.* They did not have an escort because the ship could presumably outrun anything. When they set sail, the men sang "Nearer My God to Thee."[16] Shortly after they arrived in Italy, Perry heard General Mark Clark's address to the whole regiment of around 3,500 men. Clark welcomed them to the theater and told them he had assigned them to a light sector so they could gain some experience. He said that he intended to "hurl them at the bosh" and said that the Germans were wobbling on their last legs. In many of the companies, black first lieutenants were commanding, though they had not been made captains. Upon hearing about this, Clark turned to his aide, a captain, took the bars off his collar and pinned them on Lieutenant Gandy, the commander of Company E. Clark's action led Perry to believe that they might get better treatment now.[17]

Perry (370th CT) was involved in combat for extended periods of time. Once in Italy, tensions among the officers and enlisted men continued. When he was serving in Company K Headquarters, Perry witnessed a major incident of fragging, which he described:

> When the 3rd Battalion 370th Infantry RCT entered the line the night of the 23 August 1944, we had been told to be alert. The Germans would infiltrate our lines, dressed in American uniforms and speaking proper English.
>
> The second night 24 August 1944 this incident happened at the command post of Company "K" 370th Infantry Regiment, commanded by Capt. Elmer F. Reedy (white) of Woodstock, Virginia. The soldier involved was Private James Leggett, a black rifleman in Company "K". Sergeant Waite, a white soldier of the 1st Armored Division, was returning from the latrine. Private Leggett gave the password twice and the 1st Armored Sergeant responded, "Take it easy" "Take it easy," *not* the countersign. Pvt. Leggett again gave the password and received the same response "Take it Easy," "Take it Easy."
>
> Private Leggett then fired his M-1 rifle, killing the 1st Armored Division Sergeant Waite.

Perry and another soldier, Dial Hewlett, were only ten yards from the incident. The first comment they heard by a member of the 1st Armored unit was, "We did not want them Niggers up here anyway." This shooting caused a great deal of tension between the 1st Armored and the 3rd Battalion of the 370th Infantry Regiment.[18]

A few days later, on September 1, 1944, the soldiers of the 370th went up on trucks to a little town called Pontedera, around fifteen miles east of Pisa on the Arno River. They were attached to the 1st Armored Division, a tank unit that fought in North Africa. The first night was rather quiet there. Perry was critical of the way the units constantly moved from one region to another, with the battalions spread all over the Italian countryside. They fought at distances that allowed enemy troops to outflank and expose them. An outfit might be on the coast for a couple of weeks and then suddenly be moved to the Serchio Valley, while the 2nd Battalion was sent somewhere else. The theory of using a regiment in warfare relies on using two forward-thrusting battalions and one in the rear maneuvering left or right. The soldiers of the 92nd Division did not have adequate support or continuity because they were ordered to move so frequently.[19]

The situation was complicated by the lack of an adequate number of trained "Negro infantry replacements" for those injured and killed. For example, the 442nd, the heroic Japanese American outfit (one regiment) had a larger replacement pool than all three regiments in the 92nd did. Not surprisingly, Perry and many of his fellow combatants were critical of the commanders' strategies. Adding to these problems was the fact that in the wake of D-Day in Normandy, the ammunition for the 92nd was rationed.[20]

Once when Perry's company was in Seravezza, they started climbing the steep mountain nearby and suddenly they heard somebody saying, "*Commaraden, Commaraden.*" All of a sudden everybody began to roll in place and chamber a round if they had not done so already. They spotted a German machine-gun nest manned by some Czechoslovakians who were chained to the guns. They captured the two men, and eventually took them back to their S-2 at the company headquarters. Perry's company fought for a day and a half before they ran low on ammunition. Because they could not replace it on the mountain, they just had to give up the ground.[21]

General Almond Takes Stock

Between August 24th and October 5, 1944, the 370th CT advanced about thirty miles against relatively light resistance. General Almond said that members of the 370th initially had been successful in advancing their position, but they were disappointing in their ability to remain in the position. When ordered to attack from their position in the Ligurian coastal sector west of the Serchio Valley north in order to seize Massa, they encountered fierce resistance from the Germans. They gained eight thousand yards in six days and sustained four hundred casualties, but they did not achieve their objectives.

General Almond said, "One explanation of the failure to advance and hold the advance position was the fact that Task Force 92 was attacking against the high ground of the Apennine Mountain[s], whereas from the Arno River and along the Arno River, the advance that they had made was on more even terrain and not so easily defended by the enemy." Early on, Almond blamed reverses on the terrain, but by the end of the war, he placed the blame on the Buffalo Soldiers and disregarded the German tactical advantages.[22] As the 370th CT went on the line, they were poorly supplied, had insufficient manpower backup or replacements, and some racial fragging incidents had already occurred. Soon the 371st joined the 370th on the Italian front and criticism of the 92nd intensified.

The 371st Goes on the Line

When the 371st got to Newport News, Virginia, they had to go through final examinations with equipment. When Gene Johnston took his unit to the gymnasium, they had to stand at attention, undress, run around the gym one time, and then put their clothes back on. When Gene asked about the examination, the examiners said, "That was your examination. You're going overseas." Regardless of their levels of readiness for battle, all of the members of the 92nd boarded Liberty ships bound for Italy. Along with the weapons, supplies, and equipment, the black soldiers carried their bitterness over racist treatment and memories of violence against them by angry whites. Both the black and white soldiers carried memories of wives and sweethearts, as well as hopes of surviving the war and coming home.[23]

Soon after the 371st left for Italy, Gene walked out on the stern of the ship and looked around. Suddenly through the thick fog, he saw the prow of another Liberty ship no more than three to five feet away. The crew had gone to sleep, and the ship was about to collide with theirs. Gene started yelling and woke people up. The crew of the other ship began to run around frantically and just managed to avoid the collision. At night, the Liberty ships clustered together and patrol torpedo boats ran among them. They spent thirty days or more at sea. When they got to Africa they were supposed to go ashore, but they landed at the wrong place. After a brief stop, they continued on to Italy.

When Gene and the other members of the 371st arrived in Leghorn (Livorno), Italy, on the night of October 18, 1944, the harbor was filled with ships that had been sunk. Their ship had to wind around the other ships to reach the dock. At one narrow passage, they barely missed tearing a hole in the side of the ship. The rain started pouring, making their arrival even more dismal. The rain fell so hard the soldiers could not see that the statue in the square was of four black slaves, called *Quattro Mori* (The Four Moors) sculpted by Pietro Tacca in the seventeenth century. It had been raining for two or three days and continued to rain for a week after their arrival. Gene had made friends with some cooks while on the ship. One of them ran out and brought him a whole ham in a bag, which Gene slung over his shoulder, along with his heavy gear, duffel bag, and weapons.[24]

The men had to climb down rope ladders on the side of the ship to disembark. One man kept walking on Gene's hands as he climbed down the rope, pushing him down. Angrily Gene said, "If you don't stop stepping on my hands, I will shoot you." He finally got the man's attention. Then they boarded rafts to reach the shore. There was nothing to hold onto as they stood on the rafts, so they feared that they would roll over any minute. Bright lights illuminated the harbor. When they came ashore, the soldiers boarded trucks that took them up toward the front line. Fortunately, they had their ammunition with them, because they went immediately into combat positions after going through Leghorn to Viareggio. The 370th had been fighting successfully around Massa and Pisa.[25] The 92nd Division's frontage was approximately twenty-six miles and primarily mountainous. The Buffalo Soldiers faced the Gothic Line, which the Germans had spent six months fortifying. Hundreds of mines on the beaches and in the mountains greeted them, and machine-gun nests were positioned throughout the hills.[26]

When the 92nd Division first arrived in Italy, an unknown assailant shot and killed an officer while he was asleep. This was an extreme incident, but Gene and all the other white officers were tested. One man in his company seemed to feel animosity toward him and all whites. Yet Gene generally related well to the men and never had any serious trouble. Many of the other white officers would get angry at their men, curse them out, denigrate them, and try to transfer out of the division. Then their men would quit working; in fact, they would quit doing anything.[27]

A few days after arriving in Italy, Gene was ordered to join the 10th Mountain Division in the Serchio Valley in order to be oriented. He went over in his jeep with his driver.[28] When he arrived near the front line, he had to go up the rest of the way in a 1.5-ton truck. The journey proved to be harrowing because the Germans heard the truck going up the steep incline and fired at them from the other side of the mountain. As they were grinding up the steep, winding road, a shell hit the truck. They all jumped off, and Gene felt his way in the pitch-black darkness amid constant shelling. He and the others headed up the mountain, crawled a short distance to a house built on the side of the road on a steep slope, and took cover there. Gene could tell the small space was already crowded with soldiers. They had been running in there all day, hiding from the shells. He moved slowly to keep from stepping on arms and legs of those already squeezed into the house.

After a few hours in the house, Gene crawled out and started walking to the front over the top of the ridge, about a half mile on the road to Bologna. Finally he arrived at the 10th Mountain's rear command post. When he got to the headquarters, they were glad to see him and briefed him. Gene stayed with the 10th Mountain Division for two weeks while he was getting oriented for battle. He lived on the front line at the outpost in a house that had been leveled to the ground, with a basement that had just enough crawl space to get in. The Germans fired 88s, knocking the buildings down piece by piece. A sergeant, who was quite a character, was in the house; every time a shell came in, he would check the radio wire. If the wire had been cut, he'd crawl out and come back after about an hour, having restored the connection. A few times, he fell into a cesspool right outside the building. When he came back, he smelled terrible, but that did not stop him. He faithfully kept the wire strung.[29]

The road was practically held together by wire, and there were several dead mules on the road, creating an overpowering stench. One night, a German walked right by the house without noticing the American soldiers. The Germans fired some shells when they started back down the road. Some German "Long Tom" guns, big 155-millimeter cannons, placed near the command post fired continually and shook the ground. In the daytime, Gene saw through the field glasses that the Germans had their cannons lined up in a ditch below. He could tell when they were going to fire because he saw them moving the weapons into position.[30]

After observing with the 10th Mountain Division, Gene returned to the 371st. He wrote to Alta on October 31, 1944, "from Somewhere in Italy":

> Well, darling I've just come out of the front lines and am now in a rest camp. I don't know how long I get to be here but I hope it's a few days anyway. I've been fighting with another outfit, the kind I've always wanted to be with and honestly, honey, you have no idea how proud I am of the fellows particularly those from my home state—believe me they've got the old "guts." I should know for I've seen it.
>
> Sweetheart speaking of praying—I don't [think?] I've missed a day lately praying and I'm sure that the Lord heard them even if there was a lot of noise at the time.
>
> I wonder how it would feel to hear a good old American jive orchestra swing out. I don't think I'd ever get tired of it. Honey, you just start getting your gowns out for we're sure going to swing out one of these days.[31]

Mountain and Coastal Battles

September 1944–January 1945

On a beautiful, clear, cold day near Massa, Gene Johnston shot his first German. He had a 60-millimeter mortar, and he decided to do some shooting. So he took it to the side of the ridge and laid the mortar in. He had seen some of them going into a deep cavern on the other side of the ridge, and he decided to "wake them

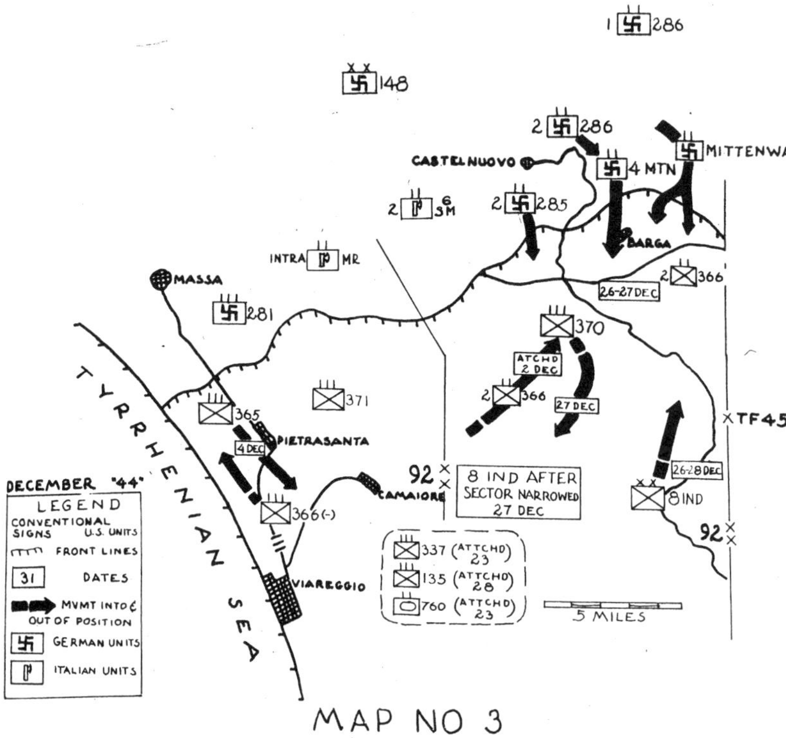

9. Map 3, Italian campaign, December 1944. Courtesy of Army Military History Institute, Carlisle, Pennsylvania.

up." He also kept seeing people emerge from the woods and enter the back of a house. After he fired his mortar, the Germans quickly spotted him and started returning fire on him. Somebody started shouting, "Stop the shooting, stop the shooting, stop the shooting." A German who had found one of the Allies' 536 radios was calling out from down in a nearby cave. Using American radios, some Germans were directing fire on them. So Gene kept firing over the dugout in order to keep the Germans from coming out.

When Gene threw a couple of grenades into the dugout, some Germans came out. One of them had a large part of his leg blown away. Gene told a sergeant, "Take these men back to the rear." Gene suspected that the sergeant killed them because he was only gone a few minutes. He later found out that the same sergeant killed a lot of prisoners; he just shot them.[32]

Again from "Somewhere in Italy," Gene wrote to Alta on November 8, 1944:

10. Sergeant Parks on horseback; Captain Eugene E. Johnston, standing. 92nd Infantry Division publication, 1942, 74–75. Courtesy of Eugene E. Johnston.

"Honey, frankly I'm a bit surprised but I'm beginning to be very proud of my men. I'm recommending some of them for decorations." Gene's company had two platoons of machine-gun sections of four guns each. All together he had eight machine guns. He also had a mortar platoon with three squads of 81-millimeter mortars, and a fifty-seven recoiling rifle platoon. When he and his company pulled into Leghorn and Seravezza, Gene was ordered to send one of his machine-gun platoons over to the eastern part of the road that led to Bologna.

Gene was up on the front continuously for more than two months and in combat the whole time, because the commanding officers wanted experienced people on the line.[33] At first, he was terrified in combat; early in his time in Italy, he came into a small town that was being heavily shelled. He was zigzagging to hide between the buildings and saw a break in the buildings. Some 88-millimeter rounds were fired over his head and were hitting just in front of him. He ran into a building and found another soldier. Gene took out a cigarette and tried to light it. His hand was shaking so much he could not even light it. So, the other soldier lit it for him. Gene stayed there about an hour. Finally, men from another company relieved them, but they did not have any ammunition.[34] But after several weeks, he faced battle more stoically.

11. Members of a Negro mortar company of the 92nd Division pass the ammunition and heave it over at the Germans in an almost endless stream near Massa, Italy. This company is credited with liquidating several machine gun nests. Ca. November 1944. Acme. 208-AA-47U-6. (african _americans_wwii_035.jpg). Courtesy of the U.S. Army, National Archives.

When Gene moved into the front line he had to take a representative from each company, and the company commander took some people with him. He would introduce himself to the men who were holding the position. They would orient him, and when he returned at night, they had guides to lead them in the dark. Sometimes the Germans found out their schedule and started shelling. It might take all night for them to get in position because they had to wait and slip in a few men at a time.[35] The 371st was right behind the 370th. The 92nd Division was fighting Germans and Italians, including the 4th Italian "Monte Rosa" Alpine Division and the 3rd Italian "San Marco" Marine Division, part of the Lombardia Corps, during the Winter Operation of December 26, 1944. In February 1945, they were fighting the Bersaglieri of the 1st Italian "Italia" Infantry Division. Often these units were fighting in concert with the Germans.[36]

Gene Johnston and his men stayed in the same place near Massa for months, and they attacked the same position six or seven times. They always attacked in the morning with heavy artillery fire. The Germans would soon counterattack and drive them off, and they would have to fall back. They attacked one morning when Gene's company was one of the two companies abreast, followed by one behind, bringing up the rear. Sometimes all three companies went on the line, but most frequently they attacked two on the line and one in reserve. Just as soon as the forward companies broke through the German line, the other company would follow.[37]

When Gene and his company were up on the mountain at Calomini in January, they had already been in several battles, and yet his men had not received their winter sleeping bags; they were still in summer bags. Most of the men had cut holes in their sleeping bags and wore them to keep warm. They looked like the soldiers at Valley Forge. They had bits of blankets wrapped around their shoes. Gene sent his sergeant back dozens of times but the supply officers would not acknowledge that his unit had never received their bags. When they had landed in Africa, his men's extra clothing and duffel bags were put in a warehouse, and they were never returned to them. So they never got their extra clothing or extra pairs of shoes and boots.

About three months later, Gene and his men were walking around with worn-out footwear. Everybody in the rear area, even the peasants who worked for them, had boots with the rough side of the leather outside. Gene's men had not received any shoes at all.[38] They had been stationed in Italy about three months when General Mark Clark came up one day. General Clark took one look at his men and said, "What happened here?" Gene told him that after they left North Africa, supply officers kept telling them that they had gotten their bags and shoes, and he had his men put in voucher after voucher to retrieve the winter clothing. No one would pay any attention to him.

Clark turned to a nearby colonel. "Do you know about this, Colonel?" "No sir." He had four full colonels with him. He said, "You have got until sundown to get a pair of boots on every man here." General Clark was furious; he could not understand why they could not get boots to the men when they had been up there all that time. Gene's sergeant called from the foot of the mountain to report that there were two or three jeep trailers loaded with boots in all sizes for them. Gene sent the men down to find boots that fit. The trip took about two hours down and three hours back. But all the men in his company were supplied with boots before dark.

After boots, Gene's men still needed winter clothes and bags. The temperatures had dropped below freezing. He sent his sergeant back to the rear to find out where they could get winter bags. The sergeant took some ammunition to exchange and came back with sleeping bags for all the men. Some of his troops were on the left flank and some on the right flank. Gene told the sergeant to deliver the sleeping bags to them all. About a week later, he found out that the sleeping bags had never reached his men because other soldiers had taken them. Gene had to intervene personally in order to get them back for his troops.[39]

Tensions existed throughout the companies, but sometimes all one could do was laugh. Jefferson L. Jordan, a second lieutenant of the 370th, had to restrain his laughter once at the ever-pervasive racial epithets. He had just reached the top of a mountain to find a typical mountain village house. He told his friends he could "see two soldiers looking down on me. They were right out of Bill Mauldin's sketches in *Stars and Stripes.* One, big, unkempt, and bearded, the other, scrawny, unkempt, and bearded. Both were quite nonchalant about it all. They were typical [white] American soldiers who had seen a lot of combat, been on the line too long, and nothing impressed them. One leaned out of his window and spoke quite matter-of-factly, 'Now who is that maroony motherfucker?'" Jordan fought to restrain his laughter, and he pretended that he had not heard the remark.[40]

In December 1944, Gene wrote to Alta again from "Somewhere in Italy": "I can only tell you I am seeing plenty of action and have been for some time. . . . Here's hoping our boy never has to go to war anywhere." Just as he had in the early fall campaign, Gene continued to praise the performance of his troops. He wrote Alta on December 4, 1944: "So far I've every reason to be proud of my men—they are the talk of the outfit—the rough training I managed to give them is paying dividends now—particularly in respect to discipline. Some have already received citations."

The men of the 92nd Division had to face the bitter winter conditions, the Punta Bianca guns, serious geographical disadvantages, and continuing racism. Jim Williams, who served in the 317th Medical Unit and then the 92nd Division, encountered racial tensions even when treating the wounded:

> One night I had duty; we were up in the mountains in Italy. And we had Command Posts set up. And they brought this soldier, white soldier in on a stretcher. And he had broken his leg. The femur was sticking up through his leg. . . . And Dr. Hawkins, Earl Hawkins, he was a settled man. Jet black. He bent over to examine him. And he looked up and said, "You take your hands off me. I don't want no nigger to touch me." Now to me, that would have been to hell with you. Let you lie there and die. But Hawkins just said, "That's all right, soldier. Just take it easy. We'll take care of you." He told

the attendant, "Get some morphine in this man before he goes into shock. Just keep him warm." And I said, "Now you see the difference in nature?" He said, "You can't treat evil with evil and get any results." And he took care of the guy. And I learned that from him.[41]

Williams remembered his encounter with a Southern racist in the restroom in Richmond, Virginia, and other racist incidents. He admired Dr. Hawkins for his handling of the situation with the wounded soldier. Joe Stephenson shared Dr. Hawkins's attitude when he confronted prejudice, and he inspired his men. When his platoon went into the line, they were detached from their division and went to the 88th Division up in the mountains. They were supposed to make a Christmas morning attack on the Germans, but the attack was called off because of the Battle of the Bulge. They went up on the line anyway and started patrol actions. The three platoons in the L Company had already done their patrol duty on the coast, which was a very safe place to be. Each platoon leader went out three nights, and then waited until their time came again.[42]

Stephenson ended up in a dangerous section in the mountains. On January 5, 1945, Schaffer and Cameron, two men who had volunteered to go on patrol with Stephenson's platoon, were wounded and died a week later.[43] After their deaths, the remaining members of the platoon, who had been together since Atterbury, all volunteered for a dangerous daylight patrol in the Serchio Valley. When Stephenson heard uncomplimentary things about the 92nd Division's performance, it made him angry because he thought of the courageous men he had known during the war.[44]

Stephenson took two platoons and two platoon leaders to Viareggio for a decoration ceremony. General Almond's flair for ceremony persisted overseas. Stephenson recalled the power of the moment. Almond gave an inspiring speech and said, "These are our heroes," referring to those about to receive awards. Each soldier went forward as his name was called and stood while Almond pinned the Silver Star or Bronze Star on his uniform. Then they shook hands and saluted. Stephenson found the occasion moving.[45]

Overall, however, Stephenson was extremely critical of General Almond's flawed tactical decisions. Stephenson believed the 92nd Division was mistreated tactically. Almond ran the 370th up and down the hills in Italy, and then he ran them through the plains when the Germans on the hills could shoot down on them. Many of the men became shell-shocked, angry, and discouraged because they would take a hill and then be displaced from it, only to repeat this eight or nine times.

A wound forced Stephenson to spend time in the hospital. When he was released, he found that his company had been transferred with Captain Rocco over to the 370th. If Stephenson had been released from the hospital a day or two earlier, he could have rejoined Captain Rocco and the platoon that he had trained with. But now he found himself with a new platoon that differed radically from the previous group.[46] Disappointingly, he was in a safe location in the hills during the final push, instead of fighting alongside men like Joseph Tull and Oscar Warren. He had a fine sergeant in his company from the beginning, but most of the men in his new company were fearful and reluctant to fight. When Stephenson told members of his company to go out on patrol, the men who were selected dragged their feet. Stephenson had to threaten them with military discipline to get them to go on patrol.[47]

Stephenson soon heard a disturbance when they were out on the patrol. He saw that Brown, a member of his platoon, had a man down on the ground with a rifle barrel in his mouth. The man said, "I'll go, I'll go." And he said, "Damn right you're gonna go or I'm gonna blow your head off." He found out that the man on the ground had tried to run away. Stephenson was appalled at the men's behavior. Although he stayed with them until the end of the war, they never bonded as the first group had.[48]

In contrast, Joseph Hairston, as the battery executive for Charlie Battery and forward observer, served in the artillery, which had a good reputation throughout the war. His friend, a platoon leader, went out on patrol with him one day. The path led around the face of a mountain, leaving them fully exposed in the daylight. They took turns leading the patrol and had just changed position when his friend stepped on a mine and was killed. Hairston blamed the commanding officers' strategy, because he did not believe they should be engaged in this type of patrol in daylight and especially without detection equipment. His first thought was that Colonel Wood and others like him were ensuring that the black soldiers would sustain 10 percent of the casualties—a promise he had made at Camp Robinson. This experience was so searing that Hairston carried a fervent hatred and anger for many years after the incident. At that moment, he wanted revenge and to kill the perpetrator of the action. A mortar attack forced him to take cover in a hole, and after the barrage, he had cooled down.[49]

Hairston had to contend with an exceptionally timid battery commander. He was so afraid that the troops became uneasy. In combat they learned the sound of the various shells. An 88-millimeter round, for example, had a flat trajectory and did not give any warning. With normal artillery, they could hear it and tell whether it was coming close or not. Every time the battery commander heard a round, he would yell "hit the ground" and start scrambling. The troops were so unnerved they were not functioning well. Then the commander simply disappeared. From the time Hairston took over the guns right after Christmas in 1944, until the end of the war in Italy on May 8, 1945, he did not see him again.[50]

Previously a mortar platoon leader, Jehu Hunter served in the 3rd Battalion of the 365th as a communications officer from August 1944 to October 10, 1945. He rose to the rank of captain and was awarded the Bronze Star. Hunter fought in the northern Apennines in Italy from November 1944 through April 1945. After the war, he felt very proud that he was an army officer and had fought to protect his country from fascism.[51] But Hunter was highly critical of Almond's bad leadership when the general sent a reinforced battalion on an assault across a coastal plain without first having secured the commanding high ground and when he ordered attacks on the same areas repeatedly without changing tactics. Poor leadership and the army's poor planning meant that the 92nd often received inexperienced or no replacements. Hunter endured both subtle and overt racial discrimination, as did other blacks. Towns or sections of towns were placed off limits to black soldiers. All of these factors led to a deterioration of morale.[52]

Hunter's baptism by fire occurred when he came under artillery attack while working with a wire crew to maintain telephone lines in the rifle companies. He took cover until it was over and then withdrew into the command post. Because he spent most of his time maintaining or replacing telephone lines, he was not involved in face-to-face combat. Overall, his battalion was successful in taking territory and repelling counterattacks.[53]

Hunter found that the infantry performed well initially as the Germans retreated to their heavily fortified stronghold behind the Gothic line. When the division made its assault on Mount Cauala, they had to fall back after fighting for three hard days and suffering four hundred casualties. The lack of adequate black replacements affected their capabilities significantly. But the division succeeded in diverting a number of enemy forces away from the Bologna area, where the 5th Army would eventually break into the Po River Valley.[54]

When Albert Burke of the 365th arrived in Italy, his responsibility for the duration was as official messenger from the division headquarters to General Mark Clark's 5th Army Headquarters in Rome. He carried special messages on an almost daily basis between Rome and Viareggio where they were stationed. For security reasons, sensitive messages were not transmitted by wire or telephone. One night, as he prepared to make a return trip, the Germans began their almost nightly shelling. The Germans could take an 88-millimeter round and pinpoint a single person if they saw him. Dodging a shell, Burke ran and jumped in a hole, but unfortunately he was wounded by shrapnel.[55]

Like Albert Burke, Edward Brooke, later a U.S. senator from Massachusetts, was a college graduate. He served in the 366th Infantry Regiment during World War II. When he reported for training, he experienced racial discrimination more dramatically than he ever had before. Segregation was practiced, and white facilities were superior to those of black soldiers. He felt resentment and bitterness such as he had never felt before in his life.[56]

On March 28, 1944, he boarded a ship bound for North Africa. Brooke's regiment landed in Casablanca and took a train to Oran, Algeria. Colonel Queen was the commander of the unit. When Colonel George Pense suggested that Queen set up a separate soldier's club for Negro soldiers, or as he called them, "these people," Queen refused. Queen's particular unit was not allowed to fight. Instead, 151 officers and 3,095 enlisted men of the unit provided security for airbases from May to November from Sardinia to the Adriatic Coast. On November 15, 1944, the 366th was attached to the 92nd Division. On November 26, General Almond welcomed them with a speech. Brooke recalled the memorable event:

> Almond stood before them one hand on his hip—the other holding a bullhorn. In an angry and condescending tone, what he told us was essentially: "Your Negro friends and your Negro press back in the States have been clamoring for you to go into combat. Well, since you asked for it, let's see how you like it. You can believe I will make you fight and suffer your share of casualties."
>
> This was a general who after the war would blame the 92nd Division's unsatisfactory performance on "the undependability of the average Negro soldier."[57]

Brooke missed fighting in the first clash in December because Colonel Queen assigned him to a special unit to work behind the German lines with Italian partisans. When he returned from that assignment, there were still plenty of battles ahead. A particular engagement at Mount Faeto convinced him that some of the racist white commanders had used their men as cannon fodder in order to teach them a lesson. The Germans knew the terrain better than his regiment and had the strategic advantage of concealed and well-placed artillery batteries on mountain peaks. The commanding officers frequently would run the troops up the same hill at the same time each day. Therefore, the Germans knew what to expect. Brooke suggested varying the order and sending up a force at daybreak instead of beginning with artillery fire. Finally, he persuaded them to permit a reconnaissance group to do just that. They were able to seize the hill because they caught the Germans by surprise.[58]

One morning, Gene Johnston and his men prepared to make a surprise attack against German machine-gun posts and fortifications. Gene had been to Rome and returned the previous night around one o'clock. A message from headquarters instructed him to attack the next morning. Upon his return, he found that he had three new officers, fresh from the replacement camp, eager to see action. They talked about what they were going to do, and one officer kept saying he was going to earn a Silver Star. Gene was more concerned about keeping them safe: "When you move from one place to another, stay down and don't take chances because they will shoot you. This is not a war game; it's the real thing." Because they were anxious to get started, they did not seem to hear anything he said. By that night, Gene did not have a single officer with him; the new inexperienced black lieutenants had either been wounded or killed.[59]

With the rest of his company, Gene went to Calomini and was assigned a new lieutenant. He instructed him to stay out of the houses because they were easy targets for German artillery shells. Gene left at noon, and before that night, the lieutenant had moved his men inside a warm building. Predictably, an artillery shell killed every one of them two weeks later.

Soon Gene moved east into the Serchio Valley.[60] Every night, some Italian workers brought mules carrying supplies up to the troops. Sometimes it would take them until after midnight before they got to their destination. The post exchange light wooden crates were supposed to contain enough supplies for an entire company of two hundred men. They contained candies, stationery, razors, razor blades, and tobacco. Everybody wanted tobacco. When Gene found out that mule drivers sometimes stole the supplies after causing the mules to fall off the mountain, he told some of the mule drivers he would accompany them on some of their supply trips. He called them all together and said, "The next time supplies are stolen, and I find out that the muleskinner was responsible for it, I am going to shoot him and leave him lying down with the mule." That stopped the theft.[61]

The 92nd Division was supported by the 12th Italian Mule Pack Company, with 240 mules and 10 horses, and the 92nd Infantry Division Provisional Mule Pack Battalion with 90 mules. The continuous support over long periods of time and the ability of these animals to negotiate difficult terrain while carrying heavy loads contributed to the advance of the Allied forces. From the end of January to March 1945, Spencer Moore was in charge of a mule pack. It was the best job he had in the 92nd. He did not have to get out of bed if he did not feel like it. He had a sergeant, a private, and fifty-five Italians working for him. He was like the mayor. Moore gave passes to the Italians to go to Pietrasanta. One day they came to him and said that one of the mules had been shot and one mule was wounded so he went up to see about it. At night, they had to go around the forward slope of a mountain, and the Germans shot at them.

None of the men had been hurt, but when they tried to get the wounded mule up, the animal made a few faltering steps and went back down. It had blood coming out of its nostrils, so they had to shoot it. Spencer said, "I am not going to shoot that mule. He didn't do anything to me." So he gave his carbine to one of the Italians, who shot the mule. That shot echoed through the village after they had the mule strung up, skinned, and cut up; the whole valley smelled of mule meat that night. Before long, Spencer was reassigned to his old outfit.[62]

Like Spencer Moore, Gene Johnston was thinking of home. He wrote Alta, "Remember, my love, you're all my future and without you I don't want to live. I know that you were meant for me and I just hope I can always make you happy." (Somewhere in Italy, December 12, 1944.) He did not fear being killed because he thought he could take care of himself. He was thinking about his baby that was on the way and the rest of his life with Alta. He also prayed. Everyone talked about their families and about when they might go home.[63] Although black and white soldiers inhabited parallel universes, they shared the danger, fear, courage, and longing for home.

Gene and his troops were in position above Lucca for a long time when they received an order from the division to attract attention by firing their machine guns, to bring all 50-caliber machine guns up to the front, and then to fire them toward the mountain. They set up the 50-caliber guns that they rarely used at the command post. The infantry weapons "shoots" began around December 12, 1944.[64] They moved frequently. They attacked or shifted from one place to another, especially in the Serchio Valley and in the area by the Cinquale Canal. Some companies had only about 100 men, well below the 187 men (and 6 officers) they were supposed to have. Gene would choose a route for his company and then pick a patrol from a squad. The next time, he would make a different squad responsible for the patrol, so that the job and the danger were equally shared. An officer from the intelligence department at headquarters oriented them. The men dreaded those patrols because they knew the enemy was waiting for them. On cold moonlight nights, they got into deadly fights.

Gene had to be constantly vigilant because when the men were out on guard, they might panic and shoot their own. One night, Gene went into the small town of Parma and, just as he feared, some soldier started shooting. He shot the dashboard of Gene's jeep. Gene went there another time, and he started yelling as he went out of the door of the command post. He said, "You son of a bitch. If you shoot me, I'll shoot back." So the man said, "I ain't goin' to shoot you." Gene knew the soldiers were very different from one another; one might be more aggressive than another. Some were not aggressive enough to be soldiers who could survive in combat.[65]

A few soldiers in Gene's company were killed, and some were wounded. They had good medical units, and antibiotics saved a lot of lives. When someone did get hit, sulfanilamide was a godsend. All the soldiers had small packages of it, a powder to sprinkle on the cut or take internally. Dr. Whitfield came up with something like that at Fort Oglethorpe. When a man had a part of his neck blown away, Gene changed his dressing every day and applied the antibiotic. The packet was a lifesaver when Gene picked up a bullet in his shoulder. One time Colonel Walker came to see Gene, and they walked the line together, checking positions. When they went to an aid station, the colonel picked up two packages of sulfanilamide powder. He handed one to Gene and kept the other. He said, "Hang on to this and if either one of us needs it we can use it."

Gene never left his company because he was afraid it would fall apart. Curt (Curtis) Ivey, a company commander, one of the first on the line, felt the same way when he was wounded. He would not leave his men because he was afraid they might take off. Gene went over to see Ivey and persuaded him to come down and get the medics to work on him. He was running a fever, but he would not leave his post.[66]

Gene was frequently on the Purple Heart Highway, the road going up to Seravezza. There was a big hill with a river running through it called the Cinquale Canal. The canal was a deep cut and had steep banks with two bridges across it. One was the main road coming up through the beach, and there was another concrete road on the beach. Gene and his men had been up there four or five times, but they could not manage to hold the location. They had attacked the ridge dozens of times, but each time, the Germans would counterattack and drive them off.

Gene Johnston learned by mail that his daughter Nancy had been born on January 11, 1945. He wrote to Alta on January 17, 1945, from "Somewhere in Italy": "Darling I am so excited I can hardly write—I received your cablegram today—Gee, I'm sure relieved that you are doing ok and everything is alright—I'll admit I

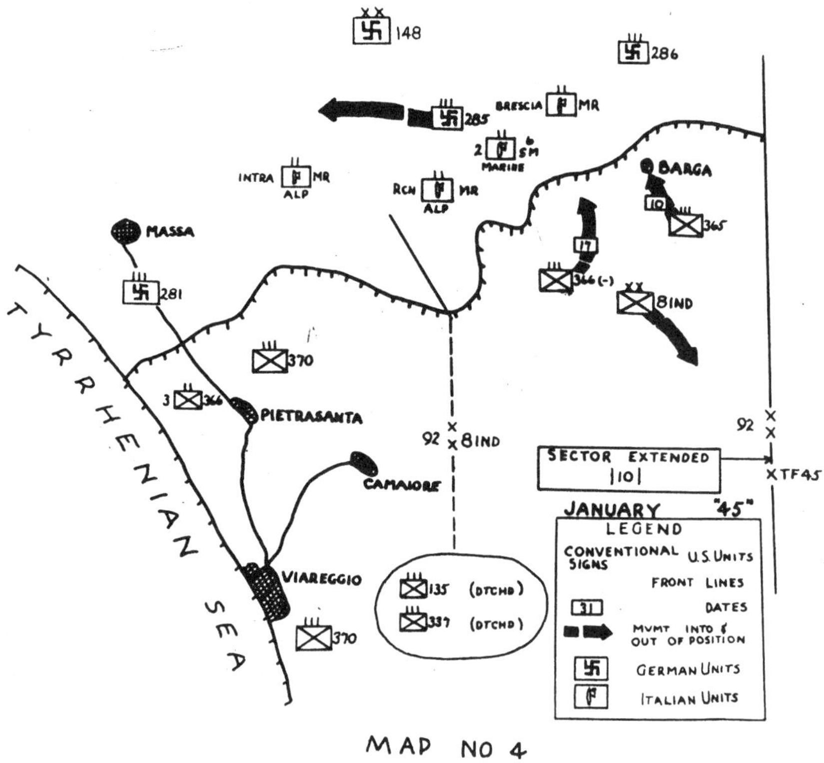

12. Map 4, Italian campaign, January 1945. Courtesy of Army Military History Institute, Carlisle, Pennsylvania.

was a bit disappointed at it being a girl but that's alright [*sic*]. I'm tickled pink. . . . Well darling I love you more than all the world and now that we have a daughter we have more than ever to look forward to when this is over." A few days later on January 21, 1945, he wrote to "tell my daughter I'm crazy about her."[67]

The joyous news did not erase the uneasiness about the course of the war for the 92nd Division. The division made gains only to lose them again as it attempted to take Massa and fight along its front in December. German forces attacked units of the 92nd, forcing them to withdraw from the area around Massa from December 26 through December 28. The 5th Army called off the Christmas Day assault, and the black and white Buffalo Soldiers advanced against German mortar and artillery; they held the towns of Barga and Gallicano. When the Germans surrounded his men in Sommocolonia, John Fox ordered artillery to fire directly on his own position, sacrificing his life. After much loss of life, by January 1,

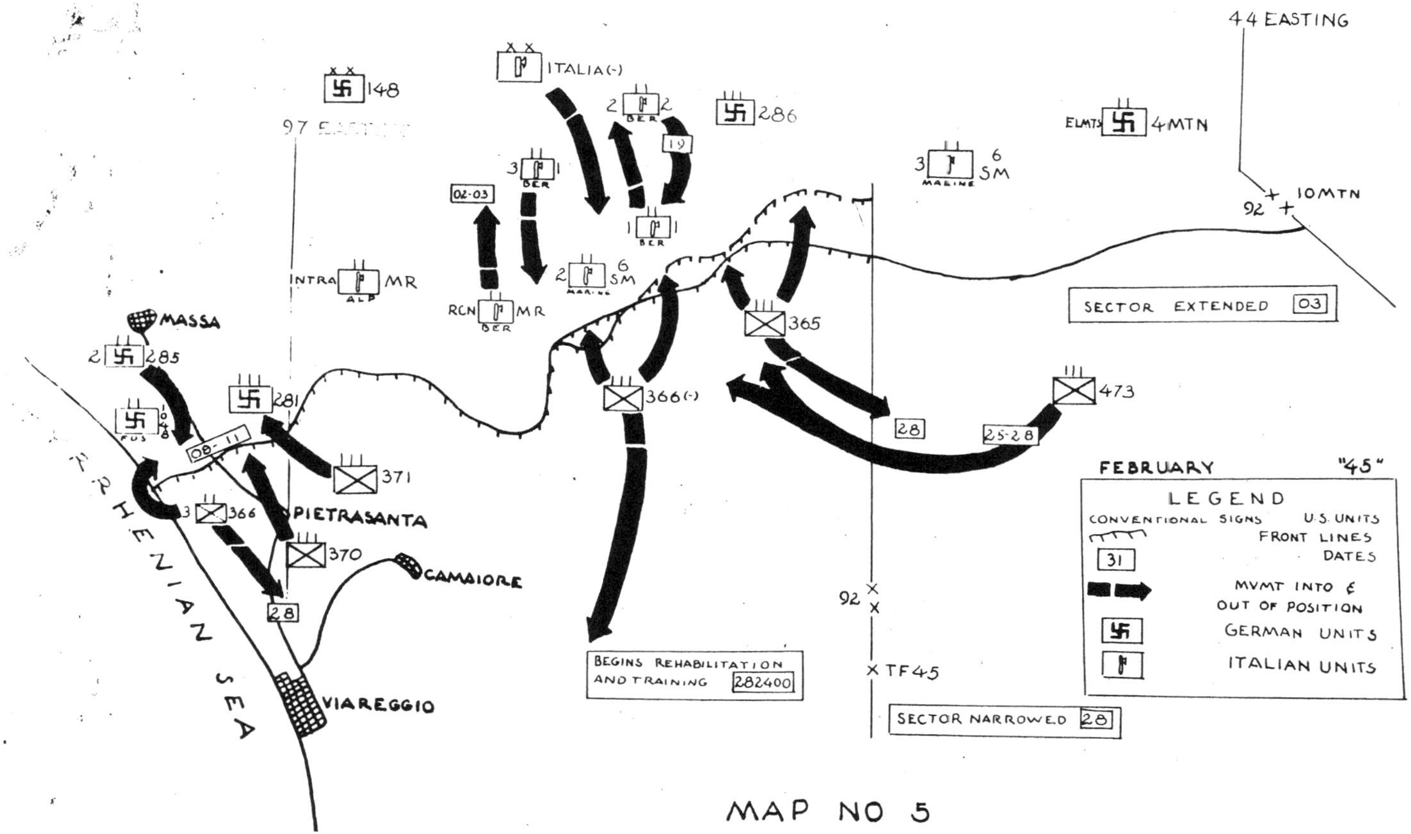

13. Map 5, Italian campaign, February 1945. Courtesy of Army Military History Institute, Carlisle, Pennsylvania.

14. This Negro combat patrol advanced three miles north of Lucca (furthermost point occupied by American troops) to contact an enemy machine gun nest. Here a bazooka-man cuts loose at the target some 300 yards distant. September 7, 1944. Edwards. 111-SC-194328.(african_americans _wwii_039.jpg). Courtesy of U.S. Army, National Archives.

1945, the Allies had essentially reclaimed their original positions. After a frustrating fall in which the 92nd took and lost the same ground over and over, they could only claim a stalemate with the Germans. Buffalo Soldiers Moore, Hunter, Perry, Johnston, Stephenson, Hancock, Brooke, and Hairston had already experienced the terrors of combat and the onset of a bitter Italian winter. As a new year began in 1945, they faced an uncertain future.

10

From Defeat to Victory

February–November 1945

> I have lived long enough to see a glorious mantle surround World War II. It was a "good war." I would say it was a necessary war, but war is never good to those who fight it or those who live through it. War is dirty, gruesome, and horrible.
>
> Edward Brooke

February Offensive (1945)

In February 1945, the 365th, 371st, and 370th assembled on the coastal plain near Pozzi and Querceta for the largest attack the 92nd would mount. Their objective was to capture Massa, but first they had to take Mount Strettoia, with hills they called X, Y, and Z. The steep mountain was 450 feet high. This engagement was unsuccessful because the Germans caught them in a trap. Complicating the operation even more, allied P-47 fighters bombed their own troops by mistake on the X, Y, Z hills.

The 92nd tried to take that ground from September 1944 to April 1945. They captured the hills and then lost them. Then they regained them and lost them again. They were up against the German commander Field Marshal Albert Kesselring, one of the most brilliant Axis tacticians. His objective was to make the Allies pay dearly for every foot of ground in Italy, and he fought them in what became one of the longest and bloodiest Allied campaigns. The mountainous terrain and harsh winter conditions were his greatest assets and the greatest disadvantages for the Allies. While the attempts on Mount Strettoia were underway, another ill-fated battle occurred on the plains below.[1]

General Almond conceived a diversionary operation. He asked Lieutenant Colonel Edward Rowny to plan an attack at the Cinquale Canal. Rowny, a West Point man, was an engineer who had been an aide to Almond and one of his favorite officers. Almond decided to put Rowny in a position where he could promote him. Seven of the division's nine infantry battalion commanders had been killed or wounded in one week. This created a critical shortage of infantry officers in the division. So he transferred Rowny from the 317th Engineers Battalion to become an infantry commander. Rowny formed a task force consisting of a tank company, a battalion, and a Special Forces outfit.[2]

An Infantry Man's Hell: Cinquale Canal

The road by the Cinquale Canal bridge was straight and built up on the sides of the bank, which ran along the beach. The whole length of the beach was lined with at least three rows of heavy mines, such that troops could not descend from the road for danger of hitting a mine.[3] Rowny's task force led the attack; he had more than twenty tanks attached to the division. The first tank went across the bridge and hit a mine; the explosion did not wreck the bridge, but it wrecked the tank, blocking the road so the others could not cross. It was just wide enough for one tank to go across at a time. Because they were under shellfire, they could not reach the bridge to clear a path. So they turned around, made a circle around the bridge, and started to go to the water's edge to avoid the mines. There they got mired down and started running over mines. Ultimately, they lost all of their tanks.

General Almond hoped that the Germans would use their reserves to stop Rowny's offensive. Then the rest of the division would be freed to attack them on higher ground. The Germans shelled the 366th heavily with mortar and artillery fire. Seven of the nine people in Rowny's command group were killed. Of 1,250 in the task force only 120 to 125 were left. Rowny thought the engagement at Cinquale Canal was a highly ingenious plan, but it was in fact a disaster. Both Almond and Rowny blamed the troops for the fiasco, but it was a failure of leadership.[4] Edward Rowny earned two Silver Stars, a Bronze Star, a Combat Infantryman Badge, and a commendation ribbon during his service in Italy. Yet because of the Cinquale Canal engagement, the 92nd Division was deemed a failure and completely reorganized.

An article in *Newsweek* of February 26, 1945, characterized the division as the "Luckless 92nd." The author derided the soldiers of the 92nd: "The most extensive and whole-hearted effort by the United States Army to give American Negro troops a role in the war equal to that of white troops has so far been more productive of disappointment and failure than of anything else. That much could be told last week about the experience of the Army with the 92nd Division, an outfit in which all the enlisted men and a high proportion of the officers are Negroes." The article referred to the assault of the Germans in December and the debacle at Cinquale Canal. Both of these engagements led to the reorganization of the division.

Reflective of the "official story" about the 92nd Division, it was based on inaccuracies and racist attitudes. The Germans launched a reconnaissance attack in December 1944 and, sensing an opportunity to destabilize the Allies, intensified the assault. After the war, the German commanding officer, Brigadier General Fretter-Pico told Allied interrogators: "The weaknesses of your deployment in the Serchio Valley in December, 1944, were that your troops were deployed on a front which was too long for the number of troops available, and your reserves were too far in the rear areas which prevented their being deployed immediately." The operations were not successful, but there were many logistical factors involved. For example, the Germans had the tactical advantage of the guns at Punta Bianca, the emplacements on the mountains above, the bad weather, and the depletion of Allied ammunition. The Allies were able to restore their lines, but the 5th Army was thrown out of balance and thus had to postpone the main effort against Bologna.[5] Moreover, the white officers like General Almond, Edward Rowny, Mark Clark, and many others were highly decorated in the Italian campaign. One can only assume that the harsh judgment of the 92nd Division's "failure" was largely racially motivated.

Soldiers of the 92nd were keenly aware of their tactical disadvantages. Captain Hondon Hargrove lamented that the battle at Cinquale Canal was an artillery man's paradise and an infantry man's hell. Bill Perry blamed it on tactical blunders. Unleashed against the 366th was the greatest single concentration of artillery fire by the Germans of the entire Italian campaign, producing the largest number of casualties experienced by the 92nd Division in the war. E Company of the 370th and the 366th were just about wiped out. Because the operation on February 1–11, 1945, at Cinquale Canal was such a colossal disaster, it was the last major offensive the 92nd made with its original units. It was evident that the Buffalo Soldiers had been hurled into a hopeless battle with little logistical support and with leadership that lacked strategic vision. The Germans had the advantage of experience as well as of their impregnable natural and man-made fortifications.

Joseph Hairston, who gave on-site artillery support, saw the battle at Cinquale Canal as evidence of a disastrous strategy:

> We lost more tanks for that size of action than any place in the whole war, because of stupidity of clearing a narrow lane through a mine field across a creek. The Germans sat up on the hill and watched them do it. And they sent the tanks down in single file. Their tanks couldn't move left or right because of the mines. And as the couple of tanks got up on the far side then

> the Germans just knocked them off so they couldn't retreat. Now that was just plain dumb. You don't use tanks that way. And yet, General Almond ends up a three-star General in the Far East Command. And he wrote that the Division had failed. I mean, his official comments were that the Division had failed to perform. And yet, generally speaking, if you are the Commander and an organization has failed, you share the responsibility. But in his, and that's what I say, it shows the racism of that period, because he's let off scot free.[6]

Gene Johnston heard about the fiasco at Cinquale Canal. He was up on the ridge above the canal and could not see clearly what was going on. Gene and his company were on the west coast, so they moved swiftly to the beach shortly after the battle.[7] He and his men pulled in right where Rowny and his soldiers had been to find their disabled tanks deserted on the beach. At night, the Germans removed the motors from those tanks. In the daytime, Gene's men used them for cover and sniped at Germans. At night, Gene sent the men out on patrol; they took dynamite with them and fired artillery rounds across the canal, blowing some holes near the Cinquale Canal for protection.[8] When they started up the road on a high bank, they anticipated the barrage from the big guns at Punta Bianca.

The 92nd Division's goal was ultimately to capture Massa. Some of the enlisted men coined the phrase, "Yassa, we a-goin to Massa." That proved quite difficult.[9] Soon the big guns at Massa started firing, and Gene knew they had to abandon Highway 1, a road that went to Genoa and Massa, because the Germans were targeting it. When he had gone about a mile and a half, he got word from the general that he was sending trucks to take them over onto the main road.[10] Shelling was heavy back and forth. Because Gene and his troops were with headquarters people at that time, he was not involved in hand-to-hand fighting. They bypassed a town near Hill Y and approached it from another direction. After they captured the town, someone started shelling it. Gene entered a house where he discovered that German soldiers were living under the floor. They had dug out a cellar where they had their bunks. When a soldier came out and surrendered, Gene took his pistol, an American-made one, and sent the prisoner back to the rear. They had attacked that town previously, but they had never been able to take it. Gene asked a captain who came down from headquarters where he was supposed to go. He was told to go into bivouac at a place on the coast and await orders.[11]

As the shelling continued, Gene moved through the front part of a town laced with mines. He asked some civilians to show him locations of the mines, but they refused. When his company captured a group of Germans, Gene lined up the German officers and asked them to locate the mines, but they laughed at him. So he said, "I'm going to line you up and let you march in front of me." One of the Germans spoke English, and said, "You can't do that. It's against the Geneva Convention." Gene said, "You are going to walk in front of me and show me where the mines are." Finally, they agreed. The American soldiers walked out right behind the German officers as they led them through the minefield, but they kept grumbling about the Geneva Convention.[12]

The 92nd Division fought with British, Indian, and Brazilian forces in the 5th Army. There were British outfits waiting in every town all the way up to France. Shortly before the war in Italy was over, in the spring of 1945, the officers in cities along the coast lived quite well. Once when Gene went down toward Viareggio to relieve a British battalion, the commander showed him all his positions: where his guns were and where to expect the action. The British officer said, "I'll tell you, old buddy, over there is my daytime position; down here is my nighttime position, and over here my combat positions." Whether there was heavy shelling or not, the British unit stopped in the afternoon to have tea.[13]

Occasionally, Gene ran into other white officers who were his friends like Roy Kealy, Curtis Ivey, Ray Zobel, Jack Gerwin, and Joe Belmore. Most of them were lieutenants. Gene used to laugh at Joe Belmore, whom he considered one of the funniest men alive. One time, Belmore came to see Gene in a small town in the Serchio Valley. Walking up the snowy mountain, Joe was sweating profusely. He frequently sat down and lay back on the snow. Gene told him, "You better cut that out or you are going to be sick." When he finally made it up the mountain, they had to carry him back down to the hospital where he remained for a long time. One day, Belmore was sitting up in the bed and a nurse told him to lie back down and behave himself. When he gave her some smart talk, she slugged him. Belmore survived the nurse and the war.[14]

Ray Zobel became the adjutant for the 371st, and he wrote to his wife every day telling her what a hard time he was having. But he was living inside a house at the regimental headquarters at Viareggio. There were no hardships for those at the headquarters at all, and they even had their own mess halls. Gene and the other soldiers did not get regular mail from home, and they could not write in the foxhole much of the time. When his father died around Christmas time in 1944, Gene was entitled to a pass to go home, but could not obtain one. Gene believed that Zobel blocked his return because he could not go home himself.

When Gene got up on the line in February 1945, where his men had attacked the same place ten times and gotten run off every time, he had to reassemble the men he had and attack that day. They managed to achieve their first objective, reaching the first hill, terraced with olive trees. They stopped on that first ridge with a radio man. The enemy was on a hill below the ridge, and the general was above them in the woods. Gene knew the Germans could see them.[15]

Around eleven o'clock on the morning of February 10, 1945, Gene and Colonel Walker were out in the open. Gene kept telling Colonel Walker that they ought to get out of there. He laughed and said, "Johnny (Gene's nickname), you're always too scared." Walker continued to walk around in the open. They were on top of a ridge near two foxholes. Their radio was in one of them. Colonel Walker and Gene were standing between the two foxholes when a mortar shell exploded near them. Gene jumped in a foxhole flat, face down, and a soldier jumped in on top of him. Gene got up and Colonel Walker was down in a foxhole that was filling up with hot dirt with smoke coming out of it. Gene dragged the colonel out and saw that his head was badly injured. He tried to pick him up, but he was too heavy to carry alone.[16]

Gene yelled for help, but men kept running off the hill to safety. Gene kept hollering, "Come help me. Help me!" Finally he got angry, pulled his .45 out, and stopped some of them. "Damn you! I'm going to kill you if you move. You're going to help me move this man." Then about a dozen men ran over to help him. He held the gun on them and told them, "By God I'm going to kill you if you don't help me get the colonel out of here."

The men took the colonel around the bend and down the mountain. Gene stayed above to organize the troops. Fortunately, the radio was still working when the general called him. Gene told the general and Major John B. Hazel that the colonel had been killed. The general asked Gene what he needed, and he said, "More troops." Gene told him that his men had disappeared, and he only had sixteen or eighteen left out of the whole company. He said, "I will send you L Company or some other company; just hang on and dig in and hold what you have."[17]

Gene was wounded. Blood covered the back of his neck and ran down his back; his entire scalp was almost torn off. But he stayed up there and tried to stop the men from coming off the hill and from running; some would still run right by him. Finally, he started organizing the line, and he talked to an artillery observer. Because this was normally the time the Germans counterattacked, he and his men were expecting it. Gene took over the battalion for a while until they sent a major to assume command.[18]

Gene went to the first aid station but not the hospital. They had an officer from the New Hebrides who ran the aid infirmary for the battalion. The medic asked him whether he wanted him to sew it or clip it; he ended up putting some clips on his scalp which had been bleeding profusely. Gene must have gotten restless in the night because when he woke the bandage was torn off, and he had to have the clips replaced. After the shrapnel had raised up his scalp, he was wounded in his arm.

Six days later, on February 16, 1945, Gene wrote to Alta from "Somewhere in Italy": "Needless to say I am still in action and expect to be (knock on wood) until this is finished for I certainly don't want my baby girl to have to go through what we're having now. There is one thing I can tell you now, probably you already know it, and that is I love you with all my heart and soul. Nothing darling can ever come between us for no one can ever take your place in my heart. I know definitely that we were meant for each other. And when this is over we'll sure 'step out' and be happy."[19]

Joe Willie Johnson, a fellow Tennessean, experienced similar longings for home. As an African American soldier of Company H in the 370th, he endured the same bitter Italian winter and the terrors of war as the white officers, but he hoped that their sacrifice would benefit all black people. He wrote to his father-in-law, Mr. Hubbard, on February 5, 1945:

> Negroes are doing their bit here, their supreme bit—not for glory, not for honor, but for I think the generation that will come. If the blood that flows here on Italy's mountain will wash from some folks' minds the stigma that has been bred there for years, then, I think that the men who have gone so bravely here will not have given their lives in vain. I think I shall see it thru, but I'm proud to be one of these few men who are fighters. The American papers call us "Tan Yanks" and other fancy names, but we find right here the best of all—the Italians call us "Americans" —just plain "Americans." That's all we want to be—and one day, I hope we will, be just plain Americans.[20]

Staff Sergeant Joe Willie Johnson Jr. had joined the army on August 18, 1942, just as he was entering his junior year of college. Like Gene, he wrote many letters to his wife from a foxhole. On February 17, 1945, he wrote to Mary Alice:

> My dearest wife,
>
> In so many days, I haven't written you a letter. I realize your anxiety, to the utmost, but I've been busy—so very busy here in this place. I know you're bound to worry, but please don't attempt to imagine what is hap-

pening to me or what is going on here. It's just torturous! . . . In a quiet hamlet one sees thick walls that would stop shrapnel, ground that would do for gun positions, a shaded, concealed way of approach, and getting supplies—instead of the well-kept home of some family, or ground that does for pretty gardens lush with flowers, vegetables, and tiny trees basking in the quiet summer's sun, its tiny branches weighted by the winter's snow. . . . As for courage in Italy, honey, I saw the kids rank first and we as soldiers respect them for it. But the desire for home, for gardens, for flowers blooming where shells have never fallen, is still the strangest here—even more than self-preservation.

. . . For now nite, dearest. I gotta go—got a job to do—and a war to win.
Forever yours,
Your husband,
Joe Willie[21]

Joe Willie wrote again about a month later on March 21, 1945, that the spring had come, with trees flowering and birds twittering, creating a glorious scene that could only be "a mockery of peace, since the war was not yet over." He closed on a somber note:

My dearest wife,

Today I'm twenty-four years of age, and yet I stand quite the youngster on the threshold of life or life's endeavor. But the complexities of life are quite vulnerable to unraveling, as I stand here with you, and that makes all else a downhill pull. What excuse on that final day shall men make for these useless, senseless days of deliberate calculative destruction? Was it done to further man's enlightenment; to further the world's progress? Have men died because of some selfish whim, or because of some beneficial ideology?

. . . Does God, in all His glory, look on us and say, "Your cause is just?" I like to think so. I like to think, honey, that men, yes men, not boys, who have fallen here have fallen for some material benefit, for some tangible progress; that the cause of our folks of Negroes, have been helped by what so few have done and are doing here . . . I'm afraid, dear, that the heralds of this respect will be too few—and that few assimilated all too soon in the maelstrom of what we have known. This is depressive, dear,—and I'm on the first phase of an exciting new journey—another year. I pray that at least part of this one will be ours.[22]

For those many months of 1944 and 1945, Mary Alice Hubbard Johnson and Alta Johnston anxiously waited for the mail and for word from their husbands. In their letters, Gene and Joe Willie tried to remain optimistic and reassuring even after searing traumas. Colonel Walker's death affected Gene more than the loss of any other friend during the war. He had nightmares about that day until his death. Over and over, he replayed the moment and regretted that he could not save the colonel.

Gene had to keep going that day. He had some good men who really fought, and on whom he could depend. They made an attack on a ridge on the eastern front. They had to get up there because they expected the Germans to attack that night. Gene waited until just before dark and a lieutenant came with about twenty men from a whole company. That was all he could find because the rest of the company had taken off.

Gene showed them where to dig in and position their guns because the Germans probably would counterattack. He showed them how to dig their foxholes, spread out, and make contact with a nearby unit. He had them all set. The next morning, when Gene checked on the unit, only ten of his twenty men remained. As soon as he had left, they had fled. During this period, General Almond decided to reorganize the whole division, and Gene joined an excellent unit. Gene had served with the 371st in F Company and M Company before the reorganization; afterward, he joined Company G of the 370th.[23]

The parallel universes of black and white soldiers were evident in the radically different perceptions of certain battles.[24] Ivan Houston, who was in Headquarters 3rd Battalion of the 370th, heard enlisted men say they had "unassed the hill." They meant that they were being fired on, or faced superior power and got back under cover. They did not view it as "melting away" or "straggling" but a "tactical retreat." Tactical retreats were often necessary because the 92nd attacked the heavily fortified German forces six or seven times before making an all-out attack on German positions.[25]

Units of the 92nd often fought all day and ended up where they started. Generally, straggling was blamed on the soldiers, and their superiors saw them as poor troops, but straggling was primarily an indication that the troops had lost confidence in their commanding officers. It would be inaccurate to overemphasize it and for it to overshadow the performance of the majority of the Buffalo soldiers who did not desert and who demonstrated courage and valor.

There was a dangerous stretch on the Purple Heart Highway coming out from Viareggio and onto an asphalt road straight to Seravezza. The Germans had stationed an 88-millimeter gun on top of the hill and would shoot at any vehicle they saw going down that road. The Americans had to drive fast to avoid getting hit by those shells. At one moment, General Almond decided to drive up the Purple Heart Highway. He took off in his jeep with his new aide. About half way up the highway, he stopped. This put them in direct line with the anti-tank guns at the top of the ridge. Despite warnings from his driver, General Almond got out of his jeep to look around. The German cannoneers started firing on him from the ridge. They tore up Almond's jeep and killed his aide. Almond's bravado endangered his men and cost one his life. When the troops found out about the incident, they assumed that Almond did not have much sense and resented his action because it cost a life.[26] The American soldiers had been driving that route for six months or more and they knew the road was in sight of the enemy.

On another occasion, General Almond endangered his men. Gene and his company were making an early morning attack and preparing to begin an attack or "jump off." Almond came out and was standing at the edge of the woods, where at that time, Gene's company was in reserve. They were the third battalion to move out and were supposed to hang back. The general got out and walked down with several young lieutenants. Evidently he was trying to show off. He started strutting through an open field toward the enemy and made the lieutenants walk along with him. He said, "Come on now; come on." Suddenly, the Germans started dropping mortar shells in among them.[27]

In addition to these sorts of incidents, Almond's segregationist policies bred resentment. He established a club on the beach in Italy for whites only. Gene never got back to headquarters, but over at Forte dei Marmi, he knew that black officers were not admitted. Gene and his men spent most of the winter near Forte dei Marmi and Seravezza on Hill X, but they were on all the hills there—X, Y, and Z, and further up the mountain. Hill X was alongside a small town back in the draw on the road leading into the mountains. Barbed wire strung across the area and minefields created dangerous conditions for any movement of troops.[28]

Rome fell on June 4, 1944, before the 92nd arrived. The Germans had used some Italian troops, but Gene rarely saw any of them. However, when he started the next attack, large numbers of armed Italian partisans wanted to join him, and they desperately needed food and ammunition. When Gene's company pulled into Viareggio one day, Simmons, one of his soldiers, began to sing *Ave Maria* in the most beautiful voice imaginable. Gene's troops and the partisans all stood perfectly still as they listened, knowing soon they would return to combat. But for that moment, the entire place was filled with such beauty and feeling. The respite was short-lived, and major changes within the division were imminent.[29]

George C. Marshall came from Washington to Italy to confer with General Al-

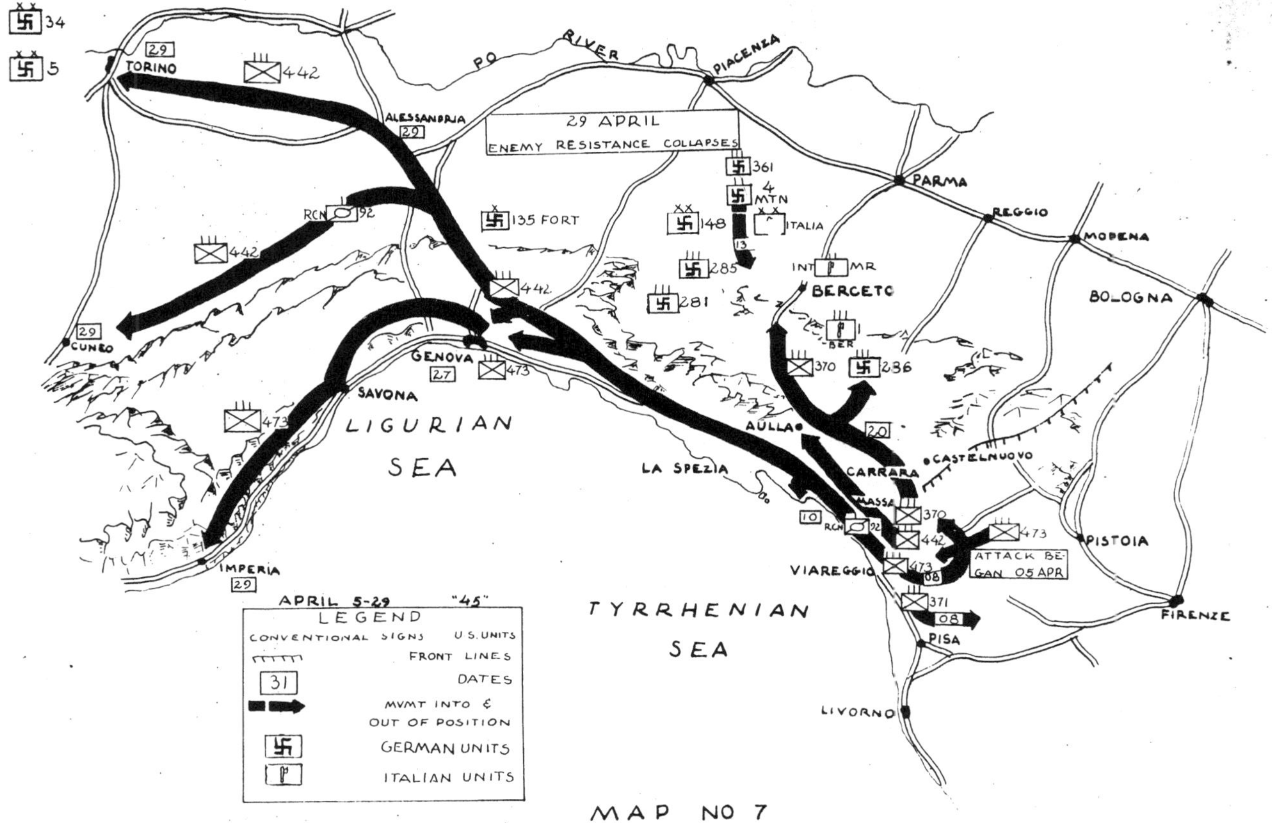

15. Map 7, Italian campaign, April 1945. Courtesy of Army Military History Institute, Carlisle, Pennsylvania.

mond. When Marshall asked him what it would "take to make this Division go," Almond stood up at the map with a grease pencil and said, "Give me something north of this line." He drew a line just south of his main battle position. He said, "My infantry regiments won't close with the enemy and won't hold their ground if they're attacked. My artillery is first rate. My logistics work well, engineer and ordnance perform excellently. I have a competent, experienced Division staff, but the infantry regiments aren't functioning well enough." General Marshall said, "I'll give you the 442nd Infantry [already famous Japanese-American Regimental Combat Team], including the 100th Infantry Battalion [composed mostly of Nisei from Hawaii]." Marshall told him he would convert the 45th Anti-Aircraft Brigade into an infantry regiment and give him that unit also. He told him to choose his best men from all his regiments and consolidate them into a new regiment. This reorganization took place before the major spring offensive.[30]

Reorganization of the 92nd and the April Operation

Second Wind (1945)

At about the middle of the war, they told Gene that General Almond had ordered a reorganization of the division, and they requested that he make a list of all the men in his company he could rely on to stay and fight on the front lines. Gene only had about sixty men in his company then. So they reorganized the 92nd Division and reconstituted the 370th. Gene joined the new 370th with a full-sized company and took his troops up on the mountain in anticipation of the final assault. His relationships with the men in his company continued to be good. After the March 2 reorganization, the 370th had 139 officers, 2,800 enlisted men, and 3 warrant officers.[31]

The final attack, called Second Wind, began. The strategy was that the newly constituted 92nd would capture Massa while the British 8th Army and U.S. 5th Army would capture Bologna, surround the German troops south of the Po River, and then capture Verona. To this end, the 92nd, 442nd, and 473rd (a white Anti-Aircraft Artillery Regiment) would jointly attack along the coast toward Genoa. Gene went with G Company to the east side of the mountain, a side he had not been on. The last time they jumped off, they were near Castle Aghinolfi. They had always attacked from the west side next to the coast. In fact, they had attacked that place at least eight times. When they went up the easier side of the slope, the Germans shot at them as they came up the mountain. This time, they attacked from the east up a steep slope that took hours to climb. Mountains X, Y, and Z were so steep that even the mules could not make it up. Gene and his men had fought on all of them. He did not know that this time he was going to be with the Japanese Americans. They had been in Italy, then were sent to France, and when needed were deployed to Italy again.[32]

The Japanese American unit was composed of the 100th Battalion and the 442nd. The 100th Battalion began as part of the Hawaii National Guard. On June 5, 1942, the unit departed with 1,432 men. After a year's training in Wisconsin and Mississippi, they were ordered to the European theater, arriving in North Africa on September 2, 1943. They went into combat in Italy on September 26 and remained until March 1944. By the time they pulled out, they were down to 521 men.[33]

The 442nd was composed of volunteers from Hawaii and the mainland, many of whom were from relocation centers. They trained from October 1943 to February 1944. Small groups had left previously to replace men from the 100th, and on June 2, the 442nd landed at Naples and moved to Anzio. The 100th and the 442nd came together on June 15, 1944, and the 100th officially became a part of the 442nd. The 442nd fought fiercely in Italy during that summer, sustaining 1,272 casualties, more than one-fourth of its strength, and then was sent to France. They spent days fighting in the Vosges Mountains and then rescued the "lost battalion," sustaining 2,000 casualties and 140 deaths, losing one-half of its original strength.

In March 1945, the 442nd moved back to Italy and engaged in the April assault. The "Go for Broke" 442nd Regimental CT was the most decorated American unit during World War II, and the most decorated unit per man and per unit in the history of the United States. In seven major campaigns, the 442nd suffered 9,486 casualties, with 680 deaths. A total of 18,000 served with the unit, winning 18,143 decorations: a Congressional Medal of Honor; 47 Distinguished Service Crosses; 350 Silver Stars; 810 Bronze Stars; and 3,600 Purple Hearts. Senator Daniel K. Inouye served in the 442nd Regimental CT in France and Italy and earned fifteen medals and citations, including the Medal of Honor. Two other participants of the Italian campaign, Edward Brooke and Robert Dole, went on to become U.S. senators.[34]

On April 1, 1945, the 370th and 442nd attacked in the Ligurian sector. The 442nd moved in at night on April 3 and remained hidden all day on April 4, and that night, several units climbed the sheer 3,000 foot cliffs of the mountain, going up the steepest part. When Gene got to the top of the mountain, he crawled up to take a look. He saw that the Japanese Americans had killed all the Germans who had come out of their bunkers. In fact, they had completely wiped them out. They chased them out of the holes that were hollowed out of the mountain, where the Germans had their guns mounted. They had shelled the Buffalo Soldiers month after month from those positions.[35]

The Japanese American soldiers moved right on as the Germans came running out of the emplacements and kept running. The members of the 442nd just stood up and shot them as they were running down the side of the mountain. They turned right and left. A group of the Japanese American soldiers fought along with Gene's company. They had a rule that they never left a buddy; when they went out on patrol they always brought his body back if somebody was killed. They accounted for every man.[36]

Gene said that the Japanese Americans were truly excellent troops, the best soldiers he ever saw. With them, the 370th broke through the Gothic line during their most important campaign. From then on, the 92nd had everything going their way. This battle was the most decisive one in the whole campaign. The men of the 370th welcomed the 442nd. The U.S. Army let the Japanese American soldiers take anything they wanted in terms of arms or souvenirs. They all had acquired German guns, rifles, and pistols. Gene sat around and talked with a number of the enlisted men. They were self-contained and extremely loyal to one another; they came up as a company and fought together. By the end of the first day, they had accomplished their objective and continued beyond it.[37]

On the eve of the major offensive in April, General Almond received devastating news. William McCaffrey was with him the night he read the letter from his wife, Margaret, that told him that his son had been killed in action, and that Tommy Galloway, his son-in-law, was missing and presumed dead. The 92nd had begun the major attack. McCaffrey had a late dinner and was reading his mail in his trailer when Almond called him over. When he entered the trailer, the general said, "I have just gotten a letter from Margaret. Tommy Galloway is missing and presumed dead and young Ned has been killed in action." His life changed in an instant. McCaffrey said, "Do you want me to call the doc to give you a shot so you'll sleep?" He said, "No, I'm going to sit here and think about things for a while." But he said, "I don't want you to mention it to the Corps. They'll find out about it soon enough. I'm going to continue to command this Division."[38]

During this major offensive in April, Gene attacked with a company at full strength. His was the last unit to be committed. They went in across a large open field and mounted the ridgeline behind the battalion that preceded them. A new lieutenant colonel, the commander of that battalion, kept calling back and talking about where he was. From the way he talked, it sounded like he had gained significant ground and had gone on past the mountain. But when Gene's men got there, his predecessor had not passed the first field. His unit was stuck, just sitting there. The commander was down in a foxhole, and Gene had to hunt for him. His men were about to get mixed up with Gene's. So Gene crawled over to the commander, and told him either he had to go ahead or Gene would have to pass him. The lieutenant colonel said, "Well, I'm not going anywhere." He never did get out of his foxhole. He had come from a Pentagon assignment, and it was the first time he had been in combat.[39]

Gene called headquarters on his phone: "I have to go ahead. I don't want to get my men mixed with his. We are just near the base of the mountain." They said, "You are not. You're up at that castle [Castle Aghinolfi near Massa]." Gene said, "No we're not. We are a long way from the castle. We're not up there yet. We are all sitting right here on the first objective on that first field." So Gene had his men attack. They went past the top line of the ridge and passed a small town right in the pocket of the mountain at the base of the ridge. Gene asked an officer from headquarters, "Do you want me to go ahead up here towards Porta [Ridge] or do you want me to turn around and clean out this town?" About that time, shells started coming in behind them. As the officer ran down the hill, he shouted that Gene should clean out the town first.[40]

Gene swung around, turned his column, and signaled his men to come back down through the back of the town. They surprised the Germans and killed many of them. They saw two tanks still burning in front of the town; the driver of one was hanging over the side burning. Every time they had been near Parma, they had fired on it, but this was the first time that they had entered the city itself.[41]

After Gene's company wiped the German troops out and cleared the town, they circled around to their position from the night before. The general finally ordered them to move on. The Germans kept shelling them, and Gene knew they were going to keep firing. They always did after they were attacked, because it made the attackers back off. This time Gene was determined to hold his ground, so he dug into a foxhole and stayed. That night, the Germans pounded the troops with artillery, and an attack seemed imminent the next morning.[42]

Without reliable radio contact, Gene and his men did not know whether to go straight ahead or go north. It was hard to keep the men alert because the Germans had pulled out, but they might come back. Finally, after waiting about two days, a light aircraft, an artillery observer plane, flew over and dropped a Coke bottle with a message from headquarters telling Gene to continue north.[43] Getting messages through was quite difficult during heavy fighting when the men were widely separated from other units. Gene's battalion commander and regimental commander had various ways of sending orders depending on the situation. They sent messages by runner, by jeep messenger when possible, and by radio when the radios were working. (The radios did not work most of the time.) On some occasions, during the last stages of the war, when they were separated by miles from their parent unit, messages were dropped by artillery liaison planes.[44]

Gene talked to a liaison officer, who told him to take his company behind the line on the coast and feed and rest his troops. He was getting ready to make a big run, so he called headquarters and was told to just hold his position and wait for orders. Meanwhile, the Japanese American soldiers in the line had moved forward almost all the way to Massa. Gene got his troops fed and rested and kept calling division for orders. When they told him to begin his attack, he led his troops up the beach road and across the Cinquale Canal where Rowny had experienced such a disaster and lost so many tanks.[45]

Gene's company went up the road with the coast on their left. Three belts of mines lined the beach, so Gene kept his men up on the road. Shells exploded in front of them, and Gene had to ease his troops, a whole company, off to the side of the road, but they kept going. He had two engineers go in front of him and check for mines with probes. Finally, they got to an intersection and stopped. He got word from division that they were sending trucks to transport the rest of the troops. The trucks took them up the main road off the beach road.[46]

Gene's Company G veered off the road and up the side of a steep mountain. Headquarters authorized the trucks for as long as needed. When the road got narrower and the terrain steeper, Gene got out and walked along in front. It was beginning to get dark and his foot struck something in the road; he stopped dead still. It was a Shu-mine. (A Shu-mine is a mine in a box, with a pin in the side of it. When the lid was pushed down, a spring on the lid pushed a pin, or held the pin down to detonate it.) Gene disarmed it by slowly lifting the lid up and on its hinges, barely breathing as he did so in the dark. Gene's company kept walking along heading north, not knowing exactly where to go, and they discovered more and more Shu-mines. One misstep and a soldier would be blown to pieces. Eventually, they had to stop and send the trucks back because the road was too steep. It started raining, and as they walked, they sank into the mud. Spotting a town down the mountain, they decided to go there until they could receive further orders.[47] When they did not find any Germans or other soldiers in the town, they moved in. The next day, Gene called in and was told to stay right there and check the road.

The End of the War

When Gene and his company arrived in one small town, the people came running out shouting, happy to see Americans. The town council wanted him and his troops to attend a meeting and banquet, where the Italians showered them with praise and showed their appreciation. They regarded them as liberators. The next day, they took Gene to see a building they used for a hospital, full of people who had lost arms or legs. The doctors had run out of anesthetic and had to amputate frostbitten limbs without it. Screams of the patients still seemed to reverberate from the walls.[48]

Thousands of partisans came out of the bushes and joined the units of the 92nd Division. Every day during the last offensive, partisans joined Gene's company. At first, he welcomed any help he could get from them, but soon he had so many of them he could not supply them with food, equipment, and ammunition, which was scarce and strictly rationed toward the end of the war.[49] Partisans were up in the mountains searching for Mussolini, and they finally caught him trying to leave the country. They stopped Mussolini's car one night and captured him when he got out of his vehicle and ran; they brought him down to Milan. Gene did not know they had caught him until he drove by the Piazzale Loreto in Milan, where a large crowd had gathered. Both Mussolini and his mistress, Clara (Claretta) Petacci, were hanging from their feet by ropes at the Esso filling station on the square.

After the war, partisans exacted revenge by going from house to house robbing and killing people. When Gene asked them why they did it, they said they were *partigianis,* meaning partisans—and they were retaliating against Nazi sympathizers. He did not try to stop them because there were too many of them. Many were wild and violent, stealing everything. The civilians said the war was over, but official word was slow in coming. After two days, Gene moved part of his headquarters down the road to the next town.

Many Germans approached Gene's unit, wanting to surrender. They had thrown their rifles away in the woods somewhere. A group of them came off a hill with their hands over their heads. They had their helmets off and their little caps on. Gene rounded up a number of prisoners, put a detail with them, and sent them down the road to a ballpark where they started assembling prisoners and feeding them. Gene also started taking his troops there to eat because they had C rations coming to them. Then they left and went straight to the mountain above Massa and started toward Genoa. The Americans had already knocked out the big guns at Punta Bianca.

After the major offensive, Gene's company went through Carrara, where they encountered blocks of marble and what appeared to be a marble road. The Germans had concealed their guns in granite quarries in the mountains, protecting them from artillery fire. From the quarries, the Germans had a clear view of the Allies on the plains below. Along the path going south, they came upon a marble shelter that the Germans had built. They found winter sleeping bags, so Gene got one, and everyone grabbed one also. Because it was cold on the mountain, he crawled in the sleeping bag to get warm. Just as he got warm something started biting him, and he discovered that the sleeping bag was full of insects. He crawled out, and threw it off, saying "Anybody can have it who wants it." About a dozen people tried to grab it. Naturally the person who got it came to regret it.

When Gene's company was in the valley near Bologna, they were in limbo for about a week or two before they went to the prison camp at Pisa. At first, it was hard to grasp that the war was over. Gene's division was spread along the highway all the way from Calomini to Leghorn (Livorno). Gene's headquarters was at Calomini and his troops were billeted in a big brick building on the side of the road. A lieutenant colonel who was a 2nd Battalion commander found a piano that he kept in his room. He played it beautifully, and when he left, the piano that had survived the war was still standing there. On May 1, 1945, Gene wrote to Alta from "Somewhere in Italy": "Gee, darling how I wish I could see you. I also wish you could see me as we pass through liberated towns—I usually have to make a speech and my interpreter passes it on. It's really something to see. You can bet I'll never let you two out of my sight for even one minute."

Three days later, on May 4, 1945, he wrote to tell her he had won a Bronze Star, and that the war was finally over: "Well, Darling it looks like the show here in this particular place is over and at last I've found time to write to you. I've just now for the first time in days had a chance to even sit down for a few minutes. Gee, I wish you could see some of the beautiful cities here. I've paraded in some pretty big cities like Massa, La Spezia, Genoa, etc. They're really beautiful. It seems so strange that right now I don't have to be listening for shells to come in or to hear a 'jerry' machine gun cracking. I do know the Lord is with me for he has proven it many times."[50]

Gene Johnston was elated that the war was over, and along with his troops, he attended ceremonies praising the American troops in town after town. As Ivan Houston, who was in the battalion headquarters in the 3rd Battalion of the 370th, said, "They loved us and showered us with hugs, kisses, and wine. Our color was no issue at all, and they were not critics."[51]

16. Negro "doughfoots" of the 92nd Infantry (Buffalo) Division pursue the retreating Germans through the Po Valley. German forces in Italy have since capitulated unconditionally. Ca. May 1945. 208-AA-49E-1-13. (african_americans_wwii_040.jpg). Courtesy of U.S. Army, National Archives.

Gene's company chased Germans in the mountains for about two weeks, following a big division that was pulling out. They did not get any sleep because they were constantly moving. As the Germans fled, they killed civilians on their path. One night, Gene kept seeing lights and hearing planes diving and motors roaring. When he and his troops took off the next day and formed a column up the road, they came across vehicles on the side of the road that the American Army Air Force had shot up. There were dead horses and dead mules that the Germans had been using to move their supplies after they ran out of gas. The horses that survived were standing there dazed.

On May 8, 1945, Gene wrote candidly to Alta expressing his weariness with war: "I've slept so long in muddy fox-holes and been so cold and gone so long without a bath or change of clothing that I'm sick of it and never want to even remember or think (about) the things I've seen." Less than a week later in a letter of May 13, 1945, from Lavagna, Italy, he told her of being wounded, but did not disclose the seriousness of his injuries: "I might as well be truthful honey, I have had a few cuts and bruises and scratches but they are ok and weren't even bad enough for me to have to be evacuated or to have a medical record made of them."[52]

At the end of the war, Almond addressed the war-weary "Officers and Men of the 92nd Infantry Division and Attached Troops." He told them: "The 92nd Division and its supporting troops have performed splendidly; without the arduous effort and unselfish cooperation on the part of each of you it would not have been possible to secure the results obtained in so short a time. . . . Following an arduous period of preparation and training, our units moved to the Italian theatre and some six months ago entered active combat. Experience has taught us much and has enabled us, during the past month, to have a part in driving a resourceful, cunning and well-trained foe from his chosen defensive position."[53]

Mark Clark commended Almond on May 1, 1945, for his occupation and clearing of Genoa, which he said would stand out as a magnificent job. Unlike his later harsh judgment of the 92nd, Clark wrote to Almond on May 5, 1945, saying, "You and your splendid division have turned in a magnificent performance in the great, final offensive of the long Italian campaign. I appreciate to the utmost your fine co-operation. Good luck to you and to your gallant officers and men." General Almond left the 92nd on August 12, 1945.[54]

Regardless of the ultimate successes of his division, General Almond still held racist views and remained highly critical of his troops. The climate of distrust, frequent reassignment of officers to different units, the dire lack of replacements, and the tactical mistakes of superiors all contributed to the performance of the 92nd.

The division commander's reputation depends on the success of the men, and General Almond's career was advanced by his command of the 92nd. He returned to the United States from Italy, and in September 1945 was assigned command of the 2nd Infantry Division at Camp Swift, Texas.[55]

In official efficiency reports, General Almond and his commanding officers (Raymond Sherman, James Notestein, J. D. Armstrong, and William P. Ennis Jr., among others) were unanimous in their harsh criticism of the 92nd Division.

Clearly, all these white commanding officers were reflecting the frustrations of the previous operations at the Cinquale Canal and the February offensive. Their evaluations of their troops became increasingly harsh. General Almond echoed these evaluations in such a way that it became a kind of litany.[56]

Certainly problems did exist, as in all units, and not all the troubles of the 92nd could be blamed on white officers; however, interpretations of actions were always filtered through a lens of racist assumptions. Reports by Almond's commanding officers were virtually identical to his. One gets the distinct feeling that they were closing ranks and creating a united front to construct a well-rehearsed script that could explain any setbacks experienced by the 92nd Division.

General McCaffrey gave a candid, balanced view of the performance of the 92nd Division and also described the racism and discrimination that the soldiers faced: "Sixty percent of the enlisted men were functionally illiterate. Eventually we decided to run reading and writing courses to teach them to read the field manuals. We failed every one of our tests the first time up. We had to get the training period extended for each phase of our training."[57] McCaffrey pointed to the black soldiers' lack of equal education and their treatment as second-class citizens. He said that they were treated as inferiors, forbidden to enter white clubs or even the downtown areas of many cities. Soldiers never really had to be literate until the professionalization of the military in World War II. Hunting and backwoods marksmanship were better skills than reading a manual in the previous wars, but the army did not know how to utilize the skills of illiterate black soldiers, and many of the officers did not have any respect for them.[58]

McCaffrey commented on the performance of the soldiers in the 92nd in the maneuvers and in combat later:

> Well, there were some things they did beautifully. Even in combat, we had wonderful engineers, first rate artillerymen, and mortar gunners who could put more rounds in the air than anybody. Where we were lacking was in the rifle companies and that was based, I think, essentially on lack of personal confidence in each other. There were many brave and effective officers, black and white, in the 92nd Division, but the chain is only as strong as its weakest link and we had some weak links in the rifle companies. If you're a rifleman in the 92nd Division, it's raining, you're on a hill in Italy and it's dark, and you start thinking: it's one o'clock in the morning, is the soldier on my right or left there or not? Some of them didn't really think the other man was still there. In a white unit, the feeling was, if I get up to leave now, that guy in the right foxhole might shoot me. In a black division, the average GI did not think his buddy would shoot him for withdrawing. There

> was no penalty of public rejection for opting out of the white man's war. It was easy for them to believe that it was a white man's war. They were treated like second-class citizens. Many of them sincerely believed they were being exploited by the white officers.[59]

Unlike Almond, McCaffrey was not racist, and he appreciated the reasons some of the soldiers preferred to go to prison rather than to war. He could see that the division lacked cohesion and unity. It was common for the soldiers to resent the authority of the white officers and interpret their demands as racist. General McCaffrey claimed that the 92nd Division had some really first-rate black officers and enlisted men. He especially admired Joe Stephenson, who was a splendid company commander and platoon leader. McCaffrey became known as someone black troops could trust; thus, he had a good reputation among them.[60]

In the last weeks of the war, the 92nd marched sixty-five miles through the Apennines from Barga to Pontremoli. Many refugees streamed down the roads, including a lot of the Italians who had left the United States before or during the war. Mussolini had said all good Italians should return to Italy. There was a constant stream coming down out of the mountains near Rapallo, many of them fascist sympathizers. They were well dressed, but their clothes were old. They had left the United States a year or two before the war and had joined Mussolini's movement.[61]

In one extraordinary episode, Gene was at Calomini up the road from Massa when Ezra Pound surrendered to him. Pound walked up behind Gene and said "I'm Ezra Pound." Gene said, "I am Eugene Johnston." Pound assumed that my father would immediately know who he was, but the name meant nothing to him. Pound said, "Could you take me to your commanding officer?" Gene was busy, so he just turned around and said, "Sergeant, take him on up there." The sergeant loaded him on the jeep and took off with him. An hour later, a captain asked Gene if he would sign that he had captured Pound. He refused and just laughed at him. The captain later received a Silver Star for Pound's capture. Gene later came to believe that Ezra Pound was a traitor. He heard that Pound had broadcast propaganda on the radio. He was not just a passive traitor; he was an active one. He felt that Pound's name should have to be accompanied by an inscription saying that he was opposed to his country.[62]

Before the war, Gene was a plans and training officer. After the war, Gene went back to headquarters as S-3 with Colonel James Notestein as his commanding officer. As a staff officer, he planned the movements of the troops. He set up the dates of the movements and all the logistics. When he was S-3, he sent out patrols every night. He briefed them on their mission and destination and waited for them all night until they reported back to him.[63] When the war ended, Gene's company went to southern Italy to perform guard duty around an air base. The whole battalion remained there the entire summer of 1945. The men's morale went up because the shooting was over, and they were having a good time. They began making plans for redeployment in September.[64]

Reburial of Christopher Columbus's Ashes

While in northern Italy, Gene witnessed the reburial of Christopher Columbus's ashes on June 6, 1945. Historians still argue over where Columbus's ashes really are. Some claim Spain, others the Dominican Republic; supposedly some of his ashes were given to Genoa by Spain. During the war, they hid the ashes in a small church. After the war, they brought them back in an urn to a church in Genoa.[65]

When they entered Genoa, the American soldiers saw a huge banner across the road that said: "Welcome Americans. One of our boys discovered your country." Gene went up to Genoa with the whole division for the reburial. Many of the men did not know what it was all about until they got there. Troops lined up in a formation on the square in the populated part of the town and paraded by the reviewing stand. When they fired some cannons, it broke the window lights all around the town.[66]

The men of Company H of the 370th Infantry Regiment, a heavy weapons company, led by Harold Montgomery, accompanied Columbus's ashes in their ornamental urn in a horse-drawn carriage. They solemnly marched into the Piazza della Vittoria, the largest square in Genoa. The tall, handsome Montgomery marched with great dignity and regal bearing. The "Wings of Jordan" Negro choir sang, and the chaplain spoke. The heat was stifling that day as the entire 92nd Division stood at attention for the long ceremony.[67] They got so stiff just standing there that when they relaxed, many soldiers hit the ground; like the clatter of dominoes falling, rifles and soldiers fell down, row by row. After the ceremony, they asked the civilians to come in and bring all their weapons.

It was late by the time the soldiers of the 92nd Division left Genoa. Gene rode in a jeep but most of the troops boarded a train. His orders were to report to Pisa, where his company was assigned to guard prisoners. During the war, the Americans stationed an observer in the top of the famous leaning tower. The tower had been fired on several times by German 88s, but they ricocheted off of it. Gene later learned that Ezra Pound had been imprisoned there after the war, and wrote the *Pisan Cantos* while incarcerated.[68] The prison at Pisa held mostly Italians and

Germans, including a dozen German women considered war criminals. Gene oversaw seventy thousand prisoners in the big wire enclosure, with double fences and guards walking about ten yards between the two fences. Hundreds of pup tents housed the prisoners. Outside the large fence there were thousands of civilians, mostly Italians, trying to locate relatives. The guards had to watch them constantly because the Italians would run up to the fence and pass something through to the prisoners. People exchanged messages with their relatives in the camp, and sometimes they gave them food. The Americans eventually turned the prisoners loose.

At the prison camp at Pisa, Gene lived in a tent and had a German orderly from Branson, Germany, a prisoner who kept his things straight and his clothes clean. The Allied forces had been collecting prisoners there since the war ended, and checking their identification papers. Most of those Germans were supposed to be enlisted men, but many were officers who had taken papers belonging to other soldiers and substituted their own pictures. They had hoped to pass as enlisted men to avoid prosecution as war criminals. Eventually, the German officers were incarcerated separately, before being transported elsewhere, some to Nuremberg. Daily bulletins reported the ongoing trials there.[69]

From Pisa, Gene wrote to Alta on August 15, 1945:

> Hooray! The thing we have been looking for so long came over the radio last night that Japan had surrendered to the conditions of the Potsdam convention. At any rate, it shouldn't be so very long now until our dreams come true. The things we planned on so long will soon be happening. Darling, I can hardly wait.
>
> One of the greatest thrills in my life though will be when I take Jeanie [Nancy] in my arms for the first time. It's hard for me to realize yet, since I've never seen her but I'm sure it won't take me long to get accustomed to it (ha). I just hope she will like me as much as I like her.
>
> . . . Darling it seems ages and ages since I left you there the last night at Huachuca—we sure have a lot of lost time to make up for. Seems like ever since we've been married we've just been meeting and then saying goodbye but honey, that's all going to be over with soon—for where I go you will go too. You're my whole future . . . we're guarding PW's here."

While still in Pisa, he wrote to her on September 3, 1945, that his score was ninety-nine points, qualifying him to be one of the first to leave, but the army delayed his departure. He confided to Alta: "If it hadn't been for the thoughts of our future those cold wet nights in the mountains in a foxhole would have been pretty hard to take. . . . Remember darling, you are my one and only and I'm living for you only."[70]

From Pisa, Gene went to a large camp in a pine forest along the beach outside Leghorn. They stayed there for about a month. The ones who had been in combat longest were supposed to go home first. Jack Gerwin, a friend of Gene's who had come over with them, could not qualify to go home yet, and he desperately wanted to go home. He was tall, handsome, and always exercising. One day they were sitting at the edge of the woods along the coast. Gerwin had captured some rabbits and had made a pen for them right outside of his tent. Gene and Jack were sitting eating lunch when they smelled smoke coming from the woods. Gerwin said, "My rabbits are over there." He took off and they heard a shot go off as a mine exploded.[71]

Gene wrote to tell Alta about the incident: "Gee, we had a terrible thing happen yesterday afternoon. Jack Gerwin walked out of his tent (right next to him) and a mine went off right beside him knocking his right eye out and splattered his whole right side with shrapnel—He is alive and will be ok except no eye. The blast from it blew me through the side of my tent, but I didn't get a scratch, my ears are still ringing though. Jack is at the 33rd hospital in Leghorn" (June 24, 1945, Viareggio, Italy). In a follow-up letter on August 14, 1945, he told her that there was some chance that Jack Gerwin might regain his sight in the eye that was injured.[72]

Gene and his unit were outside Leghorn for around three months. Gene worked on the adjutant general detail, making lists and going all over the country settling claims. All the towns had put in claims, wanting recompense for some shelling or damage. Then his troops went to Rome where they stayed another two to three months. War trials were being conducted in Rome, trying primarily officers, as well as some enlisted men. Gene's unit was assigned to the prison camp downtown, where the policy was a lot more lenient than at Pisa; they even let some German prisoners serve as trustees and drive jeeps to town with no one guarding them.[73] The members of the 92nd who were still in Italy anxiously waited to go home. One unit that got orders to leave just bundled up their gear, boarded a train, and went to the port, leaving their prisoners unguarded.[74]

Soon after Gene got to Rome, his company was sent to Bari, at the toe of Italy. The transfer of his troops upset him greatly. They ended up all over Italy on the air force fields, clearing up airfields that were used during the war. They removed the mesh, a kind of screening used to pack the earth so it would not mire up. They were also moving ramps. Out of concern for his troops' welfare, Gene drove down to Bari to see them and make sure they were getting food. It took him all day to get across to the Adriatic coast. He found his troops in a small shack they had built on the beach, seemingly "on vacation." Black soldiers were all over southern Italy as well as in the north around Bologna. Many stayed in Italy after the war.[75] In fact, Gene stayed in Italy six months after the war ended.[76]

Gene made two or three trips down to Bari. The first time he drove down there, the people ran out in every town where he stopped, stood around the jeep, and talked to Gene and his driver. They planned to stop off at one of the mess halls when they got hungry.[77] Kitchens were set up all along the highway for the U.S. Army Air Force, and they always had fires cooking. Gene and his driver Albert stopped one night to get something to eat and his driver went to every one of the kitchens, but they would not give him anything to eat because he was black. They continued on, figuring they would eat when they got into Rome.[78]

Peace brought its own dangers. After the war, Gene went with his new driver to Cannes, France. They were coming back after midnight, and when they came to a railroad crossing up in the mountains near Genoa, they took a sharp turn to the left and went across the track. The arm on one side of the track was up but the other arm came down. Gene pushed the arm up and it came right back down and they could not move the jeep off the track. The track was supposedly abandoned. There was something wrong with one of the arms, and the watchman probably had been asleep, woke up, and closed it. They heard a whistle and an electric train was coming right toward them at a high speed.[79]

Just moments before the train hit the jeep, they got off the track and jumped back the other way. Gene narrowly missed getting his leg caught and being killed. The train dragged his jeep down the track, and tore it up before it finally stopped. A man came running out where the signal was. When the gendarmerie arrived, Gene told him he had to get to the next town, where he was going to spend the night. From there he called headquarters and told them what happened, and then waited three days for a new jeep. Gene got impatient, and when someone came by in an old truck, they got on it.[80] Gene stayed in Italy until November 1945. He finally received orders to return to the states, departing on the SS *Eufaula.* He arrived in the United States on November 26, 1945.[81]

When peace came in May 1945, Spencer Moore expressed his longing to go home to his parents in June of that year:

> Dear Mom and Pop:
>
> Glad to know Europe is OK. Don't have to go to the Pacific. I can hardly remember what it's like in the States. You would be surprised at what a numb feeling I have. I guess it will take a couple of months to really realize that I am home. Well it won't be as long as it has been before

17. Arlington Cemetery, Washington, DC. Photograph courtesy of Spencer C. Moore.

all of us are back home. That will be "Victory at Home" day for all of us.
You know I have 98 points and am on the waiting list to come home.
Love,
Spencer[82]

Spencer Moore came back from the war in a Liberty ship, the *Thomas H. Bent.* On the way, they ran into a fierce storm and had to shut the engine and propeller down. Having survived the war, many soldiers wondered if they would survive the trip home, which took around twenty days. Glenn Miller's music filled the air when they landed in New York. As they came into the harbor, the United Service Organizations and boats were blowing their whistles and shooting water up in the air.[83]

Gene Johnston's war was a war of memory—whose memories survive as the official record? How do black and white soldiers remember the war differently? What are the landscapes of the memory? Along with those nightmarish memories of death, dismemberment of body and soul, and racism, there are also memories of comradeship, heroism, and courage. Fighting in a Jim Crow army, African American soldiers had to fight two wars: the war against racism and violence against them in their own country, and the war against the Nazis in Italy.

Unlike Spencer Moore and Gene Johnston, Staff Sergeant Joe Willie Johnson would not be going home. A German sniper killed him on April 10, 1945, just weeks after his twenty-fourth birthday. Before his death, Johnson had written a moving letter to his wife: "Time will immortalize the men who now lie beneath the scarred hills; time will perhaps marvel at the quietness of some trail where once the dreaded song of guns raged; small children will play on piles of rock where once a nation hung in the balance."[84]

VI LIFE AFTER WORLD WAR II

11

Coming Home

> Our motto must be: In spite of despair, hope must exist. In spite of suffering, humanity must prevail. And in spite of all the differences in the world, the worst enemy the worst peril is indifference.
>
> What unites us as human beings is the aspiration to make the world better, more compassionate, with less conflict, less hate and hardship, and with more tolerance and understanding.
>
> Elie Wiesel

The war's end was a beginning for all the Buffalo Soldiers as they attempted to adjust to the peace. Gene Johnston came back with his company on a slightly larger vessel than the one they had gone over on. He came in with the packs he had carried for so long that he was sick of them. When they landed at Newport News late in November, the first thing they did was to get on a ferryboat. They almost froze to death on that big flat boat, as the strong winds blew and the ocean spray hit their faces. Upon landing, Gene called Alta to say he was really coming home. A train backed up to the docks when they came ashore to take them to North Carolina. After arriving there and being discharged, Gene boarded a train to Chattanooga.[1]

Alta was so excited that her heart was racing. She could not understand why he had been forced to stay longer than the others. Did he *want* to come home? They had kept him in Italy longer to serve as the head of two prison camps and to work with the judge advocate general's section investigating war claims against the United States. For now, she was just grateful that he was coming home. Alta picked Gene up in Chattanooga. He was ready to get out of the army at that point and anxious to see his daughter. Nancy was just under a year old and stared at him with her big brown eyes; she smiled when she first saw him. The war was finally over. Gene took off his uniform; it would not be for long though. He and Alta moved to Cartersville, Georgia, and he started working with his brother-in-law Gale Ross, also his best friend, in a dry-cleaning business. After experiencing the action and intensity of the war, he found this job extremely boring. Before long, he became dissatisfied with the dry-cleaning business.[2]

Gene kept getting letters urging him to reenlist. Finally, he decided to do just that, and in 1948, he returned to active duty at Fort McPherson, Georgia, again to the 5th Army. Then he went to the 11th Infantry Training Regiment Company in Fort Jackson, South Carolina. White and black soldiers faced physical and psychological challenges when they returned from the war. They were not the same as before they left. Some, like Gene, reenlisted. Others took any job they could find. Many of the veterans used the GI Bill, the Servicemen's Readjustment Act of 1944, to return to school.

Other veterans of the 370th and 371st also experienced problems readjusting to American life. When Spencer Moore returned to the United States, he seriously considered remaining in the military until he encountered racist remarks at the deactivation center in Fort McClellan. A bus driver told him to go to the back. "Who are you telling to get in the back? This is America. You see the medals on my chest? I don't have to get in the back for nobody. In fact, I'm gonna sit right down here and breathe down your neck." Then an old Southern colonel got up and told them, "Well, you know, you're down here in the South, and you've got to abide by the social structure of this community." Finally, after listening to this man with a southern drawl, Moore jumped up and said, "No, sir. I don't have to do it. I'm gonna sign to go home now."[3]

When Spencer returned to New Jersey, his father came to pick him up and he called Susie, who was in Indiana. Shortly after he got home, he went to see her and his new son. After he and Susie got reacquainted in Evansville, Indiana, they went home to New Jersey and he applied for college. Spencer was accepted at Drexel Institute of Technology and Temple University. He chose Temple. He thought he might become an accountant and train to be a certified public accountant.[4]

Spencer kept having nightmares and suffered from what would come to be called post-traumatic stress syndrome. He earnestly tried, but he could not study. His father said, "Get a job doing hard work and your body will be tired and you will be able to sleep."

Spencer first got a job in a cinder block company. Then he got a job in construction as a carpenter. He said, "I could make that hammer sing." He then became the first black bus driver in South Jersey. During this time, he and his cousin decided to join the National Guard and switch from infantry to anti-aircraft, so they went to school in Texas to be trained to work at a nuclear missile site. Spencer said that his racist boss sabotaged his career, and so he left after serving twenty-one years in the National Guard. After he left the Guard, he drove an oil truck and then took the civil service test for the post office, where he worked for twenty-five years.[5]

Moore possessed a strong commitment to social justice and equal rights. As he often said, "All the traditional stereotypes about white people and all those about colored people are not true; we are all individuals. We are all hues, and features.

If the Creator had been opposed to interracial mixing he would have made it so the parts wouldn't fit."[6]

When the war ended, Joseph Stephenson and his company went to southern Italy where they performed guard duty around an air base during the summer of 1945. They began making plans for redeployment in September. Stephenson ended up with seventy-two points, but needed seventy-five to go home.[7] Stephenson demonstrated outstanding leadership of his men, valor, and dignity. Years after the end of the war, his eight-year-old grandson asked him: "Granddaddy, what would have happened to me if you had gotten killed in the war?" Joe remembered the time during the war when he was crawling up to a house. He stopped and started to stand up and look, but he paused. At the moment that he paused, a machine gun shot right over his head, and if he had not paused it would have killed him. So he told his grandson, "If I had stood up I guess we would not be here. I hope you never see anything like war."[8]

At the end of the war, Bill Perry returned to Cleveland, Ohio, married Josephine Ferrell, and used the GI Bill to continue his education. He entered a life-drawing class at Western Reserve College in Cleveland. The teacher said Perry could not register for the class because they had live models. He told him, "We use white women." Perry went home and told his father about the exchange. Evidently, the instructor did not want to cause an incident, and so when Bill went back into that class he was allowed to take it and no disruptions occurred.[9]

Along with many of his fellow soldiers, Bill Perry said that the war had a very positive impact in many ways. The Buffalo Soldiers had the opportunity to learn new skills and travel to distant parts of the country and world, which broadened their intellectual and cultural lives. Without the war, Bill Perry would never have gotten to Arizona and certainly not to Italy. In the post–World War II period, the U.S. military has sometimes been an agent of social change in the area of race and gender relations, and it has been an important vehicle of mobility for minorities.

In fact, the GI Bill enabled black soldiers to receive college or vocational education, a year of unemployment compensation, and loans to buy homes or start businesses. These measures literally transformed the nation. The GI Bill profoundly affected many black soldiers as they used it to attend college, graduate schools, medical schools, law schools, and business schools. A major impact of the war was a transformation of consciousness as African Americans encountered racism in and out of uniform. All through the war, the soldiers in the 92nd resisted racism in passive and even violent ways. Many of them came to a new consciousness about their condition of inequality, and countless Buffalo Soldiers joined the civil rights movement after the war.

After serving in the army during World War II, Medgar Evers returned to Mississippi a dramatically changed man. He had been hailed as a liberator in Europe and yet still faced racism at home. He told reporters in the 1960s: "I was on Omaha Beach. All we wanted was to be ordinary citizens. We fought during the war for America, Mississippi included. Now, after the Germans and Japanese hadn't killed us, it looked as though the white Mississippians would."[10] During a campaign against segregation in Jackson, Mississippi, Evers was killed in June 1963.

Another soldier was the victim of violence on the day he was discharged from Fort Gordon, Georgia. Isaac Woodard had served four years in the service, including fifteen months of combat in the Pacific. On his way to Winnsboro, South Carolina, in 1946, he had a verbal disagreement with the bus driver. When the driver stopped at Aiken, South Carolina, he called the police. The police beat him so severely that he was left blinded.

After a month in the hospital, Woodard appealed to the National Association for the Advancement of Colored People to investigate. The organization responded with a national campaign, a fundraiser for Woodard, and pressed the White House for an FBI investigation. After the Justice Department filed charges against Leonard Shull, the chief of police of Batesburg, South Carolina, the man who had beaten Woodward, the all-white jury in the trial found Shull not guilty.[11] Woodard was among many black veterans of World War II who came home to lead the civil rights movement. Others included Oliver Brown and Harry Briggs, both of *Brown v. Board of Education,* Percy Sutton, Coleman Young, Louis Stokes, George Brown, and William T. Coleman Jr.

Harold Montgomery was also a fighter for civil rights after the Second World War. When Montgomery returned from war, he went back to the general accounting officer to reclaim his job with the U.S. Post Office Department. When he walked into the General Accounting Office's grand, high-ceilinged lobby, time seemed to have stood still. The large plaque honoring postal employees who had served in the war did not list Montgomery or any other African American veterans. A personnel manager informed him he would not receive the pay raise given to returning white soldiers. "To hell with that," Montgomery replied. He decided to find other work and reenlisted in the army.

During World War II, Harold Montgomery had to endure the indignities of segregation, but in the 1950s and 1960s he resisted openly. He and his wife Helen Montgomery fought housing segregation in 1956–57 at Fort Ord, California. They heard about a new development in Seaside, California, not far from the base. The homes were just being built. So they went out and picked a location where they would build a model home. Montgomery was preparing to go on maneuvers when the salesman from the development came to their home on the post and said, "Mrs. Montgomery, I came to tell you that the home that you picked out has been sold." Mrs. Montgomery said, "But how can it be sold? It hasn't even been built." When they went into the office the next morning they discovered that whites owned the development and stipulated that lots would not be sold to African Americans. They went to see a senator in Palo Alto. The Montgomerys eventually had to back off because Harold already had eighteen and a half years of service and a general who had heard about the incident told him he did not want to see anything in the papers about it.

Almost a decade later when Montgomery served at Fort Bragg from 1965 to 1972, the black officers still had to sit at certain tables. Montgomery was the special staff officer, the S-3 of the first student training regiment. The white officers were at separate tables and black officers came in and just sat down, so Colonel Miller called a big meeting. He wanted to know what the troubles were. Montgomery told him: "Well, I don't know about any conversations between whites and blacks. But I'll tell you one thing, Colonel. . . . The decision you're about to make now, you think about it before you make it. Because if you make the wrong decision I'm going to fight you with the same determination I fought the enemy on the field of combat. The same enemy that tried to take my life—I'm going to fight you with the same determination." Colonel Miller decided that officers would not be seated according to race, rank, or position. In other words, he made a decision that everyone would be seated just as they came into the mess hall.

Montgomery came face to face with Southern racism when he drove through Georgia on the way back from a holiday. They were driving from Alabama to Columbia, South Carolina, where he was stationed at Fort Jackson. They were going through Danielsville, Georgia, and followed the traffic past the court house in the center of the town. Some five or six miles out of town the sheriff pulled up beside them. He told Montgomery to pull over, then asked: "Where's your license, boy?" This sheriff did not have any shoes on, and he had on a straw hat with the top cut out. He had a .45 on his hip.

After he looked at Montgomery's driver's license, he ordered him to follow him back to town. He told him that someone had reported that he was speeding through town. He said, "You come on back." When Montgomery asked the charges, he replied, "Oh we'll rig up some charges by the time you get back there." The Montgomerys followed instructions. His wife Helen was supposed to stay in the car, but she jumped out and went in the courthouse. They told him they wanted him to pay $25.00 for speeding. When he protested the sheriff said either pay the $25.00 or his wife would go to jail and her husband to the county work farm. Needless to say, he paid.[12]

After the war, Jehu Hunter also faced discrimination when he sought employment with the Pentagon. He could not find a position in his field of biology, and so he worked as a guard instead. When a colleague remarked that it must have been difficult, Hunter replied, "I just decided I would be the best guard I could be." With the help of the GI Bill, he attended graduate school from 1947 through 1948 in zoology and education and became a research biologist. Along with Lieutenant Colonel Major Clark (an African American officer, sometimes confused with Mark Clark), Jehu Hunter wrote a history of the 92nd Infantry. He offered an alternative black assessment of the 92nd Division in the Italian campaign in the book and in scholarly papers. He explained that generally black officers were immediately suspicious of any white officer because at some point most of them had been treated badly by white men. The army preferred to assign Southern white officers to black units because Southern white men presumably "knew how to handle blacks better than northern white men."[13]

Jehu Hunter joined the National Cancer Institute as a biologist in 1947 and rose to the positions of assistant director for planning in the National Institutes of Health Biological Sciences Division, chief in the Office of Planning and Analysis, and assistant director of program development at the Center for Research for Mothers and Children. He was also inducted into the Royal Society of Medicine. Hunter presented numerous scientific papers at research meetings and participated in the Eighth International Conference for Cancer Control in 1962 in the Soviet Union. He was in the reserves after World War II and was recalled to active duty in Korea in 1951, serving for eighteen months in the 28th Infantry Division. He said that he welcomed the opportunity to serve his country, and that World War II taught him that "Americans are willing to sacrifice in order to preserve their democratic ideals."[14]

Like Gene, Joseph Hairston reenlisted in the army after the war. Because of the downsizing of the army and because of racism in the military, Hairston lost his commission and was relieved from active duty shortly after he had received an excellent rating in June 1949. Black officers were being disproportionately mustered out. For a year, he taught at Virginia State College in the Reserve Officer Training Corps program. When the Korean War broke out in June 1950, he went back to active duty at the rank of captain. Hairston became an army aviator in 1946. He was anxious to earn flight pay. Even after obtaining his pilot's wings, he learned his credentials were not good enough for the adjutant at a base in North Carolina, who called the Pentagon and complained, "What do you mean sending me

18. Joseph Hairston at a Buffalo Reunion. Photograph courtesy of Carolyn Johnston.

this nigger pilot?" Hairston then went to California and was refused admission to the newly formed U.S. Air Force. In 1951, he went to helicopter training school. In the Korean War, he served as a helicopter pilot and rescued wounded soldiers. The hospitals were near the front and, therefore, soldiers had a higher survival rate as a result. Hairston was able to use his training as a medic in World War II. He received his first Oak Leaf Cluster to the Air Medal for service in Korea.[15]

When Hairston was stationed in Okinawa in 1952, the commander asked him to give a visiting dignitary an aerial orientation of the island. It turned out to be Sterling Wood, now a three-star general, who had told them to expect to incur at least 10 percent of the war's casualties. For over a decade, he had hated this man and held him personally responsible for his friend's death on that mountain in Italy. He instantly recognized him, although Wood did not remember the man in the pilot's seat in front of him. Because the general was corpulent he did not want to be constrained by the parachute, so he left it undone. Hairston thought to himself: "I have this bastard." He would parachute out, let the plane crash, and have his revenge. So he rose to about 5,000 feet and opened the door of the plane. He was ready to roll out when suddenly he heard the voice of Major Beasley, the black chaplain who always stood up for the men, quoting from First Corinthians: "Though I speak with tongues of men and angels and have not love. . . . "[16] The

19. Harold Montgomery at a Buffalo Reunion. Photograph courtesy of Carolyn Johnston.

20. Albert Burke at a Buffalo Reunion. Photograph courtesy of Carolyn Johnston.

21. A. William Perry. Photograph courtesy of Maggi Morehouse.

experience changed his life. He let go of his hatred, latched the door, and went back to flying. He landed the plane, saluted the general, and walked away. He left his hatred up there in the air.[17]

After his tours in Korea and California, Hairston was transferred to Virginia, where he was able to attend college and then law school. When he retired from the army at the age of thirty-eight, he went to work at the Labor Department and then the Treasury Department. He was the first black senior executive in the Office of Chief Counsel for the Internal Revenue Service. On behalf of an African American legal organization, he traveled to Africa and Latin America, consulting on development issues. He was involved in the civil rights movement and was one of the participants of the march on Washington, in charge of security the day Martin Luther King Jr. gave his speech on the National Mall.[18]

None of the Buffalo Soldiers, black or white, were the same after the war; they were transformed by their experiences. In parallel universes, they had experienced combat, the loss of their friends on the battlefield, as well as physical and psychological wounds. Black and white Buffalo Soldiers also experienced the consequences of racism. Many African American soldiers became involved in the civil rights movement, and many of them remained in the military for many more years and saw the end of segregation in the military forces.

22. *Left to right:* Vernon Baker and Maggi Morehouse. Photograph courtesy of A. William Perry.

23. *Left to right:* Jehu Hunter and Lieutenant General William J. McCaffrey. Photograph courtesy of Spencer C. Moore.

What should we remember about the 92nd Division? They fought and made tremendous sacrifices for their country at a time that they experienced racism both before and after they went into combat. They achieved their objectives in the Italian campaign. They belonged to one of the last segregated units in the American military. Segregation failed in the military, which prompted Harry Truman to desegregate the armed services after the war with his Executive Order 9981 on July 26, 1948. This action helped to promote equal treatment and opportunity for African American servicemen, but the actual integration of the troops took many more years. The Buffalo Soldiers deserve our gratitude and respect. They were *ordinary* men of the "greatest generation" who did *extraordinary* things and found themselves literally and figuratively on a mountain in Italy fighting for a democracy they were denied.

VII AFTERWORD

12

My Search for My Father's War

> When our parents talk about their lives, they relay what they think is best, for their sake or ours. And as their children, we hear what we want, believe what we can, and as time lengthens, pry and judge and question as our needs demand. We understand from them in that light. And when we tell our parents' tales to the world, or even to ourselves, the story is always our own.
>
> Scott Turow, *Ordinary Heroes*

As a daughter of the fortress, my search for my father's war has been in part an attempt to understand its legacy. Early in my childhood when my father spoke about his experiences in the war, he never mentioned being with black troops. Like many veterans who feel no one could possibly understand what they went through, he was reluctant to talk about those years.

I had heard certain stories many times and always asked him to tell them again. My father's frequent absences made him a stranger and emotionally inaccessible. When he retired during my high school years, I did not welcome his strict disciplinarian intrusions. When I asked permission to go out on a date with an older boy, his simple reply was, "Negative!" Then there were endless political arguments over the Vietnam War, Watergate, and religion. So, it would not be easy thirty years later to open up a dialogue with him. How would I get him to talk about the war? About himself? About his attitudes toward race? My father was pleased that I was keenly interested in the war and the 92nd Division. I was impressed by the vividness of his memories, and the entire process became a means of reconciliation for us after many years of political conflicts. I realized that this was my last chance to get to know him and understand how the war years had shaped him. Eventually, our hours of interviews resulted in a 175-page single-spaced transcript.

In the journey to find my real father, I discovered the people he cared for and fought with, the men of the 92nd Division. I learned more of him through them.[1] Telling my father's story and discovering his war meant finding the black soldiers also. Virtually every military unit has reunions, but I had difficulties finding the surviving members of the 92nd. Then I followed a thread: an internet article written by Spencer C. Moore. I discovered that he lived in Magnolia, New

Jersey, and through a member of a local historical society, I found his telephone number. He graciously invited me to their reunion in 2002, and all the ones since then. Spencer C. Moore has guided me in my search.

For the past ten years, I have been privileged to attend the 92nd Infantry Division World War II Association Reunion each year in Washington, D.C. There I met A. William Perry, another historian of the division, along with approximately one hundred other Buffalo Soldiers, many of whom appear in this book. I was touched by their openness and generosity and thrilled to hear stories of their experiences. I have gained extraordinary insights into that time from them all and developed very close friendships with some of them. Through this experience, I have encountered the beauty, gentleness, and strength of the Buffalo Soldiers in their winter years and the fairness, loyalty, strength, simplicity, and humility of my father. Until he joined the army, where he found a cause and a mission, he was an understated man with limited interests. Along with the black Buffalo Soldiers, he also found himself, literally and figuratively, in combat facing the Gothic Line in Italy.[2]

My search for my father's war led me to Chattanooga, Tennessee; Cartersville, Georgia; Fort Huachuca, Arizona; Washington, D.C.; and Italy. I explored physical and psychological landscapes as a daughter and as a historian of American history and oppressed peoples. I discovered what William Faulkner meant when he wrote in *Requiem for a Nun,* "The past is never dead. It's not even past."

13

Fort Huachuca

Driving from Tucson on August 15, 2006, I was struck by the flat, monotonous desert terrain, but I was excited to be going to Fort Huachuca, where my father and the other Buffalo Soldiers trained during World War II. I had expected to be going to a god-forsaken, barren place. I had studied the photographs of the fort and seen only a desolate landscape with mountains in the background.[1]

Suddenly the skies opened up and driving rain began—so hard I could not see a foot ahead of the windshield. The skies were shattered by bolts of lightning and ominous black clouds. The Huachuca Mountains were home to the Apaches in the nineteenth century, and Buffalo Soldiers from the fort hunted Geronimo and his people. As I came closer to Fort Huachuca, the striking beauty of the place astonished me. I learned that July and August are the "monsoon" season, and so the landscape was green and the mountains a glorious blue and purple color, unlike much of the year when it appears barren, dry, and desolate. Naturally, the fort has changed dramatically since its founding in 1877 and especially in the last sixty-five years. Many more buildings exist on the post, yet the barracks where the soldiers of the 92nd Division lived have been torn down. The former headquarters and movie theater now house the two parts of a museum.

I got lost trying to find the museum, as a gentle rain began to fall. I found myself at the cemetery where those who died while at the post over many decades are buried. A statue entitled "Mourning Hearts: A Soldier's Family" by Tucson artist Jessica McCain honors the women who waited and mourned. A soldier's widow holds a baby, and a young boy stands beside her. It is dedicated to all those surviving military family members in the U.S. Army, past, present, and future. I returned to the cemetery on my last day at the fort to pay tribute.

During the war, when my mother rented an apartment in Bisbee, Arizona, my father had to get up at 4 in the morning each day to hitch a ride across the barren landscape to the fort. Having seen pictures of Bisbee that resembled something out of *The Last Picture Show,* I imagined a ghost town that had shriveled when the mines closed. I drove to Bisbee looking for that time in my parents' lives when they were full of expectations. In Bisbee, which some people considered the end of the world, they were the happiest in their whole lives. Young, beautiful, in love, just married, even though they feared the future and separation, for them the time was one of intensity and longing.

In the place of abandoned mines, I drove into a canyon where many artists and writers now make their home. The houses dot the hills above the center of the city. My mother had spoken of a hundred steps up to their house, and I saw many houses still standing that met that description. My mother smoked Lucky Strike after Lucky Strike during those days while they were at Fort Huachuca, anxiously waiting for my father to return each day.[2]

I went there to experience the landscape and imagine what the fort was like for black and white soldiers. After doing research at the Fort Huachuca museum, I took a final drive around the base, past the abandoned Mountain View Colored Officers' Club where so many of the distinguished African American celebrities performed, and past the cemetery. Today the city of Sierra Vista stands where the town of Fry stood in the 1940s.

Now Fort Huachuca houses Military Intelligence. The old World War II barracks have been torn down, but the statue of the Buffalo Soldier at the gate reminds people of those days when the 92nd and 93rd Divisions made their home there. For me, Huachuca was a mythical place that I had heard about as a child. Now it took on a new reality. Then, suddenly, just as a cloud burst had greeted me upon my arrival, another one occurred as I headed back to Tucson to continue my search for my father's war—a war that also became my mother's war, and the war of all the wives and sweethearts of the black Buffalo Soldiers too.

14

Carlisle and the Battle for Memory

My search for my father's war led me to Carlisle, Pennsylvania, the home of the Army Military History Institute, which houses many of the records of the 92nd Division. Down the road a short distance from the Army Military History Institute are Carlisle Barracks and the Army War College, where the Carlisle Indian School once stood. General Richard H. Pratt, its founder, fought with the 10th Cavalry, the original Buffalo Soldiers. In 1879, Pratt established his school at Carlisle, having previously begun his industrial training of Indians in 1875 at the prison at Fort Marion in St. Augustine, Florida. The school became a model for many such schools throughout the United States, whose mission was to eliminate the students' native culture, language, dress, ceremonies, and spiritual beliefs and to "Americanize them."

Heavy snow blanketed the landscape and the beautiful nineteenth-century homes and red brick mansions were adorned by Christmas lights. My trip to Carlisle was essential because General Almond's role in my father's war was central. Perhaps aside from Douglas McArthur, few generals have generated such intense feelings as Lieutenant General Edward "Ned" Almond. Almond spent time at the War College and donated over 155 boxes of his papers replete with his diaries and copies of the official unit histories, correspondence, and maps. Having read his oral history conducted by his grandson, Thomas Fergusson, and having heard many stories about him, I had a pretty clear view of the man. I was in search of another, more nuanced view of him. I wanted to be able to see his human side.[1]

Almond's personal papers concerning World War II reveal the depth of his racial views. He became even more racist during and after the war than he had been before. Because of his traditional Southern upbringing, Almond believed that black people were inferior to white people, and that racial differences were intrinsic and biological. In his reports on the 92nd Division, he blamed literally every reversal in combat on the troops. He took no responsibility whatsoever for such fiascoes as Cinquale Canal or the February offensive. He did not believe African Americans could be good combat soldiers. General Almond's career rose like a meteor as he earned the admiration of George Marshall in World War II and Douglas MacArthur during the Korean War. He opposed the integration of the military services and tried to delay it in Korea.

Those black soldiers who felt exploited by white officers were angry and bitter about their treatment. Staff Sergeant David Cason Jr. said: "If the 92nd was in the same geographical position in Italy and had been told there were southern crackers up in those mountains, 'get 'em,' they would have, myself included, clawed their way up if necessary. We would have waded in our own blood up to our elbows to take them because we would have had a reason: an enemy we knew, despised, and would have enjoyed destroying. The German, what could he mean to us? Nobody bothered to make him our real enemy. . . . He [white man] treated us like boys or animals and then expected us to make Leonidas at Thermopylae Pass." Cason believed that the real enemy to the black soldier during World War II was "whitey: white American soldiers, white civilians, and the white civilian and military police."[2]

Driving out of Carlisle, Pennsylvania, the snow was melting. I had come in search of more knowledge of the 92nd Division and a more nuanced view of General Ned Almond, a more human side. Instead, I found an even more racist person than I had perceived before. Almond carried his bitterness about the 92nd Division to the end of his life. He never forgot that day at Fort Huachuca when the black soldiers booed him at the dedication of the new baseball field. Instructors at the Army War College, over which General Almond presided, later remembered him with embarrassment and shame because of his racism, which they believed had no place in the modern army.

Some of the Buffalo Soldiers lived to see the first African American president, Barack Obama, speak to the returning veterans and heads of state at Normandy on the sixty-fifth anniversary of D-Day on June 6, 2009. As the waves crashed on the beach where so many died, he said:

> For you remind us that in the end, human destiny is not determined by forces beyond our control. You remind us that our future is not shaped by mere chance or circumstance. Our history has always been the sum total of the choices made and the actions taken by each individual man and woman. It has always been up to us . . .
>
> That is the story of Normandy, but also the story of America, of the Minutemen who gathered on a green in Lexington, of the Union boys from Maine who repelled a charge at Gettysburg; of the men who gave their last full measure of devotion at Inchon and Khe San, of all the young men

> and women whose valor and goodness still carry forward the legacy of service and sacrifice. It's a story that has never come easy, but one that always gives us hope. For as we face down the hardships and struggles of our time, and arrive at that hour for which we were born, we cannot help but draw strength from those moments in history when the best among us were somehow able to swallow their fears and secure a beachhead on an unforgiving shore.[3]

One could say it is also the story of the Buffalo Soldiers.[4] General Almond would have been shocked to see an African American president speaking at Normandy. My father denied having racist attitudes, but he still hoped to avoid serving in the 92nd Division when he was first assigned duty. He struggled internally with conflicting Christian views that he held and the racist ideologies he had been exposed to during his Southern upbringing. His strong religious beliefs mitigated his Southern indoctrination. Slowly he began to understand the racism that the black soldiers faced, and he came to admire his troops.

When my father fought in Italy with the black soldiers for over six straight months, he trusted his life to them, and they to him. He empathized when they were terrified and tried to lead them with integrity and courage; he even saw them die beside him. He was aware of discrimination against his men before the war, and he remarked that even General Almond's officers' club at his headquarters near the front was "for whites only." Whereas my father spent over twenty years in the army in a career that spanned the crises in Europe, Taiwan, Cuba, and Vietnam, his time with the Buffalo Soldiers remained the most memorable and evoked the most intense feelings.

My father was not alone in having such strong reactions and being haunted by his time with the 92nd, a brief period compared to the rest of his over twenty years in the army. Yet, the impact was lasting. He was highly decorated in the war and promoted, yet prejudice against his men was also directed toward him. His perception of himself differed greatly from his view of other Southerners whom he considered racist. My father's changing racial views paralleled those of the country's as he began to realize his stereotypes did not hold up under scrutiny.

As witnessed by the valor of so many African Americans in all of the American wars and Colin Powell's brilliant career, race is not a barometer of abilities or courage. Therefore, a balanced view is needed, one that doesn't try to ignore the realities of so complicated an experience, and one that attempts to acknowledge the successes and failures of human beings in a horrific war.

15

Notes from Italy

The war in Italy officially ended on May 2, 1945, but Gene Johnston's war and the other Buffalo Soldiers' war did not actually end on that day. Their war with the Germans was officially over, but there were other wars ahead: the Cold War, the prelude to Vietnam, and the continuing war against racism. The end of my father's war was the beginning of a mystery for me. To unravel it, I boarded a plane on September 7, 2007, bound for Italy. The three stories of this book would converge there: the story of my own search for my father's war, his memoir of the war, and my discovery of the stories of the black soldiers of the 92nd Division.

I made this journey with close friends from California and France—Patricia Perez-Arce, Ed De Avila, and Jeffrey Kennedy. From Pisa, my friend Jeffrey and I drove to Ficulle, a small village in Umbria, which would serve as a home base, dropped the bags, and drove immediately to Rome to experience La Notte Bianca, *The White Night,* a time when the city is lighted, all churches and museums open and free, and traffic halted.

The city was magical; music, theater, and dance filled the streets. Rome was at its most luminous and beautiful. I had already been awake twenty-four hours when I arrived in Rome and would stay up forty-two hours straight before my head hit the pillow. La Notte Bianca was like being in a Fellini film or a carnival in Gabriel García Márquez's novels. Hundreds of events filled the city. An enormous mechanical praying mantis, breathing smoke with music blaring, came down the street near the Capitoline. Hundreds of people followed it and acrobats on five-foot pogo stilts jumped alongside it. Beauty streamed through the city.

In the Circus Maximus were hundreds of iridescent globes, an acre of light glowing, with each globe changing to many different pastel colors.

During the Italian campaign, the soldiers often spent a few days on R and R in Rome. I do not know if they were as overwhelmed with wonder as I was on La Notte Bianca, but I do know they entered another world, a world away from the war. They experienced the contrast between the horrors and rigors of the front and the pleasures of good food, of female companionship (of various sorts), and of Rome's impressive historical monuments.

Back in Umbria, we traveled to Orvieto, Siena, Assisi, Bolsena, and Castelluccio di Norcia. Ancient Etruscan ruins, Roman temples, castles, churches; silver-tinged olive trees swaying; and a landscape transformed from spring to summer—Italy is a land of extremes. A panorama of wildflowers in the spring turns into a lunar landscape with virtually no vegetation in the fall. Buffaloes, sheep and the dogs herding them, and wild horses wander through the valley down from Castelluccio di Norcia.

Soon we were on the train for Naples, and I was leaving my Italian world and entering my father's Italian world. I wanted to see the three ports: Naples, Livorno (Leghorn), and La Spezia, all critical to the 92nd Division's journey in Italy. The Naples that the members of the 370th saw as they disembarked amid sunken ships is still an active port with scores of ferries, boats, and cruise ships. Napoli is gritty, intense, lively, and reputedly under the domination of the Mafia. Some areas are a bit shabby, but the city is also grand and elegant, with buildings majestically arranged around large boulevards. I imagined the black soldiers making their way to the crater camp near Vesuvius. In March 1944, Vesuvius erupted. The soldiers were perched on the side of a volcano. Just across from Naples lay Capri, one of the most spectacularly beautiful places in the world. No wonder the emperors and the Germans wanted it for their own.

Back in Umbria, we began the journey to follow in the footsteps of the 92nd Division. Overlooking the fertile valley, the house where we stayed, Casa del Fagiano, presented a panoramic view of a castle nearby and acres upon acres of grapes bursting in the sun, ready to be harvested. The landscape contrasted sharply with the memories of war: dramatic incongruities of the beauty of the setting and the ugliness of war and killing. In 1944 and 1945, the beauty gave way to bombed villages, poverty, and death. The soldiers did not remember Italy for its beauty, and many of them would only see that many years later.

Leghorn (Livorno) was the entry point for my father's 371st Regiment. An ancient fortress stood then and still stands at the harbor. I found Livorno an unadorned city with an ancient fortress (Fortezza Vecchia). However, the port with its ancient and newer fortress possesses an understated beauty. Amid the turmoil of landing, the Buffalo Soldiers may not have noticed the bronze figures in front of the old wharf; the statue of slaves stands as an eerie and sinister reminder of oppression and slavery. I could easily imagine the scenes of Leghorn that the soldiers described—sunken ships in the harbor, and the fears they must have felt as they climbed down the ropes of the ship. Just as prostitution was a perennial temptation for the soldiers, scantily dressed prostitutes line the roads now too. Some have small recreational vehicles nearby, serving as portable brothels.

Viareggio was a staging area for the 92nd Division's missions. The 92nd Division's command post stood there under canvas and in vans next to the Principe de Piemonte Hotel. Most of the officers stayed in the hotel. Now Viareggio is a thriving vacation destination on the Italian Riviera. Resorts line the entire beachfront. The forest by the coast now obscures the view of the water along Highway A-1.

The medieval walled city of Lucca was one of the first occupied by the 92nd. Partisans within the city expelled the Germans, and when their food and water supplies were cut off, they called the Americans for help. The Americans rescued and held the city. This ancient city still retains its grandeur and the same narrow alleys and streets that the soldiers navigated. Similarly, Barga, which resembles a smaller Lucca, stands as a medieval walled city today. In the distance loom the Apuan Alps and Sommocolonia.

Castelnuovo di Garfagnana is still a crossroads. During the war, the Germans relied on the city as a major communications and supply center. The Serchio River runs through its center. As we walked through the city, we found a disturbing sight in an old cavernous area. There in the cave were scrawled Nazi swastikas. They seemed to be from our contemporary period, not the 1940s.

I searched for the Buffalo Soldiers in Italy, following the path of their struggle from Leghorn all the way through the Serchio Valley, the Po Valley, Naples, and the Apuan Alps and coastal sector, up to Genoa, La Spezia, and Milan. As our car struggled around hairpin curves with drop-offs of thousands of feet, I imagined the 92nd Division soldiers walking up these mountains carrying sixty to seventy-five pound packs—often in the mud as the bitterly cold winter approached. I imagined the mule pack that Spencer Moore commanded struggling up these narrow, steep roads. I carried a small leather notebook of my father's that he had carried during the war in which to make my notes.

The striking beauty of the landscape was always before me and I could feel the presence of my father and all the other Buffalo Soldiers as I saw what they had to confront. These black soldiers, many of whom had been poor farmers in the South, and who had not been out of their states of Alabama or Georgia, found themselves in Italy. They would be forever tied to Italy because they left their blood and their brothers there when they returned home. More than four hundred African American soldiers who were descendents of slaves lie buried there. The Buffalo Soldiers might not even know all the ways in which their lives were transformed by that experience. Sitting beneath the tower in Sommocolonia where the courageous John Fox lost his life was a very moving experience. He is buried under that tower. I remembered that Albert Burke was overcome with emotion when he returned to this place and remembered his friend, and I was overcome too.

After a long search and finding many villages that were not the one we sought,

24. Barga, Italy, 2007. Photograph courtesy of Carolyn Johnston.

we found St. Anna de Stazzema, the site of the massacre by the Germans of Italian civilians that is the subject of James McBride's wonderful novel *The Miracle at St. Anna* and Spike Lee's film of the same name. Inside the beautiful small church are the photographs of those who died in the tiny village, and the museum and monuments are an eloquent witness to those who resisted the Nazis and to the soldiers of the 92nd who came to their aid.

In the small town of Calomini, the site of a famous hermitage, we walked along narrow streets in the pristine village far up in the Apuan Alps. My father often spoke of Calomini and our journey illuminated why. The small towns of Calomini and Terrinca were some of the first villages his original unit, the 371st, occupied and liberated. Ezra Pound surrendered to him near Calomini, when my father was assigned to the 370th. Understandably, he never spoke of the stark beauty of these places because he was in combat there.

Aside from the small sign at Sommocolonia about John Fox, the footprints of the Buffalo Soldiers in Italy have been erased. A statue of the brave Japanese American soldier Sadao Munemori stands in Pietrasanta. Vernon J. Baker, another Medal of Honor recipient, participated in the unveiling of the statue of a

25. Sommocolonia, Italy, 2007. Photograph courtesy of Carolyn Johnston.

26. Sommocolonia, Italy, 2007. Photograph courtesy of Carolyn Johnston.

27. Sommocolonia, Italy, 2007. Photograph courtesy of Carolyn Johnston.

courageous man in the 100th/442nd who fought in the same offensive in 1945 and died saving his fellow soldiers. Perhaps only for the surviving Buffalo Soldiers do the memories of the battles at Cinquale Canal and Mount Cauala and on Hill X, Y, and Z stir such strong emotions. The road between Pietrasanta and Seravezza, the Purple Heart Highway, is now just a simple country road, but you can almost still hear the guns of Punta Bianca as the soldiers tried to avoid being hit by the shells when they were totally exposed on the road.

Forte dei Marmi is now a lovely beach town. During the war, the 92nd had a headquarters and officers' club there. No marker remains. Nearby the town of Massa is a simple, undistinguished little town, near Carrara and the renowned marble quarries. Above Massa and Viaregggio stood Castle Aghinolfi, where Vernon Baker destroyed three German machine-gun positions, two bunkers, and an observation post; now it stands as a silent reminder of the war. The Strettoia Hills and the Cinquale Canal are close by.

There is a monument to the Gothic line at the canal and another statue honoring the Italian resistance movement. No statue commemorates the thousands of black soldiers whose blood made the canal run red. Surrounding Cinquale

28. Cinquale Canal, Italy, 2007. Photograph courtesy of Carolyn Johnston.

29. Cinquale Canal, Italy, 2007. Photograph courtesy of Carolyn Johnston.

30. Cinquale Canal, Italy, 2007. Photograph courtesy of Carolyn Johnston.

Canal today are marinas and pleasure yachts. No longer do tanks clog the current bridge. In the background looms Mount Cauala where the soldiers fought so relentlessly. My father always seemed to come back to Cinquale Canal as a bitter memory of the war; the fiasco occurred the day before his friend Arthur Walker was killed on the mountain behind it. Ghosts still remain at the canal and in those mountains. I stood gazing at the Cinquale Canal where my father gathered his troops and headed for Hill X.

Arriving in Pisa, we saw the luminous and gleaming leaning tower and beautiful baptistery that now attract thousands of tourists. I imagined my father overseeing the prison camp there, and the cage in which Ezra Pound was incarcerated, where he composed his *Pisan Cantos.* I also could imagine Spencer Moore and the other wounded soldiers looking through the flaps of their hospital tents to see the leaning tower. Gone are the tents and the prison camp, and other traces of the Buffalo Soldiers. My friend Jeffrey and I searched for Columbus's ashes in Genoa, and any remaining evidence of the reburial of his ashes in 1945. Not a trace exists there today.

One of the things that I learned in the landscapes of the Italian campaign was that logistically the 92nd Division was in an impossible position with the Germans dug in above them. One can read about this, but it is so much more vivid when one sees the enormity of the heights involved in the mountains and the rugged terrain. The same holds true for being at Cinquale Canal.

After winding our way through the Serchio Valley and the Apuan Alps, we arrived at La Spezia and Portovenere and then finally in Milan. La Spezia is a gigantic port, and it is obvious why the naval center was so critical to the Nazis during the war. It remains an extraordinarily important port. I was not able to find the Punta Bianca guns located near the Caprione promontory in the bay of Spezia. Evidently, the Allies destroyed them at the end of the war. Because of their strategic location, they could fire straight down the Ligurian coast. My father reported that he had seen the huge shells strewn around where the guns had been after the end of the war.

This journey, which was part of my search for my own identity and place, was more importantly a return to those fields of battle where black and white and Japanese Americans "gave their best for America"—to honor them and try to understand the depth and complexity of that sacrifice. Every veteran at some point will say, "No one can understand what happened who wasn't there." Whether trying to know a parent, comprehend a war, or reach across the racial divide, there will always be a zone that is inaccessible and unknowable. But one can be a witness.

This trip brought me closer to my father and the other Buffalo Soldiers, and the mystery of their war in Italy. Retracing the steps of my father and the Buffalo Soldiers in Italy, not under fire but in the beautiful sunlight of September in Tuscany, I undertook a reverential journey—appreciating their valor, their terror, and their fears.

When I saw my parents' health fail, and sat at my mother's bedside when she died in 2000, I regretted that I had not finished my oral history with her. I also realized that I had little time left to get to know my father. The impact of our interviews on my father was profound. At one level, it aroused painful memories of the war and combat, and the racist treatment he and his men received. For many years, my father was silent about his service with the 92nd, a reticence that may have stemmed from a sense of bitterness or shame. He had ambivalent feelings about his time with the 92nd and believed that he had been assumed to be black and discriminated against in his professional career because of his association with the 92nd. As we spoke many hours about *his war,* his silence remarkably gave way to testimony. After our interviews were over, I gave him books about the 92nd Division. He eagerly read them and learned much about the broader context of his own personal experiences within the larger social and political context.

Suddenly, he understood his own contradictory feelings better and gained more respect and admiration for the black soldiers of the 92nd.

Waiting in the outskirts of Malpensa Airport at the Tre Leoni Hotel, the previous three weeks began to take shape. The search for my father's war that began on the top of the swing set in Georgia finally led me to Milan where Mussolini's disgraced body hung at the end of the war for the Buffalo Soldiers. My trip home took twelve hours, whereas my father's trip home from Italy took almost a month. As T. S. Eliot wrote in *Little Gidding*:

What we call the beginning is often the end
And to make an end is to make a beginning
The end is where we start from.[1]

16

The Buffalo Soldiers at the Capitol Rotunda

On July 23, 2008, African American veterans of many wars, the Joint Chiefs of Staff, the leadership of the House and Senate, and other distinguished guests filled the Capitol Rotunda. On the platform were Speaker of the House Nancy Pelosi, who arranged the ceremony; Secretary of Defense Robert Gates; John Boehner, Republican leader of the House; James Clyburn, Majority Whip of the House; Mitch McConnell, Republican leader of the Senate; Harry Reid, majority leader of the Senate; General Colin Powell; and Captain Spencer C. Moore and Sergeant A. William Perry, Buffalo Soldiers.

In the front rows were a number of Buffalo Soldiers of the 92nd Division, Tuskegee Airmen in red blazers, and members of all branches of the services, young and elderly. The United States Armed Forces Color Guard led by the Old Guard Fife and Drum Corps presented the colors, and the United States Army Chorus sang the National Anthem. The occasion commemorated the sixtieth anniversary of the integration of the United States Armed Forces.[1]

Spencer Moore and Bill Perry together slowly walked to the podium and spoke of their experiences in a segregated army, fighting in the Italian campaign of World War II. They paid tribute to their fallen comrades whom they remember and to the courage of Harry Truman for signing Executive Order 9981, desegregating the armed forces on July 26, 1948. Perry told the distinguished audience:

> We know that all men are created equal, but in WWII this was not the belief in the United States armed forces. A couple of months after graduation from high school I enlisted in the Army before they drafted me. I was assigned to the 92nd Buffalo Division. Our division was training at four different locations because no Congressional district would allow a division-size unit of 15,000 armed black men within their state. So we trained in Arkansas, Alabama, Indiana, and Kentucky.
>
> While we were preparing to make the world safe for democracy, we finally got together as a division when the other all Negro division moved out of Fort Huachuca in Arizona. Fort Huachuca is almost on the Mexican

border. The 92nd was stationed there for about a year and we were not allowed to take leave or get a pass for any town in Arizona. As a Buffalo Soldier the only place you could go on a pass was into Mexico.

From Arizona we went to Italy and our division took approximately 3,000 casualties. We have two Medal of Honor winners: Vernon J. Baker and John Fox, and one U.S. Senator, Edward Brooke. Our Division produced Frederic Ellis Davison, the first black person to command an Army brigade in combat and the first black person to reach the rank of major general and to command a division.

My parents had three sons in World War II, and they proudly displayed three stars in their window. When I came back at the end of World War II, I took advantage of the GI Bill, graduating from Ohio State University, and I also joined the National Guard. I was in the National Guard when Truman ordered the integration in 1948. We didn't integrate right away. It took a while and some forward-thinking leaders to have that happen. But we are here today in an integrated America.

I never dreamed that I would go back to Italy and see a statue to the Buffalo Soldiers in Sommocolonia, or participate in the film by Spike Lee based on the novel *Miracle at St. Anna* by James McBride, and that I would be standing here in the Capitol Rotunda remembering those days and those who went before me and those who still lie in the soil of Italy.

He closed with words that reverberated in the Rotunda: "What took us so long to realize that all men are created equal and for America to live up to her creed?" Spencer Moore then addressed the audience:

Good morning . . . Speaker Pelosi . . . Members of the 92nd Infantry Division and Guests. I would like to thank Speaker Pelosi and her staff for making it possible for me to be here today to be part of recognizing the anniversary of the desegregation of the military 60 years ago.

President Truman's signing the Executive Order 60 years ago to desegregate the military makes him, in my opinion, one of the greatest presidents of the 20th century. This act led to the beginning of the Civil Rights Movement and eventually civil rights for the whole country.

When I joined the New Jersey Guard in 1940, I was part of the first colored unit to be established in New Jersey. We were called to active duty in 1941 as part of the 372nd.

Because we were African Americans, they placed us the farthest from the main post so we would not be easily seen. The 372nd was made up of several segregated National Guard units throughout the East Coast.

I attended Officer Candidate School and was commissioned a 2nd Lieutenant to be part of the 92nd Infantry Division. As Bill has indicated we went to Huachuca and then Italy.

Segregation was still in effect. All Senior Officers were white, and all Junior Officers were black. In fact we jokingly called ourselves number "2s" because the black Officers Club was #2, Service Club was #2, and Officer Mess was #2, and so forth. I was 20 years old.

When we arrived in Italy one of the problems encountered because of segregation was the inability to get replacements for the 92nd Division. This caused many men to stay on the front lines for extended periods. In fact, I was wounded and I had no replacement. And then I got frostbite from my extended stay in the field. They just didn't know what to do with us.

When President Truman signed the Executive Order to integrate, I was back in the NJ National Guard and was utilizing the same armory as white National Guard troops, but we were still segregated. Once we integrated many white troops thought that they were going to have to change their social status, but eventually we integrated without any racial problems. In fact for a period of time I commanded an all-white section. In the integrated military, things progressed and made a way for many African Americans to make careers in the military.

There are three generations of Moores who have served in the armed forces—from my generation of my brother, my sister, and me through my son's and my nephews and my grandson. We have all served this nation—sometimes in segregated units, and now today in integrated units. If you want to learn more about our history in the 92nd Division you can find it in the Library of Congress.

Thank you again for allowing me the opportunity to come here to be a part of this momentous occasion.

After their speeches, they received a standing ovation. The entire ceremony was profoundly moving. Michael Moore, Spencer's son; Maggi Morehouse, whose father was in the 93rd Division; Charles Lancaster's daughter, Sharon Beckham; and I sat with the generals and admirals at the ceremony. Here we were, four children of parents in the "greatest generation," who had come together to honor our fathers in the 92nd and 93rd Divisions and the integration of the military. We are also survivors of the war. Across the aisle from us sat Albert Burke, Charles Lan-

31. *Left to right:* Congressional security officer, Spencer C. Moore, A. William Perry, Senator Mitch McConnell, and Secretary of Defense Robert Gates, July 2008, in the Capitol Rotunda. Event commemorating the sixtieth anniversary of the integration of the United States Armed Forces. Photograph courtesy of Michael Moore.

caster, and other members of the 92nd Division. Albert Burke was remembering a time when he and his fellow Buffalo Soldiers returned to Sommocolonia. In July 2000, a group of Buffalo Soldiers including Spencer Moore, William Perry, Albert O. Burke, Otis Zachary, and Richard O. Hogg returned to Italy fifty-five years after the war ended. The Italian people greeted them warmly with moving tributes to their contributions. On July 14, 2000, they toured Sommocolonia, where at least forty black soldiers (including John Fox, who ordered his own men to fire on his position because he was overrun by Austrian and German troops) had been killed on December 26, 1944.

Fox was awarded a Medal of Honor only in 1997. John Fox's widow, Arlene Fox, joined the veterans along with her sister-in-law, her daughter, and two grandchildren in the town, but she did not tour the battlefield. When walking over the battlefield, Albert O. Burke sobbed as two of his frail friends held him up. "I felt I owed it to the fellows to come back. But I don't think I want to come back here anymore." After comforting his friend, Otis Zachary also broke down and said, "Burke, I see him in the tower; I see John."[2]

When President Bill Clinton awarded the Medal of Honor to Vernon J. Baker,

John Fox, and five other black soldiers on January 13, 1997, all the living Buffalo Soldiers felt vindicated. Vernon J. Baker, a Buffalo Soldier and a Medal of Honor winner, demonstrated outstanding bravery during the April offensive. On April 5 and 6 near Viareggio, Italy, he destroyed several machine-gun emplacements, killed three Germans, attacked an enemy observation post, and killed its two occupants. With his men, he attacked two more machine-gun nests, and killed or wounded four more enemy soldiers. He then covered the evacuation of the wounded men of his company by drawing the enemy's fire. The next night, he led a battalion through enemy minefields and heavy fire.[3]

Charles Lancaster was remembering all those men who did not come home from Italy. While up on Mount Cauala in 1945, Lancaster never imagined this day in the Capitol Rotunda. I found two people who knew my father during the war: Charles Lancaster, an African American officer, and Richard Salmon, a white officer. My meetings with these two men revealed the complexity of understanding the Buffalo Soldiers. One year when the 92nd Infantry Association held their meeting in Rockville, Maryland, Spencer Moore, who graciously invited me, and Bill Perry set up their remarkable historical exhibits in one of the hotel conference rooms. A distinguished older white man came into the exhibition. Richard Salmon had not come to attend the reunion, but he had seen the sign and come in. I asked him if he had been in the 92nd and he said he was originally, and that he had been at Fort Huachuca. He knew my father, and he said he was extremely funny, in fact sometimes risqué. He said that everyone seemed to like and enjoy Gene's unique sense of humor.

I asked Richard Salmon if he knew Colonel Arthur Walker, a commanding officer who was killed next to my father, and who was a close friend of his. He said that Walker was one of the finest men he had ever known and that he always wondered what happened to him. I was able to tell him about his death in detail. Tears came to his eyes as if he were just finding out about a dear comrade. Richard Salmon had not gone to Italy with the 92nd, but rather he was sent to England. Later, he sent me an obituary of Arthur Walker that he asked me to give to my father.

In stark contrast to Richard Salmon's perception of Arthur Walker, Charles Lancaster had a completely different view. He also knew my father. When I heard he was in the 371st, I asked him if he knew Arthur Walker because I thought that would place him in my father's unit. Lancaster despised Arthur Walker because he thought he was a racist. He said some unprintable things about him and about Walker's racist remarks to him, and what he would do to him if he walked through the door—had he not been killed. Lancaster was commanding a group on the

32. Charles Lancaster at a Buffalo Reunion. Photograph courtesy of Carolyn Johnston.

mountain, and he remembered Colonel Walker's criticizing the way he was handling the offensive. Walker said something to Lancaster that deeply offended him.

Lancaster was with Captain Ivey (a white officer) when Walker ordered him to attack again on Mount Cauala. Ivey told him he needed supporting artillery. Then Walker told him: "You will attack and attack as many times as I order you to attack. I'm giving you direct orders to attack as it is unfair for the White Boys to be dying and these Niggers sitting here not doing anything." After a moment of silence, Ivey exploded. Soon after K Company withdrew, John F. Runyon's company moved in. Runyon only stayed two hours and returned to the rear area leaving his company more or less under Lancaster's command. Colonel James Notestein became angry at Lancaster when he told General Almond that he had not been up observing the company. Then he ordered him to attack the same peak that Company K had without supporting fire. Lancaster had been promoted, but after an altercation at headquarters, Notestein rescinded his promotion. Lancaster was wounded and hospitalized. His hospital was shelled, and he left during the evacuation.[4]

It was shocking to hear such a radically different view of Colonel Walker. I was afraid to ask Charles Lancaster about my father. Although I was hoping to hear that my father, unlike all those other racist white officers, was a decent, honorable person, someone to admire, I was also prepared to hear that he was just like the others. To my surprise, Lancaster said, "He was a great guy. He saved my career." Frankly, I was astonished, because I had been fully prepared to hear the same angry response to him as to Walker.

I was both relieved and reassured when he told me his story. Charles Lancaster told me how he had slugged an officer for calling him a "nigger" and been demoted from captain to first lieutenant. While awaiting court martial, he was transferred from Company F to Company M, my father's company. He was supposed to report at a certain time, but he did not, and my father covered for him and said Lancaster went to the hospital. So my father had saved his career.

Some weeks after the Buffalo reunion, Charles Lancaster sent me a copy of his orders and I recognized my father's signature by his beautiful handwriting. For many years now, Lancaster and members of his family have been warm, gracious friends. Parallel worlds coexisted during the period: the two worlds of black and white soldiers. Yet although experiences differed greatly because of race, there were distinctions and differences even within the races; some white officers respected the black soldiers and some did not. Layers and layers of surprises are in store when trying to understand such a charged situation. More than sixty years have not diminished the passion of these memories. The 92nd Division continues to evoke intense emotions from African Americans and from white Americans.

During this moving ceremony I thought of my father's final years, and how impressed he would have been by this tribute to the Buffalo Soldiers. His last years were spent being cared for devotedly by my remarkable sister Nancy Smith. For at least a decade, along with her demanding teaching job, she took care of my mother and father unceasingly and lovingly. For three years, my father was also fortunate to have a compassionate caretaker, Faheem Bengazi, an African American Muslim. He enabled my father to be able to stay in his home. At times, my father thought that he was back in the Italian campaign going up the Purple Heart Highway. He had many sleeping and waking dreams about being back in combat. Each fall at the Buffalo Soldier reunion, Spencer Moore, Bill Perry, and Charles Lancaster asked with genuine concern, "How is your father doing?" I wish he had been well enough to go to those reunions. I went in his place.

In anticipation of my father's ninetieth birthday in 2005, my sister and I planned a party and invited relatives from far and wide. Regrettably, the week of the party my father had to have emergency surgery. This occurred practically the day of his birthday, October 10. He sailed through the surgery but developed a dangerous staph infection. He was able to overcome this with the help of the strongest anti-

33. The 92nd Infantry (Buffalo) Division World War II Association, 2010. Photograph courtesy of Carolyn Johnston.

biotics available. However, this trip to the hospital would lead to other complications.

The hospital staff put two different patients with staph infections in his room. Shortly after he had come through the abdominal staph infection, he developed another on his foot. This period was one of excruciating agony and led to his death on March 12, 2006. Knowing his advanced age and that of the other Buffalo Soldiers, I rushed to finish this book, but alas, my father did not live to see its completion. Before his illness, he was able to edit the transcripts of his memoirs. In those horrific months from October to March, he returned in his mind to those battles in Italy so many years ago. Once either dreaming or hallucinating, he thought he was back on the battlefield and called his troops together to pray before they attacked.

Just as he had fought the Germans, he fought the illness with courage and stamina. He did not "go gently into that good night." In fact, at the end he kept repeating, "I need more time." In his mind, he was in Italy those last weeks, with his African American caretaker, Faheem Bengazi, attending him. He endured agonizing pain as his foot began to die an inch at a time and refused the offer of amputation of his entire leg. His toughness as an old soldier came through at the end with his ability to endure unimaginable pain. On March 12, 2006, he died. I

34. Eugene E. Johnston. Photograph courtesy of Carolyn Johnston.

have sought to be a witness to the courage and valor of my father and of the other Buffalo Soldiers.

None of the black veterans in the room could have dreamed that one day, after facing such racism and violence as members of the American military, they would stand in the Capitol Rotunda to be honored by the highest ranking officers in all the branches of service and by the leaders of the American Congress. The highest ranking black veteran in the Congress, Congressman Charles Rangel, was in the front row. Great civil rights leaders were present, along with many others who struggled and continue to struggle for equality. Albert Burke was thinking about his six-year-old granddaughter, who was studying black history in school. One day her teacher said, "All the Buffalo Soldiers are dead." She said, "No they aren't." She brought her grandfather to her class to prove that a Buffalo Soldier was still alive.

General Colin Powell closed the program with an eloquent speech paying tribute to those who have served and spoke of the debt he owed personally to all those black soldiers who came before him. Powell said the American military had been an engine of social change, and that the GI Bill was transformative for American society. In closing, the audience sang with the chorus, "God Bless America," the song often played as white, but not black troops, boarded ships for overseas combat. But on July 23, 2008, standing in the Capitol Rotunda, the black veterans received the honor and recognition long overdue. My search for my father's war came full circle there with the Buffalo Soldiers, and at the cemetery where my father received military honors.[5] Anyone who has seen a military funeral knows how poignant it can be, as young soldiers play "Taps" on the bugle and fire the salute, and the flag from the coffin is ritualistically folded and presented to the family with the words spoken, "On behalf of a grateful nation." As the officer presented the flag to my sister Nancy and me, I kept thinking of all the thousands, even millions of families who had experienced this moment, and of all those soldiers who had fallen. My father lived and died as a soldier—with integrity and courage. In my search for my father's war, I found my father.

Appendix I

Timeline of the 92nd Division in World War II

Background: Nineteenth century: The 9th and 10th U.S. (Colored) Cavalry regiments during the Indian Wars and Spanish-American War were the first to be named Buffalo Soldiers.[1]

October 15, 1942	Activated at Fort McClellan, Alabama
November 1, 1942–April 15, 1943	Individual (Basic) training
April 16–August, 1943	Unit training
August 16–January 15, 1944	Combined training
December 3–December 23, 1943	Division exercises
February 8–April 3, 1944	Maneuvers
April 17–August, 1944	Post-maneuver training and preparation for overseas deployment
July 15, 1944	370th Combat Team sailed for Europe
June 4, 1944	Rome fell to Allies
August 1, 1944	370th RCT arrived in Naples, Italy
August 24, 1944	370th RCT entered combat
October 18, 1944	371st disembarks in Leghorn (Livorno), Italy
Fall 1944	370th and 371st patrolling and harassing actions in the coastal area; occupation of Lucca. Fighting around Massa. Troops fail to take the city. They advanced into Serchio Valley with heavy losses.
December 26–28, 1944	92nd was forced to withdraw under heavy enemy attacks.
December 27, 1944	Sommocolonia bombed by American fighter bombers
January 1, 1945	Allies had reclaimed original positions after series of losses.

February 9–11, 1945	Battle at Cinquale Canal
February 24, 1945	Reorganization of 370th begins
April 1, 1945	370th and 442nd Infantry Regiment attacked in Ligurian coastal sector
April 18–29, 1945	370th took over Serchio sector and pursued enemy
April 29, 1945	Enemy collapsed
May 2, 1945	Enemy surrendered
November 16, 1945	Division left for home
November 28, 1945	Division is deactivated

Appendix II

Chronology of 92nd Division in the Italian Campaign

General Character of Operations, Almond Papers, Army Military History Institute, Carlisle, Pennsylvania

In general, the operations of the 92nd Division were characterized as follows[1]:

From August 23 to September 9, 1944: operation of the 370th Regimental Combat Team (CT) in crossing the Arno River, harassing the withdrawal of the enemy and capturing Lucca.

From September 10 to October 4, 1944: operation of the 370th Regimental Combat Team in penetrating the defenses of the Gothic Line, capturing Bagni di Lucca, and following the withdrawal of the enemy north of San Marcello.

On October 5, 1944, headquarters, 92nd Infantry Division assumed control in the coastal area.

From October 6 to October 12, 1944: limited object attack to seize Massa. Small advances were made but mission not accomplished.

From October 13 to November 15, 1944: operation on a broad front to cause maximum discomfort to the enemy by continued patrolling and harassing actions.

From October 16 to October 19, 1944: operation on a broad front by harassing and patrolling. The 366th Infantry Regiment was attached on November 28. The 365th Regimental CT was detached and attached to the 88th Division.

From December 26 to December 28, 1944: enemy attack in the Serchio Sector with four battalions. Attack penetrated positions forcing withdrawal of the 370th Infantry Regiment (minus one battalion). The 8th Indian Division (British) assumed command in the Serchio Valley on December 27, 1944.

From December 27, 1944 to February 7, 1945: harassing, patrolling and in general inflicting as much damage as possible on the enemy.

From February 8 to February 11, 1945: 92nd Division attacked in the coastal sector. Small advances were made but the mission was not accomplished.

From February 12 to April 4, 1945: widening of sector; harassing, patrolling, and preparing for spring offensive. The 473rd Infantry Regiment was attached on February 23, 1945. The 365th Infantry Regiment relieved on March 28, 1945; 442nd Infantry Regiment attached on March 25, 1945; 366th Infantry Regiment relieved division control on March 29.

From April 5 to April 24, 1945: attack on 92nd in coastal sector.

From April 24 to May 2, 1945: pursuit.

Operational Highlights 92nd Infantry Division—Italian Campaigns (August 24, 1944– May 2, 1945)

Preliminary

August 24 to October 5, 1944: 370 CT attached to 1st Armored Division under IV Corps. Participates in activities in connection with seizing and crossing Arno River; occupation of Lucca, Monticatini, and San Marcello; and penetration of Gothic Line. First enemy contact made on August 25 at 0915A.

October 1944

05 1800A—Major General E. M. Almond assumes command of Task Force 92nd (2nd Armored Group and 370th CT).

05 2000A—Field Order No. 1 announces limited objective.

06 0600A—Task Force 92nd attacks to northwest to seize Massa

12 The 2nd Armored Group seizes limited objective in left sector. The 370th makes slight gains, then enemy counter attack forces 370th back and attack of 06 is not successful.

13 Patrolling program begins.

19 1700A—Field Order No. 2 designates concentration areas for division units on the way.

22 The 370th occupies position on S slope of Mount Strettoia with one platoon reinforced

30 Road through Seravezza is opened for jeeps

November 1944

03 The 371st Infantry relieves 370th Infantry. The 370th moves to Serchio sector.

04 1000A—Division sector extended to twenty-five Easting. The 370th disbanded as separate administrative organization, comes under division control, and assumes command in Serchio.

04 2000 A—Field Order No. 3 announces mission to hold maximum enemy forces in coastal area. Exert pressure and protect 5th Army left flank.

08 The 371st occupies Azzano, Basati, Terrinca, and Levigliani.

10 The 365th Infantry comes under division control and relieves 2nd Armored Group

13 All elements of 92nd Division committed.

16–19 The 370th attacks to seize Castelnuovo. Small advances are made, but mission is not accomplished.

28 The 366th Infantry Regiment attached to 92nd Division.

December 1944

04 The 365th detached from the 92nd Division and attached to the 88th Division at Savazzo.

12 Infantry weapons shoots begin.

17 1200A—Field Order No. 4 announces attack to seize limited objectives.

22 Enemy offensive intentions in the Serchio Valley are indicated.

23 The 337th Regimental CT (85th Division) and 780th Tank Battalion attached to 92nd Division.

25 1600A—Field Order No. 5 announces defensive mission.

26 92nd Division assumes defensive roles as mission changes (to maintain line by counterattack).

26–28 Enemy attacked in Serchio sector with four battalions. Attack penetrates positions and forces 2nd Battalion of the 366th Infantry and 1st Battalion of the 370th Infantry to withdraw. 8th Indian Division assumes command in Serchio sector on December 27 at 1300A.

27 Sector narrowed.

28 The 135th Regimental CT (34th Infantry Division) attached to 92nd Division.

January 1945

01 92nd Division Mule Pack Battalion activated.

05 The 135th and 337th released.

10 0900A—Field Order No. 6 announces defensive mission. 92 Division reassumes command of Serchio sector. The 365th relieves the 8th Indian Division units East of River. Boundary extended to twenty-five east.

17 1200A—The 366th (3rd Battalion) assumes command of west bank of Serchio. The 370th begins rehabilitation program.

FEBRUARY 1945

01–05	The 365th and 366th advance in Serchio sector. The 365th occupies line: Mount Della Stella, Lama di Sotto, Albiano, Castelvecchio. The 366th occupies Hill 437, Gallicano against light opposition, Mount Faeto, Calomini, and Vergemoli. Gallicano-Vergemoli road freed by the 366th.
06	1600A—Field Order No. 7 announces attack in coastal sector.
08	The 365th withdraws from Lama di Sotto after repulsing two enemy counterattacks
09–11	The 3rd Battalion, 366th Infantry, 370th, and 371st Infantry regiments reinforced by tanks and artillery and supported by IV Corps Artillery and Engineers, attack in the coastal sector W of ninety-seven Easting. Mission not accomplished. Gain of about eight hundred yards is lost on February 14.
10	1200A—Field Order No. 8.
23	1800A—Division sector extended to forty-four Easting, including all troops therein, thus 475th Infantry Regiment comes under division control.
24	1800A—Field Order No. 9 announces the division will hold the maximum enemy force in the coastal sector and exert pressure within capabilities. Reorganization of 370th Infantry begins.
25	The 473rd to relieve the 366th.
26	0500A—The 473rd assumes command of 366th sector in Serchio.
28	2400A—The 365th, relieved from 92nd Division, assumes command of entire Serchio Valley sector. The 366th begins rehabilitation and training program.

MARCH 1945

03	The 366th begins seven-day period of extensive training in division training area.
06	The 679th Tank Destroyer Battalion attached to division. Remains in staging area via Leghorn. E Company of the 370th conducts unsuccessful raid.
12–13	The 473rd gains in the Serchio sector.
17	The 370th, as reorganized, begins intensive training and rehabilitation program.
25	The 442nd Infantry Regiment attached to the 92nd Division, effective 1800B.

29 The 366th Regiment leaves division control and assembles near Bottinoccio. The 442nd, plus attachment, closes in division concentration area and begins training program.

April 1945– May 2, 1945

03 Field Order No. 10 orders an attack in the Ligurian coastal sector. The 760th Tank Battalion attached to the 92nd Division.
05 The 370th and 442nd attack at 0500, while the 371st carries on diversionary demonstration south of the Cinquale Canal. The planned patrolling program stops in coastal sector.
08 The 370th moves to Serchio sector. The 371st leaves the division. The 473rd advances to outskirts of Massa against strong resistance.
10 The 3rd Battalion of the 370th moves to Serchio. The 442nd occupies Mount Brugiana. The 1st Battalion of the 473rd occupies Massa.
11 The 3rd Battalion of the 442nd enters Carrara without opposition. The 473rd crosses Frigido and advances 1,800 yards.
12 The 758th assumes command of sector between the 473rd and the coast.
16 The 370th occupies Fiattone.
18 Enemy withdraws in Serchio, and the 370th begins pursuit. Planned patrolling program stops in Serchio.
19 The 2nd Battalion of the 370th occupies and digs in on Mount Altissimo.
20 The 370th enters Castelnuovo di Garfagnana at 0740 without any resistance.
22 The 473rd patrol enters Sarzana.
29 Enemy resistance collapses.

92nd Infantry Division

1st Battalion	Headquarters, A, B, C, and D Companies
2nd Battalion	E, F, G, and H Companies
3rd Battalion	Headquarters, I, K, L, and M Companies
597th Field Artillery	
598th Field Artillery	
599th Field Artillery	
600th Field Artillery	
365th Regiment	
370th Regiment	
371st Regiment	

366th Regiment was attached

Spencer Moore	G, B, and A Companies, 370th Regiment
Bill Perry	K, 3rd Battalion, 370th Regiment
Kermit Hancock	B Company, 1st Battalion, 370th Regiment
Harold Montgomery	H Company, 2nd Battalion, 370th Regiment
Spurgeon Burruss	598th Field Artillery
Leonidas Williams	598th Field Artillery
Jehu Hunter	365th Regiment
Joseph Stephenson	365th Regiment
Joseph Hairston	600th Field Artillery (forward observer flew airplane)
Charles Lancaster	371st Regiment
Edward Brooke	366th Regiment
Carl Proctor	597 Field Artillery
Albert Burke	Headquarters, 92nd Division
Joe Willie Johnson	Company H, 370th Regiment
Hondon Hargrove	600th Field Artillery
Vernon Baker	C Company, 1st Battalion, 370th Regiment
Reuben Horner	E Company, 2nd Battalion, 370th Regiment
Eugene Johnston	M Company, 3rd Battalion, 371st; G Company, 1st Battalion, 370th

Notes

Chapter 1

1. See James Rada's unreleased film footage of the visit to the World War II Memorial, shot for *Deeds not Words,* October 9, 2004. Friedrich St. Florian's design with its granite and bronze recalls the old memorial traditions. Douglas Brinkley, ed., *The World War II Memorial: A Grateful Nation Remembers.* (Washington, DC: Smithsonian Books, 2004), xv. The memorial was dedicated in 1995 with the sprinkling of soil from the nation's fourteen overseas World War II cemeteries maintained by the American Battle Monuments Commission (Brinkley, 3). The film *The World War II Memorial: A Testament to Freedom* (directed by Robert Uth [Washington, DC: A Production of New Voyage Communications, PBS, 2004], DVD) illuminates the power of the site. Brinkley reminds us, "As you stand at the Rainbow Pool you realize the memorial encompasses the totality of the World War II experience in all the theaters of operation. It honors not just the young GI storming ashore at Normandy or the Admiral deciding how to best win the Battle of Midway, but the American people as a whole. . . . The Memorial salutes the tireless women who worked in textile mills to make parachutes and the world-class engineers who designed essential new parts for the B-24 bomber." The memorial honors an entire generation (Brinkley, xiv).

2. The 100th Infantry Battalion came from Hawaii's National Guard and joined the 442nd Regimental Combat Team on June 10, 1944, after the unit had already distinguished itself in Italy. The unit was then identified as the 100th/442nd Regiment Combat Team in recognition of its previous war record. Many people also referred to the unit simply as the 442nd. The Division was the largest African American unit in the army, composed of 15,000 men, and even 20,000 at one time. See Orville C. Shirey, *Americans: The Story of the 442nd Combat Team* (Washington, DC: Infantry Press, 1947).

3. Christopher Paul Moore, *Fighting for America: Black Soldiers—The Unsung Heroes of World War II* (New York: Presidio Press, 2005), xiii. In 1998, of the sixteen million who had served in uniform during the war, fewer than six million were alive; fewer than four million survived when the memorial was dedicated in 2004. See Robert Uth, "Making History on the Mall," in Douglas Brinkley, ed., *World War II Memorial,* 270.

Chapter 2

1. Stuart Yamane's moving documentary *Journey of Honor* (Kaneohe, HI: KHET Hawaii PBS, 2001) chronicles the return of Japanese American veterans to Italy in 2000.

Chapter 3

1. Interview with Eugene Johnston by Carolyn Johnston, June 15, 2003.

2. Ibid.

3. Ibid.

4. Fred Johnston was an artist who became a founding member of The Southern Highland Craft Guild. Interview with Eugene Johnston by Carolyn Johnston, June 21, 2002.

5. Interview with Eugene Johnston by Carolyn Johnston, taped in 1999.

6. Interview with Eugene Johnston by Carolyn Johnston, June 24, 2002.

7. Ibid.

8. Interview with Eugene Johnston by Carolyn Johnston, June 19, 2002.

9. Interview with Eugene Johnston by Carolyn Johnston, June 24, 2002. I have used the terms *black* and *African American* interchangeably in the book. I have used the terms *Negro* and *colored* when quoting contemporary sources that used those terms, or individuals from that period who used those terms as the respectful terms to use. Sometimes the terms were capitalized and sometimes they were not. Offensive racial epithets were also common during the period and in the documents. The more recent terms did not become standard practice until the 1960s and the civil rights movement.

10. Capt. Thomas G. Fergusson, "Reflections: Transcripts of the Debriefing of General Edward M. Almond," 25 March 1975, Edward M. Almond Papers, Archives. U.S. Army Military History Institute, Carlisle Barracks, Carlisle, PA, III-39, 170.

11. Interview with Eugene Johnston by Carolyn Johnston, June 19, 2002.

12. Ulysses Lee, *The Employment of Negro Troops. United States Army in World War II,* Special Studies Center for Military History publication 11-4 (Washington, DC: U.S. Government Printing Office, 1966), 335–336, 500–534.

13. Interview of Spencer Moore II by Reno Domenico, vice principal, Sterling High School, New Jersey, 2001. See also Charles Lancaster, "Black Soldier: 'I'll Fight No More'" (unpublished autobiography, 1986, revised in 2010), 2–3, typescript. The 92nd Division was composed of the 365th, 370th, 371st infantry regiments; four field artillery battalions: the 597th, 598th, the 599th, 600th; Headquarters and Headquarters Company; Headquarters and Headquarters Battery; the 92nd Cavalry Reconnaissance Troop; the 317th Engineer Combat Battalion; 317th Medical Battalion; 792nd Ordnance Company; 92nd Signal Company; 92nd Quartermaster Company; Headquarters Special Troops; maintenance personnel; and 92nd Military Police Platoon. See Hondon Hargrove, *Buffalo Soldiers in Italy: Black Americans in World War II* (Jefferson, NC: McFarland, 1985), 192. Units that were attached to the 92nd were the 366th Infantry Regiment, the 442nd Infantry Regiment, the 473rd Regimental Combat Team, the 785th Tank Battalion, the 679th Tank Destroyer Battalion, the 894th Tank Destroyer Battalion, and 701st Tank Destroyer Battalion, 760th Tank Battalion, 84th Chemical Mortar Battalion, and 27th Armored Field Artillery Battalion. See *The Army Almanac: A Book of Facts Concerning the Army of the United States* (Washington, DC: U.S. Government Printing Office, 1950), 510–592.

14. Interview of Spencer Moore II. See also Lancaster, "Black Soldier," 3.

15. Maggi M. Morehouse, *Fighting in the Jim Crow Army: Black Men and Women Remember World War II.* (Lanham, MD: Rowman and Littlefield, 2000), 9–10. Much of the following material was taken from oral histories with Buffalo Soldiers of the 92nd conducted by Maggi M. Morehouse and subsequently recorded in her book *Fighting in the Jim Crow Army* and from the original transcripts of the interviews in her personal archives.

16. Morehouse interview transcript. Bill Perry recently donated his collection to the Li-

brary of Congress Manuscript Division. Along with Spencer Moore, he has been devoted to the 92nd Infantry Division Association, and also to the Huachucans, an organization of World War II veterans in Cleveland, Ohio. See Bill Perry interview, Morehouse Archives; see also Morehouse, *Fighting in the Jim Crow Army,* 19, 46.

17. Lieutenant General William J. McCaffrey, USA Retired, interviewed by Lieutenant Colonel John E. Baggott. Carlisle Barracks, PA, 1997. Senior Officer Oral History Program. U.S. Army Military History Institute, McCaffrey interview, 22–24.

18. McCaffrey interview, 22–24.

19. Maggi Morehouse Archives. Albert O. Burke died in Washington, DC, on October 22, 2010, at the age of 90. *Washington Post,* October 27, 2010.

20. Maggi Morehouse Archives; see Gene Roberts and Hank Klibanoff, *The Race Beat: The Press, The Civil Rights Struggle, and the Awakening of a Nation* (New York: Vintage Books, 2006). The National Association for the Advancement of Colored People and black press were pushing hard for this. Yet, some of the new recruits hoped they would not push quite so hard. See Patricia Sullivan, *Lift Every Voice: The NAACP and the Making of the Civil Rights Movement* (New York: The New Press, 2009).

21. Conversation with Joe Stephenson: October 2004; see also Morehouse, *Fighting in the Jim Crow Army,* 19.

22. Morehouse, *Fighting in the Jim Crow Army,* 45, 118–119; Morehouse Archives, original transcript of interview. Stephenson said that evidently during the Korean War, Almond was just as mean and devilish as he could be with white troops as he was with blacks. Interview with Carolyn Johnston, October 2004.

23. William E. Alt and Betty L. Alt. *Black Soldiers, White Wars* (Westport, CT: Praeger, 2002), 79–80; Lee, *Employment of Negro Troops,* 5–15, esp. 5–6. See also Chad L. Williams, *Torchbearers of Democracy: African American Soldiers in the World War I Era* (Chapel Hill: University of North Carolina Press, 2010).

24. Alt and Alt, *Black Soldiers, White Wars,* 79–80; Lee, *Employment of Negro Troops,* 5–15, esp. 5–6. In *Black Soldiers, White Wars,* the authors round the total number of troops to four hundred thousand.

25. Alt and Alt, *Black Soldiers, White Wars,* 81, 90; for more details regarding the incident, see Gail Buckley, *American Patriots: The Story of Blacks in the Military from the Revolution to Desert Storm* (New York: Random House, 2001), 182; Lee, *Employment of Negro Troops,* 5–15.

26. Morehouse, *Fighting in the Jim Crow Army,* 130-131; for an in-depth discussion of the performance of the 92nd Division and effort to discredit them, see Robert W. Kesting, "Conspiracy to Discredit the Black Buffaloes: The 92nd Infantry in World War II," *The Journal of Negro History* 72, no. 1/2 (Winter–Spring 1987), 1–19.

27. See Army Service Forces Manual, M5, *Leadership and the Negro Soldier* (Washington, DC: United States Government Printing Office, 1944), 26. The manual that the Special Service Division of the army produced counseled the officers on how to deal with black soldiers: Officers had to be aware of beliefs, attitudes and traits most likely to cause trouble in the handling of Negro troops. For any white officer who did not understand these things, terms including *boy, darky, uncle,* and *nigger* were named as offensive, as was the pronunciation of Negro as if it were spelled "Nigra." Race-based jokes about blacks were prohibited (73). See also: Dr. Conrad Crane, the director of the Army War College in the film *Sacrificial Soldiers: The Colored Troops of the 92nd Division,* produced and directed by James Rada and his class in video production (Washington, DC: Howard University, 2005). Lee, *Employment of Negro Troops,* 254, 243; see Lee, 244, for the test score statistics for March 1941–December 1942.

AGCT Grade	White		Negro	
Total:	4,129,259	100%	440,162	100%
Group I:	273,626	6.6%	1,580	0.4%
Group II:	1,154,700	28.0%	14,891	3.4%
Group III:	1,327,164	32.1%	54,302	12.3%
Group IV:	1,021,818	24.8%	152,725	34.7%
Group V:	351,951	8.5%	216,664	49.2%
Percentage		90.4%		9.6%
AGCT Combined White and Negro Scores				
Total:	4,569,421	100%		
Group I:	275,206	6.0		
Group II:	1,169,591	25.6		
Group III:	1,381,466	30.2		
Group IV:	1,174,543	25.7		
Group V:	568,615	12.5		

The Army Service Forces Manual M5 of October 1944 recognized that race discrimination was "fatal" to military efficiency. See Daniel Kryder, *Divided Arsenal: Race and the American State during World War II* (New York: Cambridge University Press, 2000), 166.

28. Army Service Forces Manual M5: *Leadership and the Negro Soldier,* 18–19. Army General Classification Tests (AGCT) revealed the following:

20% Negroes and 74% white in Army grades I, II, II
80% Negroes and 26% whites Grades IV, V

The expenditure per Negro pupil in nine southern states was $18.82 in 1939–1940. The average for a white pupil was more than three times as great: $58.69 (30). The manual's overall conclusions were that doctrines of innate racial inferiority and superiority were not supported by scientific evidence, and that differences in the AGCT test scores of black and white soldiers did not indicate differences in innate abilities. See *Leadership and the Negro Soldier,* 33, 48, 74; Elbert L. Harris, *Let the Ammunition Roll: The Story of a Negro GI* (New York: The Exposition Press, 1948), 18–19.

See also Buckley, *American Patriots,* 258, 164. Buckley wrote, "The curious logic of southern racism required that black men be seen at once as dangerous, in order to justify repression, and as cowardly, to justify contempt and exclusion"(164).

29. Stephenson interview, Morehouse Archives; see also Morehouse, *Fighting in the Jim Crow Army,* 69–70. On the AGCT tests, "Open-minded white officers working with black troops came to distrust the AGCT as an accurate barometer of performance. The Army incorporated new screening techniques at induction centers and special training units for low-scoring draftees." Morehouse Oral history transcript, 113; RG 208, OWI stack 350; row 71, co., 12, shelf 4; entry 1, Records of the Director and Predecessor Agencies 1942–1945 box. Memo Theodore M. Berry (Liaison Officer) to Elmer Davis, July 24, 1942; attaches March 4, 1942. "Blue-print of Program for Strengthening Negro Morale in War Effort."

30. The expenditures of states on education reflected dramatic inequalities. The median ex-

penditure for African American pupils in nine southern states was $17, whereas nationally, the median state expenditure was $54 per pupil per year in the period from 1939 to 1940. Expenditures ranged from $157 per pupil in New York to $7.36 for Negro pupils in Mississippi. Jean Byers, *A Study of the Negro in Military Service.* (Washington, DC: U.S. Department of Defense, January 1950), 18–19, 52–53.

31. Interview with Spencer Moore, conducted by Carolyn Johnston, May 25, 2007.

32. Franklin, in *The War,* directed and produced by Ken Burns (Washington, DC: Florentine Films and WETA, 2007), DVD, and John Hope Franklin, *Mirror to America: The Autobiography of John Hope Franklin* (New York: Farrar, Straus and Giroux, 2005).

33. Edward W. Brooke, *Bridging the Divide: My Life* (New Brunswick, NJ: Rutgers University Press, 2007), 31, 21, 24–29, 32. Brooke received the Presidential Medal of Freedom in 2004.

34. Jehu C. Hunter and Lt. Col. Major Clark, "The Buffalo Division in World War II" (unpublished manuscript, typescript, 1985), 10, 14; Jehu C. Hunter, Veterans Survey, Carlisle, folder 4204. Hunter rose to the rank of captain and was awarded the Bronze Star.

35. Conversation between Carolyn Johnston and Charles Lancaster, October 2004, Rockville, Maryland. Lancaster, "Black Soldier," 5–6, 8–9. Colonel Sterling Wood disciplined Lancaster for "embarrassing a white officer" when he quoted the regulations to him and corrected his statement about a policy (11). Lancaster stated that Colonel Sterling Wood was assaulted seriously at Fry gate at Fort Huachuca later (13–14).

36. Henry Wiencek, *The Hairstons: An American Family in Black and White* (New York: St. Martin's Griffin, 1999), 250–253, 255, 261.

37. Ibid. Joseph Hairston joined the army in 1940 but it took three months for the recruiting officer to find a unit that would accept him because of his race. He earned $21.00 a month as a private first class. Finally, he was assigned to a medical detachment at Alexandria, Louisiana. He met his wife, Ann, there, and they have been married since 1942. After serving there, he was assigned to the 92nd Division. Conversation between Joseph Hairston and Carolyn Johnston, November 29, 2010.

38. Morehouse, *Fighting in the Jim Crow Army,* 129–130. William S. M. Banks, *From Beginnings in the SIP* (Fort Valley, GA: self-published, n.d.), 49. Maggi Morehouse Archives, interview transcript, 10. Wiencek, *Hairstons,* 260–261.

39. Wiencek, *Hairstons,* 255.

40. Interview with Eugene Johnston by Carolyn Johnston, June 19, 2002.

41. Ibid., tape 8.

Chapter 4

1. List of units in the 92nd Division: Fort McClellan, Alabama: Headquarters, 92nd Headquarter Company; Military Police Platoon; 92nd Signal Company; 92nd Cavalry Reconnaissance Troop; 92nd Quartermaster Company; Headquarter and Headquarter Battery 600th Field Artillery Battalion; 317th Medical Battalion; 317 Engineers Battalion; 792 Ordnance Light Maintenance Company. Camp Atterbury, Indiana: 365th; 597th Field Artillery Battalion. Camp Breckinridge, Kentucky: 370th; 598th Field Artillery Battalion; Light Maintenance Company. Camp Joseph T. Robinson, Arkansas: 371st; 599th Field Artillery Battalion. Edward Almond Papers, box 24A, articles by Almond Folder with clippings, 1942.

2. Almond Papers, box 24A.

3. Interview of Lieutenant General Edward Almond with Captain Thomas Fergusson, March 24–30, 1975, 163. Accessed December 2007, http://www.carlisle.Army.mil/cgi-bin/

usamhi/DL/showdoc.pr?docnum=82. I have numbered the pages consecutively as they appear in Adobe. Originally the pages were numbered in each section. Colonel Fergusson has provided a marvelous gift to researchers with his oral history of General Almond, his grandfather. There are 155 boxes of papers in his collection at Carlisle Barracks, American Military History Institute (USAMHI). Interview, 164. Almond received the following decorations: Mexican Border, Victory Medal, Silver Star—World War I, Purple Heart, German Occupation World War I, American Defense; American Theater, Equadore Estrella Abdon Calderon-1936. World War II, Distinguished Service Medal, Oak Leaf Cluster to Silver Star; Air Medal Combat Ribbon with two Oak Leaf Clusters, Order of Bath (British), Legion of Honor (French), Medal di Guerra (Brazil) (Almond Papers, AMHI Carlisle, box 3). See also *VMI Review,* Spring issue 1971, 15. Almond graduated third in his class with a BS degree in electrical engineering. He was commissioned a second lieutenant in the regular army infantry on November 30, 1916. He was the recipient of more than twenty U.S. combat decorations, numerous U.S. service ribbons and battle campaign stars. He received ten foreign decorations from seven different nations and was made a distinguished citizen of Genoa, Italy, upon its liberation by his troops in April 1945. He was wounded in the Aisne-Marne offensive, and for his service in that war, he was awarded the Silver Star and Purple Heart. He commanded the 92nd Division in the Italian campaign. He earned a Distinguished Service Medal, a second Silver Star, the Legion of Honor (French), the Order of Saints Maurice and Lazarus (Italian), and the Medal of War (Brazil). Interview, 416.

4. Almond interview, 163–165. See also interview of Lieutenant General William P. Ennis Jr., USAT Retired, interviewed by Lieutenant Colonel Miguel E. Monteverde Sr., March 14, 1984, 108. William P. Ennis, Papers Archives USAMHI, box 1, project, Senior Officer Oral History Program, tape 36. See also 84–86, 176. Ennis commanded the IV Corps Artillery in support of the 92nd in Italy. Almond; John E. Wood, the assistant division commander; and William H. Colburn Jr., the division artillery commander, were all three Virginia Military Institute graduates. See also Dale E. Wilson, "Recipe for Failure: Major General Edward M. Almond and Preparation of the U.S. 92nd Infantry Division for Combat in World War II," *Journal of Military History* 56 (July 1992), 473–488, esp. 478–479. Ennis said his black unit, the 96th Field, in Korea was one of the best battalions he had. "General Almond said we were using them before they were mentally ready for such use. We were using them as officers, using them as . . . that they just mentally weren't up to it. I think it is very different now that we have mixed them." See Ennis interview, 113, 114.

5. Morehouse Archives, original transcript of interview; interview with Carolyn Johnston, October, 2004.

6. Interviews with Eugene Johnston by Carolyn Johnston, March 16, 2002; June 19, 2002.

7. Maggi Morehouse Archives. Helen Montgomery remembered their time at Fort Huachuca. At first they lived on OK Street, and then they moved to Drury Gulch. Bill Perry stated: "In the 1st Battalion black captains commanded Companies A and C; in 2nd Battalion: Companies E and H; in 3rd Battalion: Companies I, L, and M."

8. Maggi Morehouse Archives.

9. Interview with Eugene Johnston by Carolyn Johnston, March 16, 2002.

Chapter 5

1. Interview with Eugene Johnston by Carolyn Johnston, March 16, 2002. Emily Yellin, "Women in World War II," in *The World War II Memorial: A Grateful Nation Remembers,* edited by Douglas Brinkley (Washington, DC: Smithsonian Books, 2004), 250. Approximately

1.8 million couples married in 1942, and in the first year of the war, over two hundred thousand more married than did in 1940.

2. Interview with Eugene Johnston by Carolyn Johnston, March 16, 2002.

Chapter 6

1. Mary Penick Motley, comp. and ed., *The Invisible Soldier: The Experience of Black Soldiers in World War II* (Detroit, MI: Wayne State University Press, 1975), 294, 297; Truman Gibson, *Knocking Down Barriers: My Fight for Black America* (Evanston, IL: Northwestern University Press, 2005), 157. The Mountain View Officers' Club was commonly referred to as the "Colored Officers' Club" during the time that the 92nd was at Fort Huachuca.

2. Maggi Morehouse Archives. After serving at Fort Huachuca, Madine Davis Lane went to Burma. In October 1944, 82 Negro nurses attended 150 patients at Fort Huachuca. Maintaining segregated military facilities cost a tremendous amount. Jean Byers, *A Study of the Negro in Military Service for Departmental Use, June 1947* (Washington, DC: U.S. Department of Defense, January 1950), 81–82. Huachuca's two hospitals contained 1,141 beds for a population of over 25,000, whereas Tucson had 350 hospital beds and 80,000 citizens. One of Fort Huachuca's hospitals was the only Negro-commanded and -staffed hospital in the United States. Also, it was the largest service hospital. Cornelius C. Smith Jr., *Fort Huachuca: The Story of a Frontier Post* (Honolulu, HI: University Press of the Pacific, 2000), 299. See also Darlene Clark Hine, "Black Professionals and Race Consciousness: Origins of the Civil Rights Movement, 1890–1950," *Journal of American History* 89, no. 4 (March 2003), 1279–1294; Hine, *Black Women in White: Racial Conflict and Cooperation in the Nursing Profession, 1890–1950* (Bloomington: Indiana University Press, 1989).

3. Maggi Morehouse Archives.

4. Gibson, *Knocking Down Barriers,* 156.

5. Ibid., 156–157. Bousfield added, "Almond is pretty stupid about race relations." Another chaplain of the 92nd was Chaplain Jones who was based in the 3rd Battalion Headquarters Company and who reported to Colonel Daugette. Ivan Houston wrote: "We had a joke that after anyone shared his problems with the chaplain, he would receive a TS card, meaning Tough Shit. The truth is that Chaplain Jones was a very fine officer and his presence meant a lot to the men." Ivan Houston, "Memoir" (unpublished typescript, n.d.), 85. Truman Gibson served as advisor on racial affairs to Secretary of War Henry Stimson from 1943 to 1945. See also Christopher Paul Moore, *Fighting for America: Black Soldiers—The Unsung Heroes of World War II* (New York: Presidio Press, 2005), 96–97.

6. Almond interview, 166. Almond prevailed and the entire division was assigned overseas. After more intensive training at Huachuca, the 92nd headed for Italy in the fall of the year. Almond interview, 168, 166.

7. Almond interview, 209–210.

8. Morehouse Archives, transcripts.

9. Benjamin Davis Sr. papers, Carlisle, Benjamin Davis's Visit to Fort McClellan, box 17, folder 17.

10. See Letter from Pierre V. Kieffer, March 24, 1943, for General Davis. Nevertheless, Davis gave the following ratings: post headquarters detachment: superior; military police detachment: superior; supply and service detachment: excellent; WAAC section, SCLU 1922: superior. Davis Collection, Carlisle, box 18. Joseph Stephenson asserted that the commanders at Camp Atterbury ordered integration of the mess hall and other sections in advance of

General Davis's inspection tour and resegregated them right after his visit. October 8, 2009, Buffalo Soldier Reunion, Silver Spring, Maryland.

11. Almond interview, 172.

12. Reuben Horner interview, Maggi Morehouse Archives; Almond interview, 173.

13. Letter from Truman Gibson to Dan Burley, 21 September 1943, Benjamin Davis Sr. Collection, Carlisle, box 13. Truman Gibson accompanied Benjamin Davis Sr. on his inspection tour of Fort Huachuca. Like Davis, Truman Gibson was respectful of General Almond and diplomatic in his dealings. He referred to him as one of the most highly thought of general officers in the army. John Robert Bruning Jr., *Elusive Glory: African American Heroes of World War II* (Greensboro, NC: Avisson Press, 2001), 11. Benjamin O. Davis graduated from West Point in 1936. Second Lieutenant Davis was assigned as an officer in the 24th Infantry. The 24th was a line unit, and he thought he would be serving as a combat-trained officer. He soon learned "the 24th was simply a glorified janitorial unit that trained half-heartedly for battle twice a year. As the African American soldier put it, "They [the Army] said us black troops weren't any good . . . the only thing [they thought] we were good for was to dig latrines and bury the dead." Bruning, 11.

14. Signed G. C. Marshall Chief of Staff. Collection of Benjamin O. Davis Sr., box 13, AMHI. Office of the Inspector General. General Business, War Department Policy on the treatment of Negro Personnel, 7 June 1943.

15. Collection of Benjamin O. Davis Sr., box 13, AMHI. Office of the Inspector General. General Business, War Department Policy on the treatment of Negro Personnel, 7 June 1943.

16. Davis Collection, American Military History Institute, Carlisle, box 18. Official Papers: Office of the Inspector General Inspection Tours from 24 Feb 1943 to 6 Sept 1943, 1942–17 Dec 1943, Special mission: February 1943, Truman Gibson. Edwin N. Hardy, post commander at Huachuca to Davis.

17. Gibson, *Knocking Down Barriers,* 158.

18. Moore, *Fighting for America,* 143–144. Hondon Hargrove, a black officer in the 92nd, was very tempered in his survey answers regarding Almond, and he said, "I want to avoid the pitfall of many black writers who would blame the white officers for all the division's problems. Sure there was racism, but a lot of those white men were damn fine people and damn fine officers. They carried out their duties like everyone else and they died too." Veterans Surveys World War II, Carlisle.

19. Vernon Baker with Ken Olsen, *Lasting Valor: Story of the Only Living Black World War II Veteran to Earn America's Highest Distinction for Valor, the Medal of Honor* (Columbus, MS: Genesis Press, 1997), 204.

20. *Huachuca Illustrated, a Magazine of the Fort Huachuca Museum, World War at Huachuca 1940–1949* 9(1993), 97; see videotape of interview of Reuben Horner of 17 November 1992 at Fort Huachuca. Horner did have great respect for Colonel Raymond G. Sherman.

21. *Huachuca Illustrated* 9 (1993), 89–92, 96–97; Horner and many others believed erroneously that Almond was shielded from reprisal because he was George C. Marshall's brother-in-law. I have seen no substantiation for this. Marshall's obituary in the *New York Times* does not mention Margaret Crook Almond as his sister. Horner expected Almond to be punished after Cinquale Canal, but he was not. See Horner, Morehouse Archives. Later, Reuben Horner distinguished himself in the Italian campaign. He personally destroyed a machine-gun nest. To save his men, he fought off eight separate German attacks. When he was cut off, he called on their own artillery to fire on where they were. They had captured a number of German prisoners, and they also had a lot of wounded in addition to the dead. The ammunition began to

be exhausted. So he sent one group with a little ammunition to take the prisoners and wounded back. Horner and the remaining men kept the rest of the ammunition. They made it back safely. They stayed up there and were almost rescued by the first armored tanks, but German fire power prevented it. So he and the eight men with him had to work their way back to their lines. Horner's citation was written up in such a way that he satisfied the qualification for a Medal of Honor but never received one. Back at Fort Huachuca, this future medal winner had been inspecting trash and checking uniforms at the movie theater. See Morehouse Archives.

22. Maggi M. Morehouse, *Fighting in the Jim Crow Army: Black Men and Women Remember World War II.* (Lanham, MD: Rowman and Littlefield, 2000), 46.

23. Morehouse interview; interview with Carolyn Johnston, October 2004.

24. Morehouse, *Fighting in the Jim Crow Army,* 60–61.

25. Lieutenant General William J. McCaffrey, USA Retired, interviewed by Lieutenant Colonel John E. Baggott. Carlisle Barracks, PA, 1997. Senior Officer Oral History Program. U.S. AMHI, 28.

26. McCaffrey, interview, 28.

27. Cornelius C. Smith Jr., *Fort Huachuca,* 299.

28. Gibson, *Knocking Down Barriers,* 158.

29. Almond papers, box 33, AMHI, Carlisle.

30. Almond papers, box 33.

31. General Davis interpreted the incident as an expression of overall resentment over conditions at Fort Huachuca, rather than being completely personal. In his report, Davis cited discontent over "the promotion policy of the War Department as applied to colored officers as discriminatory and unjust, and the segregation of colored officers in a regimental mess demoralizing." He also pointed out that the assignment of only black officers to the School of Application and Proficiency was an example of discrimination and punishment rather than an extension of help. Gibson, *Knocking Down Barriers,* 158–159.

32. Gibson, *Knocking Down Barriers,* 160–161. See also *Buffalo,* May 15, 1943, 12; again in April 12, 1944, 7.

33. *Buffalo,* June 17, 1944, 2; *Buffalo,* May 12, 1943, 3; *Buffalo,* May 22, 1943, 4, column, Sgt. Henry L. Philyaw; see also July 22, 1944 issue. While the *Buffalo* did not mention it, plenty of prostitutes were available right outside the post. Columns in the newspaper addressed the problem of venereal disease and implored the soldiers to protect themselves against it.

34. *Buffalo,* April 22, 1944, 2. The division had another song that preceded this song. *Buffalo,* January 9, 1943, 1. The words and music to the division song were written by Mrs. L. G. Osborne, wife of Lieutenant Colonel L. G. Osborne, adjutant general.

35. *Buffalo,* May 29, 1943, 7; May 29, 1943, 7. See also Baker, *Lasting Valor,* 74. Hondon B. Hargrove, *Buffalo Soldiers in Italy: Black Americans in World War II* (Jefferson, NC: McFarland, 1985), 6; Hargrove, 6; *Huachuca Illustrated* 9 (1993), 54. Buffalo mascot handler Sergeant Auston Valentine of Headquarters 92nd Division was previously a circus worker in civilian life. See *Buffalo,* October 15, 1943, for a great picture of Buffalo Bill and trainer. See also *Buffalo,* August 28, 1943, 5, for an article on The Heavenly Gospel singers of Company M 371st, Gene Johnston's unit. They won fame for their blended harmonies and had previously broadcast from Little Rock, Arkansas. Members included Alonzo Starks, Ferris Hollinguest, Sergeant James Hardy, Gerald Stevenson. The April 24, 1943, edition has a photograph of Edward Rowny, and the April 17, 1943, edition has one of John Flippin. *Buffalo,* January 30, 1943, announced Raymond A. Zobel's promotion to captain and Richard Salmon's promotion to first lieutenant.

36. *Buffalo,* August 1, 1943, 7; June 12, 1943, 3; August 28, 1943, 7; October 2, 1943, 7; August 12, 1944, 3; concert was on August 18; *Buffalo,* August 19, 1944, 7.

Cornelius C. Smith Jr., *Fort Huachuca,* 305. On the jukebox at Huachuca you could listen to "Chattanooga Choo Choo," "Deep Purple," and "Frenese" (309). The hospital at the fort engaged in experimental penicillin therapy (308). Jim Finley wrote, "Almost overnight the little village blossomed forth a city, up from the desert." The area of the reservation spread to 117 square miles, and the population grew to twenty-five thousand. Seventy-five thousand acres of the training grounds covered the valley and the prairie up to the mile-high old post. *Huachuca Illustrated* 9 (1993), 20, 22. See Huachuca Museum, 29 August 1944, James S. Simmons, Brigadier General USA; Chief Preventive Medicine Service to Mr. Harvey H. Bundy, Special Assistant to Secretary of War, Pentagon, RG 159 Office of the Inspector General; Gen. Correspondence. Sect. 1939–1947, Fort Huachuca, AZ Entry 26F, box 44, 1. The history of Fort Huachuca might be seen as alternating between a home for bison (buffalo) and Buffalo Soldiers. After the war in 1947, the army declared the post surplus. The War Assets Administration turned it over to the Arizona Fish and Game Department. They decided to use it as a buffalo preserve. See Cornelius C. Smith, *Fort Huachuca,* 311–312.

37. Daniel K. Gibran, *The 92nd Infantry Division and the Italian Campaign in World War II* (Jefferson, NC: McFarland and Co., 2001), 13–14, 20–26. James Rada, unreleased footage shot for *Deeds not Words.* See also Domenico interview; oral history with Spencer C. Moore, May 25, 2007, with Carolyn Johnston.

38. Elbert L. Harris, *Let the Ammunition Roll: The Story of a Negro GI* (New York: The Exposition Press, 1948), 12.

39. Gibson, *Knocking Down Barriers,* 1.

40. A. Russell Buchanan, *Black Americans in WWII (*Santa Barbara, CA: Clio Books), 1977*),* 80; Ulysses Lee, *The Employment of the Negro Troops. United States Army in World War II* (Washington, DC: U.S. Government Printing Office, 1960), 349. Daniel Kryder, *Divided Arsenal: Race and the American State During World War II (*New York: Cambridge University Press, 2000), 165; Sitkoff, Harvard. "Racial Militancy and Interracial Violence in the Second World War," *Journal of American History* 58, no. 3 (December 1971), 668–669.

41. Motley, "Sergeant Lester Duane Simons," in *The Invisible Soldier,* 44–45. For other incidents of racial violence against black soldiers see Harris, *Let the Ammunition Roll,* 12; see also Sitkoff, "Racial Militancy."

42. Morehouse Archives, interview with Joseph Hairston, transcript, 4–6. Conversation between Joseph Hairston and Carolyn Johnston, November 29, 2010.

43. Morehouse Archives, and Maggi M. Morehouse, *Fighting in the Jim Crow Army,* 119. The text of Williams's account differs slightly in the original transcript and the published version. See also Kryder, *Divided Arsenal.* Kryder wrote: "The War Department continued to investigate conditions inside the camps. In July, General Davis and Truman Gibson visited Forts Huachuca, Arizona; Bliss, Texas; and Clark, Texas, all sources of recent complaints and incidents." They interviewed a large number of enlisted men and met with camp officers. "The litany of complaints at Fort Huachuca was long and familiar: the segregation of black officers at mess, the beating of soldiers, and officer promotion practices that violated Army policy. The investigators showed little concern for conditions at Fort Bliss, since the commanding officers there had not only adjusted the racial situation with sensitivity after a disturbance in El Paso the previous month but also had sponsored the creation of an interracial committee there that had begun to address the difficult problem of community-camp relations" (151–152). "A black company of the 92nd Infantry, stationed at Fort McClellan, Alabama, appointed a committee

to meet with the commandant to discuss the reform of camp conditions. Although their initiative was refused, the technique was a familiar one by 1944 and 1945. The share of racial confrontations caused by organized protest by black soldiers rose from 3.4 percent in 1942 to 19.4 percent in 1944" (157–158, 165). See also Thomas R. Brooks, *Walls Come Tumbling Down: A History of the Civil Rights Movement 1940–1970* (Englewood Cliffs, NJ: Prentice Hall, 1974), 45; *Pittsburgh Courier's* Double V Campaign: victory at home and abroad—essentially black, racialist, or race proud without nationalist overtones; and Charles Spurgeon Johnson, *To Stem This Tide: A Survey of Racial Tension Areas in the United States* (Boston: The Pilgrim Press, 1943).

44. Sitkoff, "Racial Militancy," 670–671.

45. "Democracy" by Corporal Rupert Trimmingham, Fort Huachuca, Arizona, 1945, quoted in Steve Kluger, *Yank: The American Weekly* (New York: St. Martin's Press, 1991), 265. See also Byers, *A Study of the Negro in Military Service,* 68. Trimmingham wrote a follow-up letter:

> Dear *Yank:*
> Allow me to thank you for publishing my letter. Although there was some doubt about its being published, yet somehow I felt that *Yank* was too great a paper not to. . . . Each day brings three, four or five letters to me in answer to my letter. I just returned from my furlough and found 25 letters awaiting me. To date I've received 287 letters, and strange as it may seem, 183 are from white men and women in the armed service. Another strange feature about these letters is that most of these people are from the Deep South. They are all proud of the fact that they are of the South but ashamed to learn that there are so many of their own people who by their actions and manner toward the Negro are playing Hitler's game. Nevertheless, it gives me new hope to realize that there are doubtless thousands of whites who are willing to fight this Frankenstein that so many white people are keeping alive. All that the Negro is asking for is to be given half a chance and he will soon demonstrate his worth to his country. Should these white people who realize that the Negro is a man who is loyal—one who would gladly give his life for this our wonderful country—stand up, join with us and help us to prove to their white friends that we are worthy, I'm sure that we would bury race hate and unfair treatment. Thanks again.

A response appeared from Private Joseph Poscucci (Italian), Burma: "Cpl. Trimmingham asked: 'What is a Negro fighting for?' If this sort of thing continues, we the white soldiers will begin to wonder: What are *we* fighting for?" Kluger, *Yank,* 266–267.

Chapter 7

1. Lieutenant General William J. McCaffrey, USA Retired, interviewed by Lieutenant Colonel John E. Baggott. Carlisle Barracks, PA, 1997. Senior Officer Oral History Program. U.S. AMHI, 50. See also Paul Goodman, *A Fragment of Victory in Italy during World War II* (Nashville, TN: The Battery Press, 1993), 9.

2. Interview with Eugene Johnston by Carolyn Johnston, taped in 1999. In his letter, Gene proposed setting up a code that they could use when the mail was censored. He said she would need a "small scale map of the world with a good coordinate system whereby you can by just a few letters figure out where I am." (Letters from Eugene Johnston to Alta Johnston in 1944). While on maneuvers, Gene wrote regularly to Alta. Through many years of moves, Alta kept

Gene's letters—from Fort Huachuca, Louisiana, and Italy, as well as Taiwan and Thailand. They sustained her and kept her going. Reading them allowed her to recall the love and tenderness of those letters all over again.

On January 10, 1944, Gene wrote to Alta: "Well we (the staff) were moving up right with the men when some soldier made a mistake in his figuring and started dropping mortar shells on us—The first one fell about 25 yards from where we were, killing two enlisted men and a few minutes later another one fell about 5 yds in front of me killing another man and seriously injuring one of the captains on our staff—I have several cut places in my clothes but not a scratch—the blast from it made me deaf for an hour or so. Lucky me. Throughout it all General Almond's expression didn't change one bit—I must admit he has certainly got a lot of intestinal fortitude."

On the next day, January 11, 1944, he wrote to her again:

> If my loving you helps win the war, it should be over tomorrow. I hope I never get so hardened that I can't return to civilian life and enjoy good clean sport. Always trying to kill or maim the other fellow gets kind of old.
>
> I heard something today that made me kind of feel good—an officer who has access to the 66–1 (something we are not allowed to see) told me that I had been rated twice as "superior"—this means I have a very good chance of being promoted to Major soon. I'm not getting my hopes up however, and don't you—for it may be a long time before there's a vacancy.

Gene assured Alta that she might get to see her husband in the "dawn attack" that was going to be filmed by five newsreel cameramen from Fox, Movietone, and Paramount, among others (January 12, 1944). Later that week, he confessed to her, "I'm just an old country boy at heart though and I don't think I'll ever be absolutely happy until I get out of all this and settle down peacefully with you in our own little home. That's what I'm fighting for."

Gene often expressed his love for Alta. He wrote on January 17, 1944: "One thing I do know though for sure is that I have the sweetest and most faithful little wife in all the world, and regardless of where I may be sent I will always love her with all my life."

3. Letters from Eugene Johnston to Alta Johnston in 1944.

4. Eugene Johnston to Alta Johnston, February 4, 1944, from Knight, Louisiana. See also interview with Eugene Johnston by Carolyn Johnston, June 19, 2002.

5. Letters from Eugene Johnston to Alta Johnston, February 14, 1944, Anacore Creek.

6. Letters from Eugene Johnston to Alta Johnston, February 17, 1944, Fal, Louisiana.

7. Letters from Eugene Johnston to Alta Johnston in 1944.

8. Letters from Eugene Johnston to Alta Johnston in 1944.

This is one of many comments that he makes both during the maneuvers in Louisiana and while in combat in Italy about incompetent superior officers. On March 10, 1944, from Dusenberry, Louisiana, Gene wrote: "Maneuvers—against 75 Div. Captured their Gen. & all their staff—prisoners, vehicles, etc. & got back to our lines"—Letters from Eugene Johnston to Alta Johnston in 1944.

9. Letters from Eugene Johnston to Alta Johnston, previous letters. Last letter: March 14, 1944, 6 Miles South West Caney, Louisiana, in 1944. See also letter of March 16, 1944, Vic Burrs Ferry, Louisiana. Gene speaks of his dreams after the war of having his "jeep and trailer and hunting & fishing every chance he gets and having the best Scout troop in the country." Then he says, "I guess this all sounds kind of 'dopey' but you should hear some of the fellows sitting

around at night discussing what they intend to do after the war. Funny thing, there's just plenty of them who'll probably never live to see their dreams come true" (Letters from Eugene Johnston to Alta Johnston in 1944). Gene wrote on July 24, 1944, of his dreams for the future: "Darling, I'll probably never know how it happened that so nice and sweet a girl ever consented to marry a rough old sad sack like me. All I know is that without you to look forward to I wouldn't want to live. When I left you there at the station I left my heart and future. All I can think and dream of is the day all will be over and we can be together forever. In my heart there's an ache and lonesome feeling that sometimes is very hard to control."

10. Nelson Peery, Maggi Morehouse Archives, 20.

11. Mary Penick Motley, comp. and ed., *Invisible Soldier: The Experience of Black Soldiers in World War II* (Detroit, MI: Wayne State University Press, 1975), 263–265. See also Arthur E. Barbeau and Florette Henri, *The Unknown Soldiers: Black American Troops in World War I* (New York: Da Capo Press, 1996), 32. Barbeau and Henri described the desire to use the black man like an inferior yet have him perform as an equal. They added: "The lesson was clear. To survive, the black man would have to agree that he was an inferior brute; that he must not defend himself; that he could not lead and must not follow other black men; and that, above all, he could not advance except under the guidance of white men."

12. Letters from Eugene Johnston to Alta Johnston in 1944.

13. Interview with Eugene Johnston by Carolyn Johnston, June 19, 2002 (preceding paragraphs).

14. Maggi Morehouse Archives. Most of the towns nearby were off limits to the black soldiers. Just outside the fort, the Green Top, the favorite bar of the soldiers, drew large crowds. Right outside the camp or gate there was also a tent city where merchants came on the weekends and set up a kind of shack town (Johnston interview, 1999). Prostitutes came down from Phoenix and places like that and set up tents for the soldiers, a place that became known as The Hook. At least three hundred and fifty prostitutes were there regularly, and venereal disease was a colossal problem. Educational programs and prophylactic stations tried to reduce the incidence of disease. The venereal disease rate was 368 per 1,000 per year in 1943; in 1944, the rate dropped to 167 per 1,000 per year.

15. Interview with Eugene Johnston by Carolyn Johnston, March 16, 2002.

16. Aside from General Almond and General McCaffrey, Thomas St. John Arnold, and Edward Rowny, evidently the only other white officer who has recorded his experiences in the 92nd is John Runyon. I found John Runyon's manuscript at Carlisle. I did not recall my father's mentioning him, but some of the African American soldiers interviewed had. Runyon entered the army in October 1942. See Runyon manuscript, Veterans Survey, AMHI, box 1, pp. 1, 14, 7–9, 13. In the 98th Division at Camp Breckenridge, he was assigned to be the aide to a General Wood located at Fort Huachuca, Arizona (2–3). He was in the 371st, which was Gene's unit.

17. Runyon manuscript, Veterans Survey, AMHI, box 1, pp. 1, 14, 7–9, 13.

18. Maggi M. Morehouse, *Fighting in the Jim Crow Army: Black Men and Women Remember World War II* (Lanham, MD: Rowman and Littlefield, 2000), 16, 53–54; Morehouse Archives.

19. Conversation with Susie Moore, Rockville, Maryland, October 2003. They remained married until her death in 2004. When Spencer Moore was training at Fort Huachuca, his unit won third best squad, and the third best platoon in a competition. When he clashed with his captain, the captain gave him a poor efficiency report. He talked to a black chaplain who fought for him, but as a result, the chaplain was ordered off the post in twenty-four hours. Domenico interview.

20. Interview with Eugene Johnston by Carolyn Johnston, March 16, 2002.

Chapter 8

1. These pages on "the long wait" reflect hours of conversation that I had with my mother, Alta Johnston, about the war years. As a result of smoking those Lucky Strikes and Marlboros, her life was cut short because of congestive heart failure on July 13, 2000, at the age of eighty-one. I alone was with her when she died. We did not have a chance to finish the extensive formal oral history that we began, but we spent countless hours in conversation about her life. She kept every letter that my father sent to her both during World War II and afterward whenever they were apart. Some of these letters are quoted in this chapter. She made sure that I knew exactly where she kept them. They offer insights into their loving relationship, their hopes and dreams during the war, and Gene's experiences in the 92nd Division. Regrettably, my mother's letters to my father were not saved. Margaret Mead captured the subtleties of the women's experiences when she said that babies during the war must have felt their mothers' stress and tension as they bathed them. See Margaret Mead, "The Women in the War," in *While You Were Gone,* ed. Jack Goodman (New York: Simon & Schuster, 1946), 286–288. I have written extensively about American women and World War II in my book *Sexual Power: Feminism and the Family in America* (Tuscaloosa: The University of Alabama Press, 1992), 170–200.

2. All Americans were affected by austerity measures such as rationing, the end of civilian car production, price controls, and nearly full employment. Terry Golway, "The War on the Home Front," in *The World War II Memorial: A Grateful Nation Remembers,* edited by Douglas Brinkley (Washington, DC: Smithsonian Books, 2004), 226-237. Popular music featured war themes: "Coming in on a Wing and Prayer," "Boogie Woogie Bugle Boy," "We'll Meet Again," "When Lights Go On All over the World," and "God Bless America" by Irving Berlin, which was sung by Kate Smith continuously on the radio and became a communal prayer for Americans.

3. Interviews with Alta Johnston by Carolyn Johnston, 1990–1999.

4. Maggi Morehouse, transcript. See Wallace Stegner, *Women on the Wall* (Boston: Houghton Mifflin, 1950; repr., Lincoln: University of Nebraska Press, 1981). Stegner wrote a powerful story about women waiting during the war to hear about their husbands.

Chapter 9

1. Morehouse, interview with Spencer Moore, transcript 9–10. Much of the following material was taken from the original transcripts of the interviews in Maggi M. Morehouse's personal archives. See her book: *Fighting in the Jim Crow Army: Black Men and Women Remember World War II* (Lanham, MD: Rowman and Littlefield, 2000).

2. Oral history with Spencer C. Moore, by Carolyn Johnston, Magnolia, New Jersey, May 25, 2007; see also James Rada, unreleased footage shot for *Deeds not Words,* October 8, 9, 2004, Rockville, Maryland; see also Domenico interview.

3. Moore also recalled that "an SOB, a white officer who had been nasty, got hit by an artillery shell during the war. It wasn't clear whose shell it was." Oral history, May 25, 2007, Spencer Moore and Carolyn Johnston; James Rada, unreleased footage shot for *Deeds not Words,* October 8, 9, 2004, Rockville, Maryland.

4. Morehouse interview transcript.

5. Oral history, May 25, 2007, Spencer Moore and Carolyn Johnston; James Rada, unreleased footage shot for *Deeds not Words,* October 8, 9, 2004, Rockville, Maryland.

6. Truman Gibson, *Knocking Down Barriers: My Fight for Black America* (Evanston, IL: Northwestern University Press, 2005), 178.

7. Paul Goodman, *A Fragment of Victory in Italy during World War II* (Nashville, TN: The Battery Press, 1993), 91–92, quoted in Gibson, 178–179; Hondon B. Hargrove, *Buffalo Soldiers in Italy: Black Americans in World War II* (Jefferson, NC: McFarland, 1985), 90, 94.

8. Gibson, *Knocking Down Barriers,* 179. Hondon Hargrove, Paul Goodman, Ulysses Lee, and Vernon Baker explained the challenges of such an objective and the strategies proposed.

9. Morehouse, *Fighting in the Jim Crow Army,* 157. Domenico interview; Oral history on May 25, 2007, with Carolyn Johnston. James Rada, unreleased footage shot for *Deeds not Words,* October 8, 9, 2004, Rockville, Maryland.

10. Morehouse, *Fighting in the Jim Crow Army,* 164–165.

11. Conversation with Spencer Moore, October 2004; oral history, May 25, 2007, with Carolyn Johnston; see also Domenico interview. Moore did not see his friend whose life he saved again until forty-seven years later in 1992. When Spencer was getting together a souvenir booklet to raise money for the 92nd Infantry Association, Kermit Hancock called after the deadline was past and asked if his picture could still get in the book. Moore asked him which unit he was in. Hancock said, "B Company, the 370th." Moore said, "Do you remember your Lieutenant?" Hancock said, "Gandy." Moore said, "No, you remember the light-skinned black Lieutenant Moore?" He said, "You're talking to him." Hancock, who lived in Baltimore, came to every reunion after that until his death in 2007. During the reunion in 2003, four of Moore's sergeants attended. Spencer said, "The 92nd Association is about camaraderie, not money. Kermit Hancock was one of the ones I loved. Those who fought together, bled and those who died alongside us." Conversation with Spencer Moore, October 2004; oral history, May 25, 2007, with Carolyn Johnston; see also Domenico interview.

12. Oral history, May 25, 2007, with Carolyn Johnston; see also Domenico interview. Conversation with Spencer Moore, 2004; Maggi Morehouse, transcript; Rada, unreleased footage shot for *Deeds not Words,* October 8, 9, 2004. Ironically, sulfanilamide drugs were the discovery of German scientists: Bayer chemist Josef Klarer; Gerhard Domagk, who won the Nobel Prize in Physiology or Medicine; Heinrich Hoerlien, a Farben executive who led the team in 1939; and Fritz Mietzsch, Klarer's research partner. The first sulfonamide was called Prontosil (1932 tests). Prontosil was the first medicine to effectively treat bacterial infections in the body (http://medlibrary.org/medwiki/Sulfanilimide).

13. Conversation with Spencer Moore, 2004; oral history, May 25, 2007, with Carolyn Johnston. Even now, he still feels a twinge in that heel, reminding him of that terrifying night.

14. Conversation with Spencer Moore, 2004; oral history, May 25, 2007, with Carolyn Johnston. E. B. Sledge described incidents like the one Moore related. He wrote of his experiences in the Pacific theater: "In addition to the terror and hardships of combat, each day brought some new dimension of dread for me: I witnessed some new, ghastly, macabre facet in the kaleidoscope of the unreal, as though designed by some fiendish ghoul to cause even the most hardened and calloused observer among us to recoil in horror and disbelief" (160, 294). E. B. Sledge, *With the Old Breed: At Peleliu and Okinawa* (1981; repr., New York: Presidio Press, 2007), 160, see also 294.

15. Maggi Morehouse transcript; see also conversation with Spencer Moore, October 2004; interview with Spencer Moore, May 25, 2007, conducted by Carolyn Johnston.

16. Morehouse interview transcript.

17. Interview with Carolyn Johnston, October 2004; box 24A, Almond Papers. See also "Clark Exhorts Negro Soldiers to Win Glory," 3, box 24A, Almond Papers. In his address to the members of the 92nd Division, Clark said: "You will find when you meet the German that you have nothing to fear from him. In fact, he will be afraid of you. What could be a finer set-

ting for entrance into battle than the Germans wobbling on their last legs, with the Allied forces in France and Russia closing in on him, and we ready again to bloody his nose here. Take this opportunity, as I know you will, to cover yourselves with glory. Good luck to you and God bless you."

Hondon Hargrove, who wrote a splendid account of the 92nd Division and the Italian campaign, claimed that "German generals whose forces opposed the 92nd have flatly stated that it was the most misled division they ever encountered." See Hondon Hargrove, in Mary Penick Motley, comp. and ed. *The Invisible Soldier: The Experience of Black Soldiers in World War II* (Detroit, MI: Wayne State University Press, 1975), 319–326. Charles Brown, another soldier in the 92nd (1st Battalion, B Company, 1st Platoon), summarized the sentiment of many of his fellow soldiers: "One could not help but get the impression that Clark took the 92nd reluctantly. . . . When you tell the general he must take waiters, busboys and shoeshine boys, he doesn't want them to begin with. The social reflection of the Negro in the United States has some of its greatest effect on the military mind; they are used to the superior-inferior situation." Motley, *The Invisible Soldier,* 272, 279.

18. Conversation with Bill Perry, October 2004; William S. M. Banks also reported several incidents of "fragging" while the units were doing overnight field exercises even earlier. He said that several white officers were badly beaten and disfigured. See interview of Jim Williams by Maggi Morehouse, Maggi Morehouse Archives.

19. Maggi Morehouse Archives; interview of Bill Perry with Carolyn Johnston, October 2004.

20. Maggi Morehouse Archives.

21. Maggi Morehouse Archives; interview with Carolyn Johnston, October 2004.

22. Captain Fergusson summarized the troop movements. The general was in the Arno-Florence area of the 5th Army by November 1. Almond interview, 180, 182.

23. Interview with Eugene Johnston by Carolyn Johnston, taped in 1999.

24. Interview with Eugene Johnston by Carolyn Johnston, June 21, 2002.

25. Interview with Eugene Johnston by Carolyn Johnston, June 21, 2002, and 1999 tape.

26. John Runyon, a white officer, gave his view from the line. Runyon was in the 371st, so he was in the same outfit as Gene Johnston. He described the formidable terrain: "The Germans had spent six months preparing the defenses of the Gothic line. Personnel trenches were dug between machine gun posts. The Germans had dugouts, reinforced outposts with mines, trenches, and hundreds of mines on the beach and in the mountains. Reinforced concrete resisted any bombing (19). On the beach alone after the war the Americans uncovered four hundred mines, some of which were prepared to destroy tanks (20). The Germans also had the advantage that they could use vehicles to deliver supplies. The Americans had to use mules because of the steep grade" (21). John Runyon, typescript manuscript, Veterans Surveys WWII, AMHI, Carlisle, PA. Almond wanted Runyon to be his aide, and then he would be promoted to lieutenant colonel. Runyon turned it down. Runyon won two Distinguished Service Crosses, one from the United States and one from Italy; the Silver Star; the Bronze Star; and the Combat Infantry Badge.

27. Ulysses Lee, *The Employment of Negro Troops. United States Army in World War II,* Special Studies Center for Military History publication 11-4 (Washington, DC: U.S. Government Printing Office, 1960), 553; interview with Eugene Johnston by Carolyn Johnston, June 21, 2002.

28. In that same area, Almond's chief of staff of the regiment was killed shortly after his ar-

rival in Italy. See McCaffrey interview, 32–33. Colonel Frank Barber was killed in his jeep driving over to see his friend Colonel Champeny, commander of one of the 34th Division's Regiments in the eastern part of Italy, north past Bologna. He was killed by German artillery on his way back. Almond then called McCaffrey and said, "I'm going to have to ask you to be acting Division Chief of Staff." McCaffrey ended up as the permanent one because of something that had happened previously during the maneuvers in Louisiana. Another candidate for the position had publicly embarrassed Almond at that time. Thus, Almond told McCaffrey, "You will be the permanent Chief of Staff of this Division." So, he was promoted to full colonel that February 1945, just a few years out of West Point. When Almond was designated as the commander of the 92nd Division, he only had one month of experience in such a position. He had held staff positions previously, not positions commanding combat units. McCaffrey interview, 34, 36, 29.

29. Interview with Eugene Johnston by Carolyn Johnston, June 21, 2002, and 1999 tape.

30. Interview with Eugene Johnston by Carolyn Johnston, June 29, 2001, and June 21, 2002.

31. Interview with Eugene Johnston by Carolyn Johnston, June 29, 2001, and June 21, 2002. Letter from Eugene Johnston to Alta Johnston, October 31, 1944, Somewhere in Italy. One night Gene did not hear any noise, but he heard something on his radio: "They're closing in on me now." The man said he wanted to call fire down on his own people. Gene learned later that it was John Fox on the radio. Fox was posthumously awarded the Medal of Honor. Interview with Eugene Johnston by Carolyn Johnston, June 21, 2002, and 1999 tape.

32. Interview with Eugene Johnston by Carolyn Johnston, June 19, 2002; June 29, 2001; and June 2000.

33. Interview with Eugene Johnston by Carolyn Johnston, March 16, 2002, and June 21, 2002. The lack of adequate ammunition was a real problem during the time. In addition, the 92nd Division sometimes received used and less effective, less accurate shells.

34. Interview with Eugene Johnston by Carolyn Johnston, March 16, 2002, and June 21, 2002.

35. Interview with Eugene Johnston by Carolyn Johnston, taped in 1999.

36. Interview with Eugene Johnston by Carolyn Johnston, March 16, 2002, and June 21, 2002.

37. Interview with Eugene Johnston by Carolyn Johnston, taped in 1999.

38. Ibid.

39. Ibid.

40. Motley, *The Invisible Soldier*, 282.

41. Morehouse Archives, oral histories.

42. Morehouse Archives, original transcript of interview.

43. Morehouse Archives, original transcript of interview. Interview with Carolyn Johnston, October 2004.

44. Morehouse Archives, original transcript of interview. His time with them ended on February 5, 1945, when he was wounded by a mine. He received a Bronze Star and a Purple Heart, as well as a Blue Combat Infantry Badge. Interview with Carolyn Johnston, October 2004.

45. Morehouse Archives, original transcript of interview. Interview with Carolyn Johnston, October 2004.

46. Ibid.

47. Ibid.

48. Ibid.

49. Morehouse Archives. Conversation between Joseph Hairston and Carolyn Johnston, November 29, 2010.

50. Maggi Morehouse Archives; here is an account of another scared white officer.

51. Jehu C. Hunter, captain, U.S. Army Reserve Retired, "Between a Rock and Hard Place: Reflections on the Performance of the 92nd Infantry Division in the Italian Campaign," August 1944–April 1945, 10, 14 (prepared for presentation at the 1992 Conference of Army Historians); Veterans Survey, Carlisle, folder 4204. He retired in 1962.

52. Veterans Survey, Carlisle, AMHI; Hunter, "Triumph and Tribulation; Reflections on the Combat Experience of the 92nd Infantry Division in North Italy," August 1944–April 1945.

53. Veterans Survey, Carlisle, AMHI; Hunter, "Triumph and Tribulation." After the war with the help of the GI Bill, Hunter went to graduate school and became a research biologist.

54. Jehu C. Hunter, captain, U.S. Army Reserve Retired, "Between a Rock and Hard Place," 2, 4, 5. Along with Lieutenant Colonel Major Clark (an African American officer, sometimes confused with Mark Clark), Jehu Hunter wrote a history of the 92nd Infantry. He reflected on the performance of the 92nd Division in the Italian campaign in the book and in scholarly papers.

55. Morehouse Archives. Albert Burke was fighting to get back home. Burke served with Lieutenant Fox, who received the Medal of Honor. But Burke also believed that there were more men than Fox who were up there who should have gotten awards, and they died there in Sommocolonia. World War II Memorial conversation, and James Rada, unreleased footage shot at World War II Memorial for *Deeds not Words,* October 9, 2004.

56. Edward W. Brooke, *Bridging the Divide: My Life* (New Brunswick, NJ: Rutgers University Press, 2007), 21–22, 24–29, 31–32.

57. Ibid., 26, 24–29, 31–32.

58. Brooke paid tribute to the contributions of the African American soldiers: "They fought and died for our country and to free Europe even though they had little hope that the discrimination they faced would at all lessen when the war was won and they went home. They, too, were part of the greatest generation." See Brooke, *Bridging the Divide,* 31, 21, 24–29, 32. The 366th was disbanded on March 28, 1945, and the men transferred to various quartermaster units and to two engineering services battalions. Brooke was hurt and humiliated by this action.

59. Interview with Eugene Johnston by Carolyn Johnston, March 16, 2002.

60. Interview with Eugene Johnston by Carolyn Johnston, June 2003.

61. Interview with Eugene Johnston by Carolyn Johnston, taped in 1999.

62. Interview with Spencer Moore conducted by Carolyn Johnston, May 25, 2007. See also box 38, Almond Papers.

Report in Almond Papers states: "Supplying troops situated in the high mountainous Apennines of Italy without roads presented a serious logistical problem. Our answer to it was the formation of the 92nd Division Mule Pack Battalion on 17 Nov. 1944. During the attack starting 5 April 1945 and to the cessation of hostilities on 2 May 1945, approximately 2,288 tons of supplies were transported by the Mule Battalion. During the operation of the Battalion 8 men were seriously wounded and 18 mules were killed. Narrow trails high up in the mountains, scarcely a foot wide in some places, were a constant hazard and several mules were lost when they fell off of these trails into deep canyons."

63. Letter, Eugene Johnston to Alta Johnston, Somewhere in Italy, December 12, 1944. Interview, June 5, 2003.

64. Interview with Eugene Johnston by Carolyn Johnston, June 29, 2001.

65. Interview with Eugene Johnston by Carolyn Johnston, June, 19, 2002, and July 4, 2002.

66. Interview with Eugene Johnston by Carolyn Johnston, tape 5, June 2003.

67. Interview with Eugene Johnston by Carolyn Johnston, June 26–27, 2002. Letters from Eugene Johnston to Alta Johnston, June 19, and January 21, 1945, Somewhere in Italy.

Chapter 10

1. Ivan J. Houston, *Black Warriors: The Buffalo Soldiers of World War II,* with Gordon Cohn (New York: iUniverse, Inc., 2009), 154–157. See also Carlo D'Este, "Victory in Europe," in Douglas Brinkley, ed., *The World War II Memorial: A Grateful Nation Remembers* (Washington, DC: Smithsonian, 2004), 91, 94.

2. Edward Rowny, *Engineer Memoirs* (Alexandria, Virginia: U.S. Army Corps of Engineers, 1995), 10–11.

3. Ibid., 12–13.

4. Ibid.

5. For the full text of the *Newsweek* article, see "Fighting Fronts," and "The Luckless 92nd," *Newsweek,* February 26, 1945, 34. See also Paul Goodman, *A Fragment of Victory in Italy during World War II* (Nashville, TN: The Battery Press, 1993), 67–69, 72–73.

6. See Hondon B. Hargrove, *Buffalo Soldiers in Italy: Black Americans in World War II* (Jefferson, NC: McFarland, 1985), 130–136; Henry Wiencek, *The Hairstons: An American Family in Black and White* (New York: St. Martin's Griffin, 1999), 265–266, 255; Maggi Morehouse Archives, transcript of interview with Joseph Hairston conducted by Maggi Morehouse, 20. Conversation between Joseph Hairston and Carolyn Johnston, November 29, 2010.

7. Interview with Eugene Johnston by Carolyn Johnston, June 26–27, 2002.

8. Interview with Eugene Johnston by Carolyn Johnston, taped in 2001.

9. Hill X was 450 feet high; Hills Y and Z were another 100–200 feet above X. Ivan Houston wrote about the phrase that some enlisted men coined—"Yassa, we a-goin to Massa." Ivan Houston, "Memoir," 88–100.

10. Interviews with Eugene Johnston by Carolyn Johnston, June 29, 2001; June 26–27, 2002; and June 2003.

11. Interview with Eugene Johnston by Carolyn Johnston, June 29, 2001; June 26–27, 2002; and June 2003.

12. Interview with Eugene Johnston by Carolyn Johnston, June 29, 2001.

13. During the night of November 8–9, 1944, Captain Curtis J. Ivey, the commanding officer of Company K, was severely wounded by mortar fire. He refused to leave his company. The unit sustained heavy casualties (ten wounded and one killed), but he succeeded in getting his men on the objective. The enemy also sustained heavy casualties. Only after he had been able to consolidate the position did he allow them to bring him down the mountain and evacuate him. Hargrove, *Buffalo Soldiers in Italy,* 34. See also Almond Collection, box 27A for copies of awards for Silver Star, Bronze Star, etc.

Major Louis J. Beasley, January 15, 1945: "For meritorious service in combat on 1 November 1944 in Italy; entered military service from Atlanta, GA, Feb. 21." Bronze Star to Roy L. Keely, 371st: "For heroic achievement in action on Dec. 5, 1944 in Italy entered military service from Ada, Ohio. Bronze Star to Jack E. Gervin: "For meritorious service in combat from 1 Nov. 1944 to January 15, 1945; entered military service from Edward, Mississippi."

I had hoped to find more on these white officers who were friends of Gene's. A few records do exist of their battle decorations, but those are the remaining traces of them.

14. Interview with Eugene Johnston by Carolyn Johnston, June 29, 2001.

15. Interview with Eugene Johnston by Carolyn Johnston, June 21, 2001.

16. Interview with Eugene Johnston by Carolyn Johnston, June 2000.

17. Ibid.

18. Interview with Eugene Johnston by Carolyn Johnston, July 4, 2002.

19. Interview with Eugene Johnston by Carolyn Johnston, taped in 2001. Letter from Eugene Johnston to Alta Johnston, February 16, 1945, Somewhere in Italy.

See Almond Papers, box 26b. Silver Star awarded posthumously to Arthur H. Walker for gallantry in action November 18, 1944, in Italy, Mrs. Ira Walker, wife, 934 North Campbell St., Tucson, Arizona, notice of Bronze Star. April 23, 1945, general orders number 16. Eugene E. Johnston, 01293262, captain, Infantry 371st, for heroic achievement in action on February 10, 1945, in Italy, entered military service from Chattanooga, Tennessee. An award to John Hazel from Findley, Ohio.

20. Letter, Joe Willie Johnson to Mr. Hubbard, 5 February 1945, Somewhere in Italy, folder 1493, World War II letters, 1940–1946, Western Historical Manuscript Collection—Columbia, Missouri. Michael Polley called this collection to the attention of Maggi Morehouse and subsequently to me.

21. Letter, Joe Willie Johnson to Mary Alice Hubbard Johnson, 17 February 1945, Somewhere in Italy, folder 1493, World War II letters, 1940–1946, Western Historical Manuscript Collection—Columbia, Missouri.

22. Letter, Joe Willie Johnson to Mary Alice Hubbard Johnson, 21 March 1945, Somewhere in Italy, folder 1493, World War II letters, 1940–1946, Western Historical Manuscript Collection—Columbia, Missouri.

23. Interview with Eugene Johnston by Carolyn Johnston, taped in 2001; Johnston interview, June 21, 2001.

24. When I first heard my father speak of this straggling, my heart sank because I had a very positive view of the division and felt their performance was courageous and unfairly criticized. I have come to accept the ambiguities and complexities of the situation. Nevertheless, stories of Gene Johnston, Joe Stephenson, Spencer Moore, and a number of scholars regarding straggling honestly acknowledged the very real problem. Desertion was not simply a problem for the 92nd but for the black and white Allied soldiers in the Italian campaign. See Thomas C. Childers, *Soldier from the War Returning: The Greatest Generation's Troubled Homecoming from World War II* (Boston: Houghton Mifflin Harcourt, 2009), 53; Rick Atkinson, *The Day of Battle: The War in Sicily and Italy, 1943–1944*. Volume II of the Liberation Trilogy (New York: Henry Holt and Company, 2007), 508. See also John Peaty, "The Desertion Crisis in Italy, 1944," *RUSI (Royal United Services Institute) Journal* 147, no. 3 (June 2002), 76–83. During World War I, desertion and cowardice were punished by capital punishment. This practice was abolished between World Wars I and II. Desertion and being absent without leave (AWOL) were at their peaks in Italy in the autumn and winter of 1944. The 8th Army's Field General Courts Martial convicted 2,237 men for desertion and 840 for absence between January 1944 and January 10, 1945. There were 1,788 convictions for desertion and absence, or 536 a month. The figures did not include those who were not apprehended, those who did not surrender, or those who were acquitted (76). Investigations by the Adjutant General's Department concluded that the main cause was prolonged action, which was greatly increased by close contact with the enemy. According to their investigator, there were "two broad categories: the 'deliberate,' who preferred disgrace and imprisonment to the continued dangers of battle; and the 'involuntary,' men with nervous breakdowns who would often welcome a second chance to prove themselves." The study was inconclusive because the sample group was limited to sixteen prisoners (77). Dur-

ing World War II, the army only executed one deserter, Ernie Slovik, during the Battle of the Bulge. U.S. Armed Forces Desertion rates: 1944: 6.3%; 1945: 4.5%. See *The Oxford Companion to American Military History,* edited by John Whiteclay Chambers II (New York: Oxford University Press, 1999), 212.

25. Houston, with Cohn, *Black Warriors,* 120. After serving in the army from 1943 until 1945, Houston returned from the war and completed his BS degree in 1948 from the University of California at Berkeley. He went on to a highly successful and distinguished career. He served as the chief executive officer of Golden State Mutual Life Insurance Company from 1970 to 1990. He has worked tirelessly for racial equality for his entire life. He headed one of the nation's largest African American businesses. His book is a superb work on the 92nd Division that illuminates his experiences and the major engagements in the Italian campaign. The phrase "melting away" had been used to describe desertion in battles between Sparta and Athens 2,500 years ago. In response to criticism that the 92nd failed to take and control Mt. Cauala and later the city of Massa, Houston said:

"My response to those comments is that officers and platoon leaders were being killed and wounded trying to lead men who all their lives had been treated as second-class citizens. Those same men and their children displayed plenty of determination and guts during the later civil-rights marches, sit-ins, and in subsequent wars when military segregation was history" (Houston, *Black Warriors,* 119–121). Lieutenant Colonel John Phelan reported on October 17, 1944: "During my period of observation, I have heard of just as many acts of individual heroism among Negro troops as among white. There is no reason to believe that there is any greater lack of individual guts among them." Phelan was killed in action during the last campaign of the war. See Daniel K. Gibran, *The 92nd Infantry Division and the Italian Campaign in World War II* (Jefferson, NC: McFarland and Company, 2001), 58.

26. Interview with Eugene Johnston by Carolyn Johnston, June 19, 2002; March 16, 2002; and July 4, 2002. First Lieutenant Jesse Wooten was killed. See Goodman, *A Fragment of Victory in Italy,* 56, for a description of the incident also.

27. Interview with Eugene Johnston by Carolyn Johnston, June 19, 2002, and March 16, 2002.

28. Interview with Eugene Johnston by Carolyn Johnston, July 4, 2002. See also Hondon Hargrove, "Il Corsaro: A Story of War and Friendship," *Michigan History* 64, no. 1 (January/February 1980), 14–17. In the article, Hargrove tells of a partisan with whom he developed a friendship and who helped the American troops. He went back to find him after the war in June 1977 and found his sister near Massa. Veterans Surveys World War II, Carlisle.

29. June 29, 2001. One is reminded of the extraordinary version of *Ave Maria* that Aaron Neville sang in the aftermath of Hurricane Katrina in New Orleans.

30. McCaffrey's description of the meeting, McCaffrey interview, 52. See also McCaffrey's views on the 442nd, McCaffrey interview, 68.

31. Interview with Eugene Johnston by Carolyn Johnston, June 29, 2001; June 21, 2002; and June 26–27, 2002. Gene had a view of both the heavy weapons and of rifle platoons. Artillery had a fine reputation all through the war, and the rifle platoons garnered the most criticism. See also Houston, *Black Warriors,* 165.

32. Interview with Eugene Johnston by Carolyn Johnston, June 29, 2001; June 21, 2002; and June 26–27, 2002; see also Houston, *Black Warriors,* 171–174.

33. *Commission on Wartime Relocation and Internment of Civilians, Personal Justice Denied: Report of the Commission on Wartime Relocation an Internment of Civilians* (Washington, DC: Government Printing Office, December 1982), 256.

34. *Personal Justice Denied,* 257–258.

Second Lieutenant Daniel K. Inouye received a battlefield commendation on November 1944. On April 21, 1945, leading his platoon on Mt. Musatello in Italy he was wounded in his right arm and right leg. His arm had to be amputated. He was promoted to captain, but was not released from the hospital until 1947. Thirty-three thousand Nisei served in World War II. *Personal Justice Denied,* 252–253. See also, *New York Times,* August 23, 2010, adapted from *National Journal's Almanac of American Politics*: Matt Bai, "The Way We Live Now: 10–29–01; Encounter; Hyphenated Americans," *New York Times,* October 28, 2001. Lieutenant Robert Foote, a white officer, served in Company K, 3rd Battalion of the 442nd. The 442nd had mostly white officers. See his memoir, Robert Hutchinson Foote, *Connecticut Yankee in Nisei King Company's Court: With the Japanese American 442nd RCT in World War II* (Ithaca, NY: The Internet-First University Press, 2005).

Stuart Yamane made a film entitled *Journey of Honor* (2001) to commemorate the veterans of the 100th Battalion and 442nd and their return in 2000 to Italy. His father, Masakichi, who he had scarcely known due to divorce and alcoholism, was a decorated veteran. He came to know his father and understand the significance of the World War II mementos his father left him. In a beautifully conceived film, he follows the veterans as they travel to Pietrasanta for a Liberation Day ceremony, to Mt. Folgorito for a reunion with the Alpini, the Italian Mountain Corps, who guided the Allied troops in the area. With the Alpini's assistance, they were able to break through the Gothic Line, which had previously been impenetrable. Then they visited the Sicily-Rome American Cemetery and Memorial in Nettuno, Italy, and Monte Cassino. Yamane said, "This is a story of memory and how we remember. . . . It is a call to remember the human side of heroism and the true meaning of being an American." *Journey of Honor,* directed by Stuart Yamane (Kaneohe, HI: KHET Hawaii Public Television, 2001). Documentary film.

35. Interview with Eugene Johnston by Carolyn Johnston, July 4, 2002.

36. Interview with Eugene Johnston by Carolyn Johnston, June 29, 2001, and March 16, 2002.

37. Interview with Eugene Johnston by Carolyn Johnston, June 21, 2001, and July 4, 2002. During this spring offensive, Vernon Baker, a Medal of Honor winner, demonstrated outstanding courage. Baker had attended OCS and became a 2nd Lieutenant. When he trained in the South, he was beaten and harassed by white men. He demonstrated heroism in combat in Italy on many occasions, especially on April 5, 1945. That day Vernon Baker and his weapons platoon of twenty-five men were ordered to participate in the fourth attack on Castle Aghinolfi. Exposed on Hill X, Baker knocked out two machine gun nests of Germans, a third gun in a bunker, an observation post, and three machine gun nests, and severed dozens of communication wires. He and his platoon were only 300 yards from one of the most heavily defended German positions in Italy. Baker killed a German who threw a grenade at him; he then ran down the slope and into a German bunker, clearing it with a Tommy gun. Machine guns from the castle opened fire on them. Finally, Baker wiped out the entire German platoon. Nineteen of his twenty-six men died that day. Since no African American in World War II had received a Medal of Honor, a review committee was formed in 1997 to investigate whether racism had prevented deserving recipients from receiving medals. Fifty-two years after the war, Vernon Baker and seven other African Americans who fought in World War II received the Medal of Honor, thanks to President Bill Clinton and the review board. Baker was the only one still living. He died on July 13, 2010, at the age of 90 in his home near St. Maries, Idaho.

See John Robert Bruning Jr., *Elusive Glory: African American Heroes of World War II* (Greensboro, NC: Avisson Press, 2001), 18–28, and Richard Goldstein, "Vernon Baker, Belated Medal of Honor Recipient, Dies at 90," New York Times, July 15, 2010.

38. Not only did McCaffrey feel compassion for General Almond, he resolved not to advise his own son as Almond had his to go to West Point, to join the infantry, and to have a rifle company. Later, McCaffrey's daughter Patty's husband Dave was killed in Vietnam on August 24, 1964. When his own son, Barry McCaffrey, who has had a distinguished career as a highly decorated general, was growing up, McCaffrey refrained from advising him at all about his military choices. That evening with General Almond had been a searing and poignant lesson for him. McCaffrey interview, 45 47.

39. Gene Johnston recalled that a number of white officers, even high-ranking ones, were cowards during the battles. Some of them refused to lead, hid in foxholes, and so it is little wonder that there were some issues of "straggling." This is a critical insight because it may help to explain another dimension of the problem.

40. Interview with Eugene Johnston by Carolyn Johnston, June 2002.

41. Ibid.

42. Ibid.

43. Interview with Eugene Johnston by Carolyn Johnston, July 4, 2002.

44. Eugene E. Johnston, papers, essay, "Where Is Heaven?" He compared the importance of knowing where one is by referring to the experiences he had during the war. He added, "And after all isn't the question of heaven just as important to everyone now, because it is a case of life and death also?" Messages were always written on a standard message blank, most of which would read "Continue the attack to such and such town or place," followed by a map coordinate. Gene's first reactions to these messages were always the same. Where *is* this place? *What* is the place? And *who* is there? Hopefully, there were no Germans. These questions were extremely vital to him because they were playing a game of life and death.

45. Interview with Eugene Johnston by Carolyn Johnston, July 4, 2002.

46. Ibid.

47. Ibid.

48. Ibid.

49. Ibid.

50. Ibid. Letter from Eugene Johnston to Alta Johnston, May 1, May 4, 1945, Somewhere in Italy.

51. Houston, "Memoir," 124; *Black Warriors,* 203.

52. Interviews with Eugene Johnston by Carolyn Johnston, June 19, 2002, and July 4, 2002. Letter from Eugene Johnston to Alta Johnston, May 8, 1945, Somewhere in Italy.

53. Almond Papers, box 9, May 8, 1945.

54. Box 10, Almond Papers. In Gail Buckley's book, *American Patriots* she reminds us that later in Korea, Almond acted out his racism by resegregating already successfully integrated units; he also refused to approve medals for black soldiers. Buckley, 349. See also *The Best of Yank The Army Weekly 1942–1945,* selected by Ira Topping (New York: Arno Press, 1980). Notes from Eisenhower and Harry S. Truman.

From Rome, Sgt. Fred Rosen, a *Yank* correspondent, July 1944 issue, 9–10. See Steve Kluger, *Yank* (New York: St. Martin's Press, 1991). A correspondent for *Yank* wrote:

> Together they comprised the last bunch of guys who went to war willingly, who abdicated youth for loyalty, puppy love for national pride, and home cooking for stuff that came in a tin and was indistinguishable in every way from camouflage paint. Yet they embraced it whole heartedly and went nonetheless; by whatever means and down whatever roads would take them there, lying about their ages and memorizing eye charts in advance the same way they'd only yesterday memorized the fundamentals of plane ge-

ometry so that the medics wouldn't discover how nearsighted they really were. Or how undernourished. Gangly arms hung alongside Depression-stunted legs and underdeveloped chests were incongruously flanked by biceps the size of basketballs. Nobody had to tell these guys that life was tough. They'd already figured that out. (xi)

55. Almond interview, 210.

56. Almond Papers, Carlisle, box 41. After Notestein had criticized his men rather harshly, he went on to point to a number of men who had performed heroic actions, including Lieutenant Marcellus Mars, First Lieutenant James Parrish, Second Lieutenant Theodore Smith, and First Lieutenant Hubert M. Moman, as especially demonstrating leadership and courage. In his February 23, 1945, report, he mentioned Gene. He said that one section of heavy machine guns, Company M, under faltering leadership, failed to advance under moderate enemy fire, until led forward by Captain Johnston, the company commander. James Notestein, February 23, 1945, to Almond. J. D. Armstrong, the commanding officer of the Headquarters 365th Infantry, wrote his efficiency report on February 21, 1945. He singled out those of valor like Joseph Stephenson, who he says had been recommended for the Silver Star. He reported that 90 percent of his colored officers of his command measured up well in all respects when committed to combat. Almond Papers, box 40.

Writing in July 1945, Almond claimed that his experience of three and one-half years in an attempt to create a combat infantry division comprising only negro units convinced him that it is a failure. He acknowledged individual cases of valor or outstanding performance, but "such cases are the exceptions; the Dr. Carvers, Booker T. Washingtons, and Marian Andersons of the Negro Race; they do not represent the average ability of the negro in combat." Almond Papers, box 41. For extensive reports by all of Almond's officers, see Almond Papers, boxes 40–41.

57. McCaffrey interview, 28.

58. Ibid., 36. Almond even continued to claim that there were no segregated clubs in Italy. He said that there were areas where white officers by choice would congregate as friendly gatherings and would get together of their own choice but not as an official club. Almond, who had antipathy for the Negro newspapers, charged that they were the ones to claim there was segregation overseas. Almond acknowledged that two officers clubs were established in Viareggio. One had a small orchestra and the other one had the division band. The former had a dress code. He called the one that did not have a dress code the "shirttail one." He said that a black officer and an Italian woman would show up each night in the club that had the orchestra. He said this demonstrated that segregated officers' clubs did not exist in Italy, and this had no relation to the morale and the performance of black officers. He said that very few Negro officers attended the one club, but a different mixed couple attended each night.

59. McCaffrey interview, 51.

60. Ibid., 62, 59, 60, 119.

After some one hundred court-martial cases were pending, they came up with an alternative solution. They wanted to discourage men from going AWOL, deserting, or refusing to fight. So they stopped the general court-martial, and instead sentenced them to a summary court-martial and 30 days confinement in the forward area (59). They were in a dangerous location and thus the word got out quickly that disobedience or desertion would put them in perhaps more danger and not guarantee them a fast trip home. Evidently this strategy worked quite well. McCaffrey interview, 60.

See also Carlo D'Este, "Victory in Europe" in Brinkley, *World War II Memorial.* Este wrote: "During the final Allied offensive in Italy, the specially trained 10th Mountain Division won several key positions leading to the Po Valley and the all Nisei 442nd Regimental Combat Team whose soldiers were among the most highly decorated of any unit in the Army, performed brilliantly" (99). "Between 400,000 and 500,000 troops fought in the Italian campaign as part of the largest Allied multinational force of WWII. Of the 312,000 Allied casualties, 189,000 (60%) were sustained by the U.S. 5th Army. Of 31,886 Allied troops killed in action, 19,475 were American. For 602 days, from Salerno to the foothills of the Alps, the U.S. Army fought some of the bitterest battles of World War II during what has mostly been a forgotten campaign"(99). See also Ron Field and Alexander Bielakowski, *Buffalo Soldiers: African American Troops in the US Forces 1866–1945* (New York: Osprey Publishing, 2008), for excellent photographs of the Italian campaign.

61. Interview with Eugene Johnston by Carolyn Johnston, June 19, 2002.

62. Interview with Eugene Johnston by Carolyn Johnston, July 4, 2002, and June 19, 2002. "Ezra Pound American indicted for treason. Living in Rapallo since 1916 Captured by 92nd Division Cpt [Gene Johnston]. On November 15 he sails after 13 months." On November 26, Gene returned to the United States. Box 40, 5th Army Book of Facts Top Secret, Edward M. Almond Major General. Bill Perry (a member of the 3rd Battalion) also remembered Pound's surrender and said that he heard that the 2nd Battalion of the 370th encountered Ezra Pound (Morehouse Archives). Gene Johnston would not find out for a long time who Pound really was. There was a big controversy about Pound when they brought him back to an asylum in the United States. He was a good friend of T. S. Eliot, the famous poet. Eliot nominated Pound for the Bollingen Prize, given by the Library of Congress and the U.S. government for the best poet. Many critics considered Ezra Pound and T. S. Eliot the two greatest poets of the twentieth century. A controversy arose over whether he should get the prize because he was a traitor. So people all over the country were divided one way or another about whether he should get it. Pound was sent to St. Elizabeth's Hospital in Washington, DC, which was a federal institution for the criminally insane. He was there for twelve years and released in 1958. However, a lot of people said he was not insane, but rather he was just a fascist during the war. Pound ended up getting that prize, even while he was incarcerated in the asylum. It was very controversial. See also Christopher Paul Moore, *Fighting for America: Black Soldiers—The Unsung Heroes of World War II* (New York: Presidio Press, 2005), 272, for commentary on another "traitor," Axis Sally.

63. Interview with Eugene Johnston by Carolyn Johnston, June 19, 2002.

64. Interview with Eugene Johnston by Carolyn Johnston, October 2004.

65. Interview with Eugene Johnston by Carolyn Johnston, June 19, 2002.

66. Rowny, *Engineer Memoirs,* 14.

67. *Washington Post,* Sunday, May 30, 2004, by Nurith C. Aizenman. For an account of the ceremony with Montgomery and Company H in Genoa, see Houston, *Black Warriors,* 189–190. Montgomery and some of his fellow members of the 92nd were invited back to Genoa in 1995 for a celebration.

68. Interview with Eugene Johnston by Carolyn Johnston, March 16, 2002. During this time, Alta was under great financial strain. Because she could not afford a dentist, she lost all her teeth.

69. Interview with Eugene Johnston by Carolyn Johnston, 2002. Letter from Eugene Johnston to Alta Johnston, August 15, 1945, Pisa.

70. Letter from Eugene Johnston to Alta Johnston, August 15, 1945, Pisa. The love letters that Gene Johnston wrote to Alta Johnston during World War II, 1944–1945, were the only contact she had for those long months. These beautiful letters reveal much about my father's love and longing for my mother during the war. They also are revealing about the attitudes that he

had toward his troops. Throughout the months after they arrived in Italy, he wrote often about how proud he was of his men. His letters offer us glimpses of the war through offhand comments like "I have gotten a few scratches" to convey his being wounded but minimizing it so my mother would not be worried. Because of the letters' loving tenderness, it is understandable that my mother would carefully pack them away during the scores of moves that they made and always know just where they were. Those were the memories she cherished from the time period, not those agonizing hours waiting for the mail or perhaps a telegram announcing her husband's death in battle.

71. Interview with Eugene Johnston by Carolyn Johnston, 2002.

72. Letters from Eugene Johnston to Alta Johnston, June 24, 1945, Viareggio, and August 14, 1945. Interview with Eugene Johnston by Carolyn Johnston, taped in 2001. See also *Buffalo,* large format, August 14, 1944; December 4, 1943, 4. A notice about Jack Gerwin read: "Capt. Jack Gerwin commanding Co. A, 371st received a degree in veterinary science from Miss. State College in 1940. He became one of the most successful commanders in 371st. He has been the commander for a year of Co A since Nov. 25, 1942. His company has received best in Regt on many occasions. He was inducted into the Army in April 1941, and then entered OCS in June 1942." Alta and Jack Gerwin's wife were good friends. They had driven back from Huachuca together.

73. Interview with Eugene Johnston by Carolyn Johnston, June 19, 2002, and March 16, 2002.

74. Interview with Eugene Johnston by Carolyn Johnston, July 4, 2002; June 21, 2002; and March 16, 2002. After the war was over, Gene visited a concentration camp in Germany. For years afterward, he was haunted by the sight of the people who had suffered unspeakable horrors there.

75. Interview with Eugene Johnston by Carolyn Johnston, July 4, 2002; June 21, 2002; and March 16, 2002.

76. Interview with Eugene Johnston by Carolyn Johnston, March 16, 2002.

77. Interview with Eugene Johnston by Carolyn Johnston, tape 11, 2001, and June 21, 2002.

78. Interview with Eugene Johnston by Carolyn Johnston, tape 11, 2001; June 21, 2002; and June 29, 2001.

79. Interview with Eugene Johnston by Carolyn Johnston, taped 2001.

80. Interview with Eugene Johnston by Carolyn Johnston, taped 2001.

81. Interview with Eugene Johnston by Carolyn Johnston, July 4, 2002.

82. Maggi M. Morehouse, *Fighting in the Jim Crow Army: Black Men and Women Remember World War II* (Lanham, MD: Rowman and Littlefield, 2000), 185.

83. Conversation between Carolyn Johnston and Spencer Moore, Washington, DC, October 2003; oral history, May 25, 2007, with Carolyn Johnston.

84. Letter, Joe Willie Johnson to Mary Alice Hubbard Johnson, 1945, Somewhere in Italy, folder 1493, World War II letters, 1940–1946, Western Historical Manuscript Collection—Columbia, Missouri.

Chapter 11

1. Interview with Eugene Johnston by Carolyn Johnston, June 29, 2001.

2. Interview with Eugene Johnston by Carolyn Johnston, July 2000.

3. Conversation between Carolyn Johnston and Spencer Moore, Washington, DC, Oc-

tober 2003; oral history, May 25, 2007, with Carolyn Johnston. See also Maggi M. Morehouse, *Fighting in the Jim Crow Army: Black Men and Women Remember World War II* (Lanham, MD: Rowman and Littlefield, 2000), 195–196. Spencer Moore's collection is a very rare one. He has been collecting for over fifty years. His collection includes not only memorabilia from the 92nd Division but also an extraordinary array of photographs, many of which he took during and after the war. He also has photographs of the Buffalo Soldiers at each of their reunions and of their return to Italy in 2000. One of his photographs shows a sign reading, "This Street Off Limits to 92nd Division Troops." He has excellent troop pictures, pictures of Spencer and his brother and friends, the entrance to Fort Huachuca, and a picture of him with friends on R and R in Rome with a sax playing "Body and Soul." He donated the collection to the Library of Congress, Manuscript Division. See James Rada, unreleased footage shot for *Deeds not Words,* October 8, 9, 2004, Rockville, Maryland. Of all the Buffalo Soldiers, I have many more interviews of Spencer Moore on which to draw than others. He and William Perry have both been absolutely critical to this book. Of all the members of the 92nd, I have spent the most time with them.

4. Conversation between Carolyn Johnston and Spencer Moore, Washington, DC, October 2003; oral history, May 25, 2007, with Carolyn Johnston.

5. Oral history on May 25, 2007, with Carolyn Johnston; James Rada, unreleased footage shot for *Deeds not Words,* October 8, 9, 2004, Rockville, Maryland. Conversation between Carolyn Johnston and Spencer Moore, Washington, DC, October 2003. For a superb book on the experiences of returning veterans, see Thomas C. Childers, *Soldier from the War Returning: The Greatest Generation's Troubled Homecoming from World War II* (Boston: Houghton Mifflin Harcourt, 2009).

6. At the age of eighty-eight, he still had an astonishing memory and mental sharpness, a twinkle in his eye, and a spring in his step. Oral history on May 25, 2007, with Carolyn Johnston; James Rada, unreleased footage shot for *Deeds not Words,* October 8, 9, 2004, Rockville, Maryland. Conversation between Carolyn Johnston and Spencer Moore, Washington, DC, October 2003.

7. Morehouse Archives, original transcript of interview; interview with Carolyn Johnston, October 2004.

8. Morehouse Archives, original transcript of interview; interview with Carolyn Johnston, October 2004.

9. Maggi Morehouse Archives; interview with Carolyn Johnston, October 2004; Morehouse, *Fighting in the Jim Crow Army,* 204. He and his wife Jo still reside there.

10. Juan Williams, "For Some, the Battle Began When the War Ended," *International Herald Tribune,* August 3, 1995, 2.

11. See Patricia Sullivan. *Lift Every Voice: The NAACP and the Making of the Civil Rights Movement* (New York: The New Press, 2009), 319–320.

12. Morehouse Archives, transcript of interview with Harold Montgomery conducted by Maggi Morehouse.

13. Veterans Surveys, Carlisle, AMHI; Jehu C. Hunter, "Triumph and Tribulation; Reflections on the Combat Experience of the 92nd Infantry Division in North Italy August 1944-April 1945." Hunter noted that the infantry performed well initially as the Germans retreated to their heavily fortified stronghold behind the Gothic line. When the division made their assault on Mount Cauala, they had to fall back after fighting for three hard days and suffering four hundred casualties. The lack of adequate black replacements impacted their capa-

bilities significantly. But as Hunter pointed out, the division succeeded in diverting a number of enemy forces away from the Bologna area where the 5th Army would eventually break into the Po River Valley. See also Jehu C. Hunter, captain, U.S. Army Reserves Retired, for presentation at the 1992 Conference of Army Historians: "Between a Rock and Hard Place: Reflections on the Performance of the 92nd Infantry Division in the Italian Campaign," August 1944–April 1945, 2, 4, 5. See also, Robert Bock, "Colleagues Mourn SIDS Research Pioneer Hunter," Milestones, *NIH Record,* January 27, 2006.

14. *Washington Post,* December 19, 2005. He died on December 7, 2005. See also Maggi Morehouse Archives.

15. Henry Wiencek, *The Hairstons: An American Family in Black and White* (New York: St. Martin's Griffin, 1999), 268–269, 261, 270–272, 249. Conversation between Joseph Hairston and Carolyn Johnston, November 29, 2010.

16. Wiencek, *The Hairstons,* 268–269, 261, 270–272, 249. Conversation between Joseph Hairston and Carolyn Johnston, November 29, 2010.

17. Wiencek, *The Hairstons,* 268–269, 261, 270–272, 249. Conversation between Joseph Hairston and Carolyn Johnston, November 29, 2010. Years later, he would learn the fascinating story of his family, the Hairstons. One of his great grandfathers was white. His great-grandmother had a relationship with a white overseer of the Hairston plantation. They lived in the same house for a lifetime. Even more extensive search revealed the complex interrelationships of the ways in which Joseph Hairston was directly descended from the white plantation owner, "Saura Town" Peter Hairston, and his slave Sally Blag.

18. Wiencek, *The Hairstons,* 268–269, 261, 270–272, 249. Conversation between Joseph Hairston and Carolyn Johnston, November 29, 2010. In fact that day during the speech, he was on top of the memorial watching for any possible disruptions or fights that might break out.

Chapter 12

1. About twelve years ago, I decided to write a book with my father about his World War II experiences. At the time I began this venture, I was finishing up a book on Cherokee women that was a way to honor my mother and her background, as well as to explore a neglected area of scholarship that held great meaning for me personally. After my mother's death in 2000, my father became much less communicative. As we began to work together on this book, we had endless conversations and hours of taping; he became intensely engaged with life again. My understanding of him unfolded, and it was clear to him that I greatly admired his courage and contributions during the Second World War. I also realized how transformed we both were by that experience. See Johnston, *Cherokee Women in Crisis: The Trail of Tears, Civil War, and Allotment* (Tuscaloosa: The University of Alabama Press, 2003).

2. Their voices and those of their fellow soldiers are critical to this book. I interviewed the Buffalo Soldiers from 2002 to 2007. I also drew on Maggi Morehouse's extensive oral histories with the African American soldiers in both the 92nd and 93rd Divisions, those in the Veterans History Project of the Library of Congress, and at the U.S. AMHI at Carlisle. When Spencer Moore and Bill Perry wanted to find a home for their collections, I was able to negotiate for them to place them in the Manuscripts Division of the Library of Congress, where they will have the widest possible accessibility and unparalleled care of the materials. Those of us who are children of the fortress share a legacy that shapes us. In her book *Military Brats: Legacies of Childhood Inside the Fortress* (New York: Harmony Books, 1991), Mary Edwards Wertsch

discusses the impact of the frequent moves, and the ways in which we experience a diversity of predicaments and people. Among the useful traits we acquire are independence, willingness to take risks, and flexibility. We know how to read people quickly, initiate new projects, get along with almost anyone, and bounce back from disaster. Most of all, military brats learn to use change as a medium. As children, military brats are not in control of when and how change enters their lives, but typically they teach themselves how to profit from it anyway. But somewhere inside, we will always be children of warriors, marked forever by the transient life we led. To a degree, this means accepting that we must live with contradiction. Part of us will always want to move on; the other part yearns to stay. See Wertsch, 252–253, 282, 395–396.

Chapter 13

1. This part is based on my visit to Fort Huachuca in 2006. So much of the history of the 92nd Division has often been distorted or erased from the official record. It was gratifying to see the archives in the Fort Huachuca Museum and to see that as of 1993, items from Joe Stephenson's collection had been added to the collection.

2. My visit to Fort Huachuca in 2006.

Chapter 14

1. In my search for my father's war, I met General Almond's grandson, Colonel Thomas Fergusson, when he and his wife attended a 92nd Division reunion. The members welcomed him graciously. Fergusson spoke movingly at the banquet one evening about his search for the grave of his father, Major Thomas Galloway, who was killed in the war in France, and how he had finally found it along with his parachute that those in the village had kept. Everyone knew what no one said, and another circle closed. The 92nd Infantry Division WWII Association and Appendix to *Congressional Record* vol. 92, part 9, January 14, 1946–March 8, 1946. See also Ulysses Lee, *The Employment of Negro Troops. United States Army in World War II,* Special Studies Center for Military History publication 11-4 (Washington, DC: U.S. Government Printing Office, 1966), 5–15, on 92nd Division in World War I. See Dale Wilson, "Recipe for Failure: Major General Edward M. Almond and Preparation of the U.S. 92nd Division for Combat in World War II," *Journal of Military History* 56 (July 1992), 473–488. Colonel Fergusson is a gracious, erudite, impressive person. The major source of this chapter is the interview at AMHI of General Ned Almond with his grandson, Thomas Fergusson. See also AMHI Carlisle Indian School Archives.

2. Mary Penick Motley, comp. and ed., *The Invisible Soldier: The Experience of Black Soldiers in World War II* (Detroit, MI: Wayne State University Press, 1975), 269–270.

3. President Barack Obama, Commemoration of 65th Anniversary of D-Day, June 6, 2009.

4. Major George E. Knapp, *Buffalo Soldiers at Fort Leavenworth in the 1930s and early 1940s* (Fort Leavenworth, KS: Combat Studies Institute, U.S. Army Command and General Staff College 1991), 52–53. In interviews of 10th Cavalry Buffalo Soldiers, Knapp recorded the following statements by Chief Warrant Officer Harry H. Hollowell and Elmer S. Robinson in the 1930s and 1940s. Hollowell said: "it makes you feel so good on the inside that we made it—broke the ice—made possible for them (contemporary black soldiers) to be in that position. They are reaping the benefits of the hard knocks that we made the sacrifices for . . . that we

went through" (52). Sgt. Elmer E. Robinson said: "I feel that the contribution that we made as black soldiers made it possible for some of the people to be in the position that they are today because we took so many of the hard knocks . . . the embarrassments and everything."

Chapter 15

1. In her beautiful book *Lose Your Mother: A Journey along the Atlantic Slave Route* (New York: Farrar, Straus, and Giroux, 2007) about the Atlantic slave trade and her journey to Ghana, Saidya Hartman wrote: "The rebels, the come, go back, child, and I are all returnees, circling back to times past, revisiting the routes that might have led to alternative presents, salvaging the dreams unrealized and defeated, crossing over to parallel lives. The hope is that *return* could resolve the old dilemmas, make a victory out of defeat, and engender a new order. . . . Loss remakes you. Return is as much about the world to which you no longer belong as it is about the one in which you have yet to make a home" (100). See also Thomas Stearns Eliot, *Four Quartets* (London: Faber and Faber, 1944).

For information on Shelley's drowning near Livorno, and the slave sculpture, see *www.noehill.com/med/med2001/pisa.asp*, accessed October 19, 2007; *www.livornonow.com/sightseeing_in_livorno_out_and_about_in_via_grande*, accessed October 19, 2007. For information on Christopher Columbus, see *www.columbusnavigation.com/death.shtml*, accessed October 19, 2007.

After describing my experiences in Italy to my niece, Patricia Smith, she said, "Both memory and landscape may shift and change over time, but the legacy of hope and experience endures this ebb and flow of time."

Chapter 16

1. This ceremony in the Capitol Rotunda was the result of Speaker Nancy Pelosi's initiative. My best friend in graduate school, John Lawrence, was her chief of staff, and in the fall of 2007, we spoke about the upcoming anniversary of the integration of the military services. I suggested that the occasion might be an appropriate time to honor black veterans, especially the Buffalo Soldiers. John consulted the Speaker. Speaker Pelosi, a strong advocate of veterans' rights and benefits and the architect of a GI Bill, sponsored the event.

2. Alessandra Stanley, "On a '44 Battlefield, a Salute for a Black Hero," *New York Times,* July 16, 2000, 1, 6. Solace Wales, an American writer who spends time in Marin County, California, and in Sommocolonia, invited them and arranged a ceremony. James McBride, the Pulitzer-winning writer, took care of everything. They met in Pisa. When Moore came home from Italy through Munich, the Germans in the airport had machine guns. Immediately, he was taken back to the time of the war.

3. Christopher Paul Moore, *Fighting for America: Black Soldiers—The Unsung Heroes of World War II* (New York: Presidio Press, 2006), 269–270. In addition to the Medal of Honor, Vernon Baker received a Purple Heart and a Bronze Star. Vernon J. Baker, *Lasting Valor: Story of the Only Living Black World War II Veteran to Earn America's Highest Distinction for Valor, the Medal of Honor,* with Ken Olsen (Columbus, MS: Genesis Press, 1997), 272–273. The president also awarded the Medal of Honor posthumously to six other black soldiers: Private George Watson, 29th Quartermaster Regiment; Sergeant Edward A. Carter Jr., 12th Armored Division; Private Willy F. James Jr., 104th Infantry Division; Sergeant Ruben Rivers, 761st Tank Battalion; First Lieutenant Charles L. Thomas, 103rd Infantry Division; and First Lieutenant

John R. Fox, 92nd Infantry Buffalo Division (282–284). The authors of *The Army Almanac* wrote:

> On April 30, 1945, General Clark announced that the long, seemingly endless campaign that began in September 1943 on the beaches at Salerno had ended. Nearly one million Germans in Northern Italy and Western Austria lay down their arms in unconditional surrender on May 2, 1945, at 2 p.m. Heinrich von Vietinghoff-Scheel and the Allied Mediterranean Commander Field Marshall Sir Harold R. L. G. Alexander signed the surrender at the royal palace of Caserta on April 29.
>
> By that time the 92nd had lost almost one fourth of its men through casualties. Three hundred and thirty died in action, two thousand two hundred and fifteen were wounded, and six hundred and sixteen were missing in action. Heroes included Private Woodall I. Marshal: Silver Star; Vernon J. Baker: Viareggio, April 5, 6, 1945; Charles F. Gaudy, Jr. Posthumously awarded Silver Star, October 12, 1944; Lt. Theodore O. Smith killed; Feb. 11, 1945, one month after he received a Silver Star; First Lt. John M. Madison: Silver Star: February 8, 10, 1945; First Lt. Wm. E. Porter, Silver Star. The 92nd received 12,096; 2 Distinguished Service Crosses, 1 Distinguished Service Medal; 16 Legion of Merit Awards; 7 Oak leaf clusters to Silver Stars 95; 6 Soldier's Medals; 728 Bronze Stars, 1891 Purple Hearts, 7996 combat infantry badges. It also received 205 commendations. The division came home during the latter part of 1945. Landing in Boston, New York, and Norfolk, only 4,000 were left of 12,000 because of transfers, discharges, and deaths.

The Army Almanac: A Book of Facts Concerning the Army of the United States (Washington, DC: U.S. Government Printing Office, 1950), 510–592.

4. Charles Lancaster, "Black Soldier: 'I'll Fight No More'" (unpublished autobiography, 1986, revised in 2010), 36, 39, 45, 51, 74, typescript. Lancaster stated: "I believe that Capt. Johnston saw me and chose not to place me under arrest but give me enough time to get away as the report that I saw later stated that the officer reported as ordered but was taken to the hospital for treatment" (51). Eventually, Lancaster got his rank back, and then lost it again. He served in the 125th Quartermaster Battalion, 110th Quartermaster Battalion, and the 117th Quartermaster Battalion after his stay in the hospital. Charles Lancaster married his wife, whom he had courted for seven years, while he was on a three-day pass. They had three hours together before he had to go back to Camp Patrick Henry, Virginia. He would not see her for two years. Twenty-four hours later, he was on a transport heading overseas. His wife worked for the Navy Department during the war. After the war and a difficult adjustment, Lancaster and his wife ran a business in Washington, DC, for thirty-five years. They had four children and five grandchildren (32). Lancaster wrote: "It hurts deeply to know what the Black Soldier has gone through yet he's not fully recognized to this day" (27).

5. The extent of the racist attitudes is reflected in the ways in which the troops were sent off to war. A reporter in the black press wrote that the army band played "God Bless America" when the white soldiers boarded the troopships. Then when "Negroes went up to board the band switched to the Darktown Strutters' Ball." See Jay David and Elaine Crane, *The Black Soldier from the American Revolution to Vietnam* (New York: William Morrow and Company, 1971), 153. The way they came home from war could also be clouded by racism. Bruce M. Wright earned his first Purple Heart in the third-wave assault on Omaha Beach and his second one and a Bronze Star in Germany when he fought in the Battle of the Bulge in December 1944. When he was on his way home, he marched onto the ship wearing his decorations and a

white Navy officer sneered, "I didn't know niggers were fighting." Wright was so enraged that he left the ship and went AWOL in Paris. Eventually after returning to the United States in chains, he ended up as a New York State Supreme Court judge. See Gail Buckley, *American Patriots: The Story of Blacks in the Military from the Revolution to Desert Storm* (New York: Random House, 2001), especially the caption on Bruce M. Wright's photograph in book's inset of photographs.

Appendix I

1. The timeline of the 92nd Division in World War II was derived from these sources: Paul Goodman, *A Fragment of Victory in Italy during World War II* (Nashville, TN: The Battery Press, 1993), 196; 92nd Infantry Division WWII Association and the Appendix to *Congressional Record,* vol. 92, part 9, January 14, 1946 to March 8, 1946; Robert Hodges: indianamilitary.org/02uninfdiv/Assault.htm, accessed June 2002; *The Army Almanac: A Book of Facts Concerning the Army of the United States* (Washington, DC: U.S. Government Printing Office, 1950), 510–592.

Appendix II

1. The chronology of the 92nd Division in the Italian campaign is based on details in General Edward Almond Papers, AMHI, Carlisle, PA.

Bibliography

Abdul-Jabbar, Kareem, and Anthony Walton. *Brothers in Arms: The Epic Story of the 761st Tank Battalion, WWII's Forgotten Heroes.* New York: Broadway Books, 2004.

African Americans and World War II: 50th Anniversary of WWII. Commemorative issue. *Journal of Negro History* 51–57, nos. 1–12 (Dec. 1993).

Afro-American Historical and Genealogical Society. Jean Sampson Scott Greater New York Chapter. *African-Americans in the Military: World War I and World War II.* New York: AAHGS-NY Writers Group, 2008.

Allen, Robert L. *The Port Chicago Mutiny.* New York: Amistad, 1993.

Alt, William E., and Betty L. Alt. *Black Soldiers, White Wars.* Westport, CT: Praeger, 2002.

Ambrose, Stephen E. *The Good Fight: How World War II Was Won.* New York: Athenaeum Books for Young Readers, 2001.

The Army Almanac: A Book of Facts Concerning the Army of the United States. Washington, DC: U.S. Government Printing Office, 1950.

Army Service Forces Manual M5: Leadership and the Negro Soldier. October 1944. Washington, DC: United States Government Printing Office, 1944.

Arnold, Thomas St. John. *Buffalo Soldiers: The 92nd Infantry Division and Reinforcements in World War II, 1942–1945.* Manhattan, KS: Sunflower University Press, 1990.

Astor, Gerald. *The Right to Fight: A History of African Americans in the Military.* Novato, CA: Presidio Press, 1998.

Atkinson, Rick. *The Day of Battle: The War in Sicily and Italy, 1943–1944.* Volume II of the Liberation Trilogy. New York: Henry Holt and Company, 2007.

Badoglio, Pietro. *Italy in the Second World War: Memories and Documents.* New York: Oxford University Press, 1948.

Baird, Emma Marie. "The Negro American Soldier in War and Peace." MA thesis, University of Virginia, 1950.

Baker, Vernon J. *Lasting Valor: Story of the Only Living Black World War II Veteran to Earn America's Highest Distinction for Valor, the Medal of Honor.* With Ken Olsen. Columbus, MS: Genesis Press, 1997.

Banks, William S. M. *From Beginnings in the SIP.* Fort Valley, GA: self-published, n.d.

Barbeau, Arthur E., and Florette Henri. *The Unknown Soldiers: Black American Troops in World War I.* New York: Da Capo Press, 1996.

Bielakowski, Alexander, and Raffaele Ruggeri. *Buffalo Soldiers: African American Troops in World War II.* New York: Osprey Publishing, 2008.

Binkin, Martin, and Mark J. Eitelberg. *Blacks and the Military.* With Alvin J. Schexhider and Marvin M. Smith. Washington, DC: Brookings Institute, 1982.

Birdwell, Michael. "Celluloid Soldiers." *American Historical Review* 106, no. 2 (2001), 593–594.

Blum, John Morton. *V Was for Victory: Politics and American Culture during World War II.* New York: Harcourt, Brace, Jovanovich, 1976.

Botjer, George. *Side Show War.* College Station: Texas A & M University Press, 1996.

Boyd, W. Y. *World War II. Infantry Soldier: The Horror Endured by a U.S. Infantryman.* New York: Celeb Publishing, 1995.

Brandt, Nat. *Harlem at War: The Black Experience in WWII.* Syracuse, NY: Syracuse University Press, 1997.

Brinkley, Douglas, ed. *The World War II Memorial: A Grateful Nation Remembers.* Washington, DC: Smithsonian, 2004.

Brokaw, Tom. *An Album of Memories: Personal Histories from the Greatest Generation.* New York: Random House, 2001.

———. *The Greatest Generation Speaks.* New York: Random House, 1999.

Brooke, Edward W. *Bridging the Divide: My Life.* New Brunswick, NJ: Rutgers University Press, 2007.

Brooks, Thomas R. *Walls Come Tumbling Down: A History of the Civil Rights Movement 1940–1970.* Englewood Cliffs, NJ: Prentice Hall, 1974.

Brown, Earl Lewis, and George R. Leighton. *The Negro and the War.* New York: AMS Press, 1972.

Brown, Lee. *Strong in the Struggle: My Life as A Black Labor Activist.* With Robert L. Allen. Lanham, MD: Rowman and Littlefield, 2001.

Bruning, John Robert, Jr., *Elusive Glory: African American Heroes of World War II.* Greensboro, NC: Avisson Press, 2001.

Buchanan, A. Russell. *Black Americans in WWII.* Santa Barbara, CA: Clio Books, 1977.

Buckley, Gail. *American Patriots: The Story of Blacks in the Military from the Revolution to Desert Storm.* New York: Random House, 2001.

Buckley, Roger Norman. *The British Army in the West Indies.* Gainesville: University Press of Florida, 1998.

Byers, Jean. *A Study of the Negro in Military Service.* Washington, DC: U.S. Department of Defense, January 1950.

Carroll, Andrew. *War Letters: Extraordinary Correspondence from American Wars.* New York: Scribner, 2001.

Carver, Field Marshal Lord Michael. *The Imperial War Museum Book of the War in Italy, 1943–1945.* London: Sidgwick and Jackson, 2001.

Chafe, William. *Remembering Jim Crow.* New York: New Press, 2001.

Chambers, John Whiteclay II. *The Oxford Companion to American Military History.* New York: Oxford University Press, 1999.

Childers, John. "The Buffalo Soldiers at Ft. Huachuca, 1913–48." MA thesis, California State University, Dominguez Hills, 1997.

Childers, Thomas C. *In the Shadows of War: An American Pilot's Odyssey through the Camps of Nazi Germany.* New York: H. Holt, 2003.

———. *Soldier from the War Returning: The Greatest Generation's Troubled Homecoming from World War II.* Boston: Houghton Mifflin Harcourt, 2009.

———. *Wings of Morning: The Story of the Last American Bomber Shot Down Over Germany in World War II.* Reading, MA: Perseus Books, 1995.

Clairday, Robyn, and Matt Clairday. *Postcards from World War II.* Garden City Park, NY: Square One Publishers, 2002.

Clark, Mark. *Calculated Risk.* New York: Harper and Brothers, 1950.

Clinton, Catherine. *The Black Soldier 1492 to the Present.* Boston: Houghton Mifflin, 2000.

Collins, Julia. *My Father's War: A Memoir.* New York: Four Walls Eight Windows, 2002.

Commission on Wartime Relocation and Internment of Civilians. Personal Justice Denied: Report of the Commission on Wartime Relocation and Internment of Civilians. Washington, DC: Government Printing Office, December 1982.

Converse, Elliott V., III. *The Exclusion of Black Soldiers from the Medal of Honor in World War II.* Raleigh, NC: Shaw University, 1995; repr. Jefferson, NC: McFarland and Company, 1997.

Cooper, Michael L. *The Double V Campaign: African Americans and World War II.* New York: Dutton-Lodestar Books, 1998.

Dalfiume, Richard M. *Desegregation of the U.S. Armed Forces: Fighting on Two Fronts 1939–1953.* Columbia: University of Missouri Press, 1969.

Daugerty, James Harden. *The Buffalo Saga.* Bloomington, IN: Xlibris, 2009.

David, Jay, and Elaine Crane, *The Black Soldier from the American Revolution to Vietnam.* New York: William Morrow and Company, 1971.

Davis, Benjamin O., Jr. *An Autobiography: American.* London: Smithsonian Institution Press, 1991.

D'Este, Carlo. *World War II in the Mediterranean, 1942–1945.* Chapel Hill: Algonguin Books, 1990.

Donaldson, Gary. *The History of African Americans in the Military.* Malabar, FL: Krieger Publishing, 1991.

Dunbar, Harry B. *A Brother Like Me: A Memoir.* Wilmington: Queenhyte Publishers, 1995.

Eales, Anne Bruner. *Army Wives on the American Frontier.* Boulder, CO: Johnson Books, 1996.

Earley, Charity Adams. *One Woman's Army: A Black Officer Remembers the WAC.* College Station: Texas A&M University Press, 1989.

Edgerton, Robert B. *Hidden Heroism: Black Soldiers in America's Wars.* Boulder, CO: Westview Press, 2001.

Eliot, Thomas Stearns. *Four Quartets.* London: Faber and Faber, 1944.

Fergusson, Capt. Thomas G. "Reflections: Transcripts of the Debriefing of General Edward M. Almond." 25 March 1975, Edward M. Almond Papers, Archives. U.S. Army Military History Institute, Carlisle Barracks, PA.

Field, Ron, and Alexander Bielakowski. *Buffalo Soldiers: African American Troops in the U.S. Forces 1866–1945.* New York: Osprey Publishing, 2008.

"Fighting Fronts," *Newsweek,* February 26, 1945, 34.

Finkle, Lee. *Forum for Protest: The Black Press during World War II.* Cranbury, NJ: Associated University Presses, 1975.

Fiscus, James W. *Critical Perspectives of Non-Fiction Writing.* New York: Rosen Publishing Group, 2005.

Fisher, Ernest F., Jr. *Cassino to the Alps.* 1977; repr., Washington, DC: Center of Military History, U.S. Army: Superintendent of Documents, U.S. Government Printing, 1993.

———. *Guardians of the Republic: A History of Noncommissioned Officer Corps of the US Army.* New York: Ballantine Books, 1994.

Fletcher, Marvin E. *America's First Black General: Benjamin O. Davis, Sr. 1880–1970.* Lawrence: University Press of Kansas, 1989.

Foner, Jack D. *Blacks and the Military in American History: A New Perspective.* New York: Praeger, 1974.

Foote, Robert Hutchinson. *Connecticut Yankee in Nisei King Company's Court: With the Japanese American 442nd RCT in World War II.* Ithaca, NY: The Internet-First University Press, 2005.

Forsberg, Franklin S., and the editors of *Yank. The Story of World War II as Written by the Soldiers.* New York: Greenwich House, 1984.

Fowler, Arlen L. *The Black Infantry in the West, 1869–1891.* Norman: University of Oklahoma Press, 1996.

Franklin, John Hope. *Mirror to America: The Autobiography of John Hope Franklin.* New York: Farrar, Straus, and Giroux, 2005.

Franks, Lucinda. *My Father's Secret War: A Memoir.* New York: Hyperion, 2007.

Freedman, Lawrence ed. *War.* New York: Oxford University Press, 1994.

Fussell, Paul. *The Great War and Modern Memory.* New York: Oxford, 1975.

———. *Wartime: Understanding and Behavior in the Second World War.* New York: Oxford University Press, 1989.

Gates, Henry Louis, Jr. *Colored People.* New York: Vintage Books, 1994.

Gatewood, Willard B., Jr. "Black Americans and the Military." *Reviews in American History* 3, no. 1 (March 1975), 31–36.

Gawne, Jonathan. *Finding Your Father's War: A Practical Guide to Researching and Understanding Service in the World War II US Army.* Philadelphia: Casemate, 2006.

Gibran, Daniel K. *The 92nd Infantry Division and the Italian Campaign in World War II.* Jefferson, NC: McFarland and Company, 2001.

Gibson, Truman. *Knocking Down Barriers: My Fight for Black America.* Evanston, IL: Northwestern University Press, 2005.

Glusman, John A. *Conduct under Fire 1941–1945: Four American Doctors and Their Fight for Life as Prisoners of the Japanese.* New York: Viking Penguin, 2005.

Goodman, Jack, ed. *While You Were Gone.* New York: Simon & Schuster, 1946.

Goodman, Paul. *A Fragment of Victory in Italy during World War II.* Nashville, TN: The Battery Press, 1993.

Goodwin, Doris Kearns. *No Ordinary Time: The Home Front in World War II.* New York: Simon and Schuster, 1995.

Graham, Dominick, and Shelford Bidwell. *The Tug of War: The Battle for Italy, 1943–1945.* New York: St. Martin's Press, 1986.

Green, Anne Bosanko. *One Woman's War: Letters Home from The Women's Army Corps 1944–1946.* St. Paul: Minnesota Historical Society Press, 1989.

Gunther, John. *Inside U.S.A.* New York: New Press, 1947.

Hall, Gwendolyn Midlo. *Love, War, and the 96th Engineers (Colored) The World War II New Guinea Diaries of Captain Human Samuelson.* Urbana: University of Illinois Press, 1995.

Hargrove, Hondon B. *Buffalo Soldiers in Italy: Black Americans in World War II.* Jefferson, NC: McFarland, 1985.

——— "Il Corsaro: A Story of War and Friendship." *Michigan History* 64, no. 1 (January/February 1980), 14–17.

Harpur, Brian. *The Impossible Victory: A Personal Account of the Battle for the Po River.* New York: Hippocrene Books, 1981.

Harris, Elbert L. *Let the Ammunition Roll: The Story of a Negro GI.* New York: The Exposition Press, 1948.

Hartman, Saidya. *Lose Your Mother: A Journey along the Atlantic Slave Route.* New York: Farrar, Straus, and Giroux, 2007.

Hastie, Judge William H. *African Americans in the Military.* 46 reels of microfilm. Subject file edited by Robert E. Lester; guide by Eric H. Doss. Bethesda, MD: UPA Collection, LexisNexis, 2006.

———. *World War II, and the Black Soldiers.* Westport, CT: Greenwood, 1988.

Hausrath, Alfred H., project director. *Utilization of Negro Manpower in the Army: A 1951 Study.* The Operations Office of the Johns Hopkins University, unclassified, edition. McLean, VA: Research Analysis Corporation, 1967.

Hemphill, Paul. *Leaving Birmingham: Notes of a Native Son.* Tuscaloosa: University of Alabama Press, 1993.

Heywood, Chester D. *The Story of the 371st Infantry.* Worcester, MA: Commonwealth Press, 1928.

Higginson, Thomas Wentworth. *Army Life in a Black Regiment.* 1869; repr., New York: W. W. Norton, 1984.

Hine, Darlene Clark. "Black Professionals and Race Consciousness: Origins of the Civil Rights Movement, 1890–1950," *Journal of American History* 89, no. 4 (March 2003), 1279–1294.

———. *Black Women in White: Racial Conflict and Cooperation in the Nursing Profession, 1890–1950.* Bloomington: Indiana University Press, 1989.

Hobbs, Glynn B. *From Sicily to the Alps: Personal Accounts and Recollections of World War II in Italy.* Claremont, South Africa: Mallard Publishers, 1999.

Hogan, Cpl. Charles A., and Cpl. John Welsh III. *Puptent Poets of the Stars and Stripes Mediterranean.* Edited by Lt. Ed Hill. Naples, Italy: *Stars and Stripes,* 1945

Hogan, Eva B. *The Last Buffalo: Walter E. Potts and 92nd "Buffalo" Division in WWI.* Austin, TX: Eakin Press, 2000.

Hope, Richard O. *Racial Strife in the Military: Toward the Elimination of Discrimination.* New York: Praeger, 1979.

Horne, Lena, and Richard Schickel. *Horne.* Garden City, NY: Doubleday, 1965.

Houston, Ivan J. *Black Warriors: The Buffalo Soldiers of World War II.* With Gordon Cohn. New York: iUniverse, 2009.

———. "Memoir." Unpublished manuscript, n.d.

Huachuca Illustrated, A Magazine of the Fort Huachuca Museum, World War at Huachuca 1940–1949 9 (1993).

Hunter, Jehu C., and Lt. Col. Major Clark. "The Buffalo Division in World War II." Unpublished manuscript, 1985. Typescript.

Huntington, Samuel P. *The Soldier and the State: The Theory and Politics of Civil-Military Relations.* Cambridge, MA: Harvard University Press, 1957.

Inouye, Daniel K. *Journey to Washington.* Englewood Cliffs, NJ: Prentice Hall, 1967.

James, C. L. R. (Cyril Lionel Robert). *Fighting Racism in WWII.* New York: Monad Press, 1980. Distributed by Pathfinder Press.

Jefferson, Robert F. *Fighting for Hope: African American Troops of the 93rd Infantry Division in World War II and Postwar America.* Baltimore, MD: Johns Hopkins Press, 2008.

———. *93rd: Making the Men of the African American Servicemen in the Years of the Great Depression and the Second World War 1935–1947.* Ann Arbor, MI: University Microfilms, 1995.

Jeffries, John W. *Wartime America: The World War II Home Front.* Chicago: Ivan R. Dee, 1996.

Johnson, Charles S. *To Stem This Tide: A Survey of Racial Tension Areas in the United States.* Boston: The Pilgrim Press, 1943.

Johnson, Jesse J. *Black Armed Forces Officers, 1736–1971—A Pictorial History.* Hampton, VA: n.p., 1971.

Johnson, Marilynn S. *The Second Gold Rush: Oakland and East Bay in World War II.* Berkeley: University of California Press, 1993.

Johnston, Carolyn Ross. *Cherokee Women in Crisis: The Trail of Tears, Civil War, and Allotment.* Tuscaloosa: The University of Alabama Press, 2003.

———. *Sexual Power: Feminism and the Family in America.* Tuscaloosa: The University of Alabama Press, 1992.

Kesselring, Albert. *Kesselring: A Soldier's Record.* Introduction by SLA Marshall. Westport, CT: Greenwood Press, 1953.

Kesting, Robert W. "Conspiracy to Discredit the Black Buffaloes: The 92nd Infantry in World War II." *Journal of Negro History* 72, no. 1/2 (Winter–Spring 1987), 1–19.

Kluger, Steve. *Yank: The American Weekly.* New York: St. Martin's Press, 1991.

Knapp, Major George E. *Buffalo Soldiers at Fort Leavenworth in the 1930s and Early 1940s.* Fort Leavenworth, KS: Combat Studies Institute, U.S. Army Command and General Staff College, 1991.

Kryder, Daniel. *Divided Arsenal: Race and the American State during World War II.* New York: Cambridge University Press, 2000.

Lamott, Anne, *Bird by Bird: Instructions on Writing and Life.* New York: Anchor Books, 1995.

Lancaster, Charles. "Black Soldier: 'I'll Fight No More.'" Unpublished autobiography, 1986, revised in 2010. Typescript.

Leckie, William H. *A Narrative of the Negro Cavalry in the West.* Norman: University of Oklahoma Press, 1967.

Lee, Ulysses. *The Employment of Negro Troops. United States Army in World War II.* Special Studies Center for Military History publication 11-4. Washington, DC: U.S. Government Printing Office, 1966.

Lemke-Santangelo, Gretchen. *Abiding Courage: African American Migrant Women in the East Bay Community.* Chapel Hill: University of North Carolina Press, 1996.

Lewis, Norman. *Naples '44: A World War II Diary of Occupied Italy.* New York: Carroll and Graf Publishers, 1978.

Linklater, Eric. *The Campaign in Italy.* 1951; repr., London: Her Majesty's Stationery Office, 1977.

Litoff, Judy Barrett, and David C. Smith. *Since You Went Away: World War II Letters from American Women on the Home Front.* Lawrence: University of Kansas Press, 1991.

———. *American Women in a World at War: Contemporary Accounts from World War II.* Vol. 1. Wilmington, DE: Scholarly Resources, 1997.

"The Luckless 92nd," *Newsweek,* February 26, 1945, 34.

Lutz, Catherine. *Home Front: A Military City and the American 20th Century.* Boston: Beacon Press, 2001.

MacGregor, Morris J., and Bernard C. Nalty. *Blacks in the United States Armed Forces: Basic Documents.* Vol. 7, *Planning for Postwar Employment of Black Personnel.* Wilmington, DE: SRI Publishing, 1977.

MacGregor, Morris J. *Integration of the Armed Forces, 1940–1965.* Washington, DC: Center of Military History, U.S. Army, Superintendent of Documents. U.S. Government Printing Office, 1981.

Macmillan, Neil, ed. *Remaking Dixie: The Impact of World War II on the American South.* Jackson: University Press of Mississippi, 1997.

Marcus, Robert D., David Burner, and Anthony Marcus. *America Firsthand.* 7th ed. Vol. 2. Boston: Bedford / St. Martin's, 2007.

Mathews, Tom. *Our Fathers' War: Growing Up in the Shadow of the Greatest Generation.* New York: Broadway Books, 2005.

Mauldin, Bill. *Bill Mauldin's Army: Bill Mauldin's Greatest World War II Cartoons.* New York: Sloane, 1949; repr., Novato, CA: Presidio Press, 1984.

———. *Up Front.* New York: Henry Holt and Company, 1945; repr., New York: W. W. Norton, 2000.

McCutcheon, Marc. *Everyday Life from Prohibition through World War II.* Cincinnati, OH: Writer's Digest Books, 1995.

McGowen, Tom. *Lonely Eagles and Buffalo Soldiers: African Americans in World War II.* New York: Franklin Watts, 1995.

McGuire, Philip. *He Too Spoke for Democracy: Judge Hastie, World War II, and the Black Soldier.* New York: Greenwood Press, 1988.

———. "Judge William Hastie and Army Recruitment 1940–1942." *Military Affairs* 42, no. 2 (April 1978), 75–79.

———. *McGuire Collection of Letters from Black Soldiers 1941–1946.* n.p.: Philip Publications, 1944–1946.

———. *Taps for a Jim Crow Army.* Santa Barbara, CA: ABC-CLIO Press, 1983.

McKissack, Patricia, and Frederick McKissack. *Red-Tail Angels: The Story of the Tuskegee Airmen of World War II.* New York: Walker and Company, 1995.

McWhorter, Diane. *Carry Me Home: Birmingham, Alabama: The Climactic Battle of the Civil Rights Revolution.* New York: Simon and Schuster, 2001.

Meyer, Robert, Jr. *The Stars and Stripes: Story of World War II.* New York: David McKay Company, 1960.

Miller, Kelly. *The World War and Human Rights: Authentic History of the Negro in the World War.* Washington, DC: A. Jenkins, 1919.

Miller, Robert H. *Buffalo Soldiers: The Story of Emanuel Stance.* Parsippany, NJ: Silver Press, 1995.

Moon, Elaine Latzman. *Untold Tales: Unsung Heroes, An Oral History of Detroit's African American Community, 1918–1967.* Detroit, MI: Wayne State University, 1994.

Moore, Brenda. *To Serve My Country, To Serve My Race: The Story of the Only African American WACs Stationed Overseas during WWII.* New York: New York University Press, 1996.

Moore, Christopher Paul. *Fighting for America: Black Soldiers—The Unsung Heroes of World War II.* New York: Presidio Press, 2006.

Morehouse, Maggi M. *Fighting in the Jim Crow Army: Black Men and Women Remember World War II.* Lanham, MD: Rowman and Littlefield, 2000.

———. "Black Citizen Soldiers." PhD diss., University of California at Berkeley, 2001.

Mormino, Gary. "GI Joe Meets Jim Crow: Racial Violence and Reform in WWII Florida," *Florida Historical Quarterly* 73, no. 1 (July 1994), 23–42.

Motley, Mary Penick, comp. and ed. *The Invisible Soldier: The Experience of Black Soldiers in World War II.* Detroit, MI: Wayne State University Press, 1975.

Mullen, Robert W. *Blacks in America's War.* New York: Monad Press, 1913.

Myrdal, Gunnar. *An American Dilemma.* Vols. 1 and 2. 1944; repr., New Brunswick, NJ: Transaction Publishers, 1996.

Nalty, Bernard C. *Strength for the Fight: A History of Black Americans in the Military.* New York: The Free Press, 1986.

"The Negro Soldier Betrayed," Editorial (censuring Truman Gibson), *Crisis* 52, no.4 (April 1945), 97.

Nelson, Dennis D. *The Integration of the Negro in the US Navy.* New York: Farrar, Straus, and Young, 1951.

Nichols, Lee. *Breakthrough on the Color Front.* Colorado Springs: Three Continents Press, 1993.

Office of War Information. *Negroes and the War.* Washington, DC: Office of War Information, 1943.

Oleck, Howard. *Eye Witness WWII Battles.* New York: Belmont Books, 1963.

O'Neill, William L. *A Democracy at War: America's Fight at Home and Abroad in World War II.* New York: Free Press, 1993.

Orgill, Douglas. *The Gothic Line: The Italian Campaign, Autumn, 1944.* New York: W. W. Norton, 1967.

Osur, Alan M. *Blacks in the Army Air Forces during World War II: The Problem of Race Relations.* Washington, DC: U.S. Government Printing Office, 1977.

Ottley, Roi. *New World a Coming: Inside Black America.* Boston: Houghton Mifflin, 1943.

Parillo, Mark P. *We Were in the Big One: Experiences of the World War II Generation.* Wilmington, DE: Scholarly Resources, 2002.

Parker, Robert W. *What'd You Do in The War, Dad?* Santa Fe, NM: Rio Grande Publishing, 2005.

Peaty, John, "The Desertion Crisis in Italy, 1944," *RUSI (Royal United Services Institute) Journal* 147, no. 3 (June 2002), 76–83.

Peery, Nelson. *African American Liberation and Revolution in the United States.* Chicago: Workers Press, 1992.

———. *Black Fire: The Making of an American Revolutionary.* New York: The New Press, 1994.

Potter, Lou, with William Miles and Nina Rosenblum. *Liberators: Fighting on Two Fronts in World War II.* New York: Harcourt Brace Jovanovich, 1992.

Pound, Omar, and Robert Spoo, eds. *Ezra and Dorothy Pound Letters in Captivity 1945–1946.* New York: Oxford University Press, 1999.

Putney, Martha S. *Blacks in the United States Army: Portraits through History.* Jefferson, NC: McFarland and Company, 2003.

———. *When the Nation Was in Need: Blacks in the Women's Army Corps During World War II.* Metuchen, NJ: Scarecrow Press, 1992.

Pyle, Ernie. *Brave Men.* Lincoln: University of Nebraska Press, 2001.

———. *Here Is Your War.* New York: Henry Holt and Company, 1943.

Reagon, Bernice. *Southern Exposure* 1 (Winter 1977), 177.

Reddick, Lawrence. *Blacks and U.S. Wars.* New York: National Urban League, 1976.

Reef, Catherine. *African Americans in the Military.* New York: Facts on File, 2004.

Report by the Supreme Allied Commander Mediterranean: The Italian Campaign 12th December 1944–2nd May 1945. By Field Marshal The Viscount Alexander of Tunis. London: His Majesty's Stationery Office, 1951.

Ricks, Lucille. *A Buffalo Soldier's Legacy.* Tucson, AZ: Buffalo Soldier Press, 1993.

Roberts, Gene, and Hank Klibanoff. *The Race Beat: The Press, the Civil Rights Struggle, and the Awakening of a Nation.* New York: Vintage Books, 2006.

Roe, Frances M. *Army Letters from an Officer's Wife.* New York: D. Appleton and Company, 1909; repr., Lincoln: University of Nebraska Press, 1981.

Rosignoli, Guido, *The Allied Forces in Italy, 1943–45.* New York: Sterling Publishing Company, 1989.

Rowny, Edward. *Engineer Memoirs.* (Alexandria, Virginia: U.S. Army Corps of Engineers, 1995).

Russell, Buchanan A. *Black Americans in World War II.* Santa Barbara, CA: Clio Books, 1977.

Schoenfeld, Seymour. *The Negro in the Armed Forces: His Value and Status, Past, Present, and Potential.* Washington, DC: The Associated Publisher, 1945.

Schubert, Frank. *Voices of the Buffalo Soldier: Records, Reports, and Recollections of Military Life and Service in the West.* Albuquerque: University of New Mexico Press, 2003.

Scott, Emmett Jay. *Scott's Official History of the American Negro in the World War.* Chicago: Homewood Press, 1919.

Shelton, Richard. *Going Back to Bisbee.* Tucson: The University of Arizona Press, 1992.

Shepperd, G. A. *The Italian Campaign, 1943–45: A Political and Military Re-assessment.* New York: Frederick Praeger Publishers, 1968.

Shirey, Orville. *Americans: The Story of the 442nd Combat Team.* Washington, DC: Infantry Journal Press, 1947.

Silvera, John D. *The Negro in World War II.* New York: Arno Press and the New York Times, 1969.

Sitkoff, Harvard. "Racial Militancy and Interracial Violence in the Second World War." *Journal of American History* 58, no. 3 (December 1971), 661–681.

Sledge, E. B. *With the Old Breed: At Peleliu and Okinawa.* 1981; repr., New York: Presidio Press, 2007.

Slonaker, John. *The U.S. Army and the Negro.* Historical Research and Reference Division. Special Bibliography 2. Carlisle Barracks, PA: U.S. Army Military History Research Collection, 1971.

Smith, Cornelius Cole. *Fort Huachuca: The Story of a Frontier Post.* Honolulu, HI: University Press of the Pacific, 2000.

Smith, Graham. *When Jim Crow Met John Bull. Black American Soldiers in World War II Britain.* New York: St. Martin's Press, 1987.

Starr, Chester G. *From Salerno to the Alps: A History of the Fifth Army 1943–1945.* Washington, DC: *Infantry Journal Press,* 1948.

Stegner, Wallace. *Women on the Wall.* Boston: Houghton Mifflin, 1950; repr., Lincoln: University of Nebraska Press, 1981.

Steinman, Louise. *The Souvenir: A Daughter Discovers Her Father's War.* New York: Plume, 2002.

Stevens, John D. *From the Back of the Foxhole: Black Correspondents in World War II.* Journalism Monographs 27. Lexington, KY: Association for Education in Journalism, 1973.

Stiles, T. J. "Buffalo Soldiers," *Smithsonian* 29, no. 9 (1998), 82–95.

Stillman, Richard J., II. *Integration of the Negro in the U.S. Armed Forces.* Santa Barbara, CA: Praeger, 1968.

Stokesbury, James L. *A Short History of World War II.* New York: William Morrow and Company, 1980.

Strawson, John. *The Italian Campaign.* New York: Carroll and Graf Publishers, Inc., 1988.

Sullivan, Patricia. *Lift Every Voice: The NAACP and the Making of the Civil Rights Movement.* New York: The New Press, 2009.

Takaki, Ronald. *Double Victory: A Multicultural History of America in World War II.* Boston: Little, Brown, and Company, 2000.

Terkel, Studs. "*The Good War.*" New York: Ballantine Books, 1984.

Tobin, James. *Ernie Pyle's War: America's Eyewitness to World War II.* 1997; repr., New York: Free Press, 2006.

Topping, Ira, ed. *The Best of Yank The Army Weekly, 1942–1945.* New York: Arno Press, 1980.

Truscott, Lucian K. *Command Missions: A Personal Story.* New York: E. P. Dutton, 1954.

Turow, Scott. *Ordinary Heroes.* New York: Warner Books, 2005.

Tuttle, William M. *Daddy's Gone to War: The Second World War in the Lives of America's Children.* New York: Oxford University Press, 1993.

Wallace, Robert. *The Italian Campaign—World War II.* New York: Time-Life Books, 1978.

Warren, Lt. Col. James C. *The Freeman Field Mutiny: Tuskegee Airmen's Story.* San Rafael, CA: Donna Ewald Publishers, 1995.

Watson, Elwood. *Pimps, Wimps, Studs, Thugs, and Gentlemen: Essays on Media Images of Masculinity.* Jefferson, NC: McFarland and Company, 2009.

Weir, William. *Encyclopedia of African American Military History.* Amherst, NY: Prometheus Books, 2004.

Welliver, Warman. "Report on the Negro Soldier," *Harper's Magazine,* April 1946, 332–339.

Wertsch, Mary Edwards. *Military Brats: Legacies of Childhood Inside the Fortress.* New York: Harmony Books, 1991.

West, Jack V. *A Soldier's Story about the Forgotten Italian Front, World War II by David J. West as told by Jack V. West.* Effingham, IL: J. V. West, 1999.

White, Walter F. *A Man Called White: The Autobiography of Walter White.* Athens: University of Georgia Press, 1995.

Wiencek, Henry. *The Hairstons: An American Family in Black and White.* New York: St. Martin's Griffin, 1999.

Williams, Chad L. *Torchbearers of Democracy: African American Soldiers in the World War I Era.* Chapel Hill: University of North Carolina Press, 2010.

Wilson, August. *King Hedley II.* New York: Theatre Communications Group, 2005.

Wilson, Dale E. "Recipe for Failure: Major General Edward M. Almond and Preparation of the U.S. 92nd Division for Combat in World War II." *Journal of Military History* 56(July 1992), 473–488.

Wilson, Ruth Danenhower. *Jim Crow Joins Up: A Study of Negroes in the Armed Forces of the United States.* New York: William J. Clark Press, 1945.

Wright, Kai. *Soldiers of Freedom: An Illustrated History of African Americans in the Armed Forces.* New York: Black Dog and Leventhal, 2002.

Wynn, Neil. *The Afro American and the Second World War.* New York: Holmes and Meier Publishers, 1976.

Yellin, Emily. *Our Mother's War: American Women at Home and at the Front During World War II.* New York: Free Press, 2004.

Films

Burns, Ken, dir. *The War.* Washington, DC: Florentine Films and WETA, 2007. DVD, 15 hours.

Capra, Frank, dir. *The Negro Soldier.* Washington, DC: U.S. War Department, 1944. VHS, 43 min.

C-Span. *Sixtieth Anniversary of the Integration of the Armed Forces.* Washington, DC: National Cable Satellite Corporation, 2009. DVD, 60 min.

Don't Be a Sucker. Hollywood: Warner Bros. U.S. War Department, 1947. VHS, 18 min.

Kuwornu, Fred, dir. *Inside Buffalo: The Story of unsung heroes of the 92nd Division in World War II.* Rome: FKKFILMZ, 2009. DVD, 59 min.

Lee, Spike, dir. *Miracle at St. Anna: The Untold Story of Courage and Brotherhood.* New York: 40 Acres and a Mule Filmworks, 2008. Touchstone/Disney DVD, 2009, 160 min.

Rada, James, dir., writer, and producer. *Deeds not Words: Buffalo Soldiers in World War II.* Washington, DC: James Rada, 2010. DVD, 39 min.

Uth, Robert, dir. *World War II Memorial: A Testament to Freedom.* Washington, DC: New Voyage Communications, PBS, 2004. DVD, 60 min.

Yamane, Stuart, dir. *Journey of Honor.* Kaneohe, HI: KHET, Hawaii PBS, 2001. DVD, 60 min.

Primary Sources

Army Military History Institute

Carlisle Barracks, Pennsylvania

General Edward Mallory Almond Papers, 155 boxes

Benjamin O. Davis Sr. Papers

Lt. General Robert P. Ennis Jr. Papers

Veterans Surveys World War II

See Colonel Jesse A. Brewer (ASTP), 370th; Charles Graham, HQ; Rufus Winfield Johnson, Lt. Col. RET; Edgar S. Piggott, 370th (ASTP).

Signal Corps Photographs World War II, 92nd Division

Unit Histories and Other Records Pertaining to the 92nd Infantry Division

Proceedings of the First Conference on Black Americans in World War II, 9 September 1992. U.S. Army Military History Institute, Strategic Studies Institute, Black Employment Program Committee, Carlisle Barracks, PA

Second Conference on Black Americans in World War II, 8–9 September 1993. http://www.loc.gov/vets/

Fort Huachuca Museum, Fort Huachuca, Arizona

Manuscript Collections on Buffalo Soldiers from the nineteenth century through the twentieth century

Photographic Collection

Western Historical Manuscripts Collection—Columbia, Missouri.

World War II, Letters, 1940–1946. (CO068),

Library of Congress

Manuscripts Division

Gibson, Truman K., 1912–2005

Truman K. Gibson Papers, circa 1900–1994. 900 items.

Spencer C. Moore's Collection and A. William Perry's Collection now reside in the Library of Congress. LC Control No.: mm2007085384

United States Army 92nd Infantry Division Collection, 1926–2007 (bulk 1942–2000).

Veterans History Project

Oral Histories: www.loc.gov/folklife/vets (If you have not already done so, interview your parents and relatives and deposit the tapes and transcripts in the Library of Congress. This website contains the instructions.)

LIST OF INTERVIEWEES

Lorenzo Bell, Isham George Benton, Lester Brownlee, William Cullen Bryant, Irwin Conley, George A. Connor, Howard Cuff, Albert Curley, Donald R. Daugherty, Elwin Davidson, William Henry Davis, Van Dominick, Nathaniel Dula, John Curtis Foster Jr., Virgil M. Fulwider, Campbell Gonzalez, Luther Edward Hall, Charles L. Henson, Frank E. Hodge, Louis Hunt, Israel James, John Thomas Johnson, Robert Madison, Ernie Maynard, James Wilbert Milton, Spencer Moore, Robert E. Moran, George E. O'Connor, William Perry, Robert Reid, George T. Ridout Sr., Christopher Roberson, Calvin Anthony Shields, Roscoe Tyson Spann, Charles Whaley, Cecil Ward White, George Willis, Charles Whitfill in 92nd—382nd

Maggi Morehouse Archives, Aiken, South Carolina

Maggi Morehouse

LIST OF INTERVIEWEES

William S. M. Banks, Ogelsby Barrett, John Beavers, Sam Broadnax, (Tuskegee Airman), Albert Burke, Roland Dix, Ruth Earl, Howard Fletcher, Arthur Goodwin, Felix Goodwin, Allen Green, Joseph Hairston, Charles Hanson, Dennett Harrod, Arnett Hartsfield, Cleother Hatchcock, Howard Hickerson, Levi Hill, Reuben Horner, Jehu Hunter, Fred Hurns, Ezell Jackson, Lawrence Johnson, Charles Lancaster, Madine Davis Lane, Mrs. Robert (Leatrice) Madison, Robert Madison, Mick Marsall, William "Ted" McCullough, Dorothy McIver, I. P. McIver, Thomas McKinney, Cullen McKissock, Harold Montgomery, Mrs. Helen Montgomery, Mrs. Susie Moore, Spencer Moore, Bill Payne, Nelson Peery, A. William Perry, Alex Pitcher, Edward Price, Joseph Stephenson, Allen Thompson, W. E. "Burg" Turner, Woodrow Walton, Fred Watt, Charles Wesly, Edgar Whitley, Clyde Whitted, Hank Williams, Jim Williams, Mrs. Jim Williams

Recently many of these oral histories have been digitized and are available at the German Historical Institute's website: *http://www.aacvr-germany.org/AACVR.ORG/*

The National Archives and Records Administration, College Park, Maryland

Record Group (RG) 107: Records of the Secretary of War

RG 165: Records of the War Department, General and Special Staffs, Office of the Chief of Staff

RG 94: Records of the Adjutant General

RG 153: Judge Advocate General

RG 159: Inspector General

RG 395: U.S. Army Overseas Operations and Commands, 1898–1942

RG 407: Records of the Army Adjutant General; World War II Operational Reports, 1940–1948

Photographs of African Americans in World War II

James Rada, film archives, Ithaca College, Ithaca, New York

Index

Page numbers in italics refer to figures